CO-OWNERSHIP OF ACTION:

TRAJECTORIES OF ELEMENTS

JN064263

ふるまいの
連鎖：
エレメントの
軌跡

CO-OWNERSHIP OF ACTION:
TRAJECTORIES OF ELEMENTS

First published in Japan on August 10, 2020

Supervisor:
Kozo Kadowaki

Publisher: Takeshi Ito
TOTO Publishing (TOTO LTD.)
TOTO Nogizaka Bldg. 2F, 1-24-3 Minami-Aoyama
Minato-ku, Tokyo 107-0062, Japan
Sales:
Telephone: +81-3-3402-7138
Facsimile: +81-3-3402-7187
Editorial:
Telephone: +81-3-3497-1010
URL: https://jp.toto.com/publishing

Book Designer: Rikako Nagashima+Hiroyuki Inada / village®
Editor: Jiro Iio / speelplaats co., ltd.
Printer: Sannichi Printing Co., Ltd.

ISBN978-4-88706-386-0

INDEX

目次

0:
INTRODUCTION
イントロダクション

Introduction
Kozo Kadowaki
(Architect and construction studies)

This book serves as the catalog for the exhibition *Co-ownership of Action: Trajectories of Elements*, presented at the Japan Pavilion as part of the 17th International Architecture Exhibition of the Venice Biennale.

Held in Italy's Floating City on the Adriatic Sea, the Venice Biennale currently offers an Art Exhibition in odd-numbered years and an Architecture Exhibition in even-numbered years. The Biennale has a long and august history, and its format is fittingly traditional. The unit of participation is the nation, with each country selecting artists to represent their homeland and planning its own exhibition in competition with other countries. The approach is similar to that of a world's fair or the Olympics. In fact, the very first Venice Biennale was held in 1895, the year before the first Summer Olympics took place in Athens.

For the 2020 Architecture Exhibition, I was asked to serve as curator of the exhibition at the Japan Pavilion. Joining me in the planning were architects Jo Nagasaka, Ryoko Iwase, Toshikatsu Kiuchi, Taichi Sunayama, and Daisuke Motogi, designer Rikako Nagashima, and editor Jiro Iio. Research for the project was conducted by Norimasa Aoyagi, a historian of Japanese architecture; Aya Hiwatashi, an urban historian; Naoyuki Matsumoto, an expert on wooden structures and construction methods; and Tetsu Makino, a specialist in building preservation and restoration. Architectural curator Kayoko Ota has served as advisor on production of the overall exhibition. Participation not only by those directly engaged in the creative side of the exhibition, but also by researchers, editors and others in supporting roles, is, I believe, a significant feature of the team carrying out this project. Our plan to dismantle a typical Japanese wooden house, bring the parts to Venice, and exhibit them at the Biennale emerged from the collaboration among these multitalented members.

Bringing a Japanese house to Venice: phrased like that, the point of this project may no doubt elude many, and quite understandably. To be honest, even those of us on the planning team have yet to fully grasp its significance. While preparing for the exhibition we had to contend with daily bouts of self-doubt as we pushed our audacious scheme forward. This compulsion to carry on with a project whose meaning remained unclear felt a bit like putting the cart before the horse. As time went on, we experienced the sensation that we were not pursuing a plan so much as the plan was pursuing us. And yet it is this very reversal of cause and effect that has revealed new creative possibilities to us. The essays and dialogues in this book are our attempts to explore and articulate those possibilities.

The meaning of movement

So far this may seem like a rather vague accounting of our project. However, I think the most effective way to explain the exhibition is to review how it came to be, rather than try to convey its "meaning." Allow me to go back to its very inception over a year ago.

The project began with the delivery of a letter from the Japan Foundation, the organizer of the Japan Pavilion exhibition at the Venice Biennale, in late February 2019. The exhibition plan is selected through a competition among candidates for the position of curator; this letter informed me that I had been nominated as one such candidate. Since one of the key criteria in the competition is the composition of the exhibition participants, I had to move quickly to pull a team together. Thus the membership of our team was decided before we had any idea what our project would be about. We held our first meeting only a month after the letter. However, I already had an idea that the exhibition should deal directly with material objects rather than attempt to convey concepts through models and drawings, as at a typical architectural exhibition. The architects and designers I invited to join the team all concurred with this approach.

Jo Nagasaka's diligent way of working with objects in his architectural practice made him one of my most trusted allies in this effort. Each of his works is the product of a singular conversation among the objects, people, and places specific to that project. Nagasaka creates the impression that he is letting the work itself speak about its unique set of circumstances. The first thing he said to me was that it would be a shame if visitors to the exhibition were left unaware of the costs incurred in the transport of objects—whatever they might be—all the way from Japan to Venice. An analysis of public proposals for past competitions showed that shipping and travel costs did indeed make up a large proportion of the total budget. It would be interesting, we thought, to make the transport budget a part of the exhibition.

It further occurred to us that transport and movement in general have become an increasingly frenetic aspect of contemporary society. Not so long ago the arrival of a package was cause for excitement, but today all manner of daily necessities are delivered to our door, and receiving packages is just a part of our everyday routine. Not only things, but people, too, move about with abandon—whether commuting to work and school or traveling abroad, which is now more commonplace than ever. Without even realizing it, we have become a society of "great migrations," living in a tumultuous world of endless movement. If we can give visible form to this phenomenon, it should provide us with one means of graphically expressing the state of society today. This is the line of thinking that yielded one of the core concepts of our project: making movement itself visible.

Working with wooden houses

Our resolve to "make movement visible" notwithstanding, we found it difficult to decide just what it was we should be moving. Our breakthrough came with a challenge from Rikako Nagashima: "Buildings generate huge amounts of waste. As architects, what do you propose to do about that?" Exhibitions, too, produce waste, of course—all the more so when the exhibition purports to deal with objects, as ours does. If we wanted to face Nagashima's challenge squarely, we needed to recycle things we'd normally discard and make this an exhibition that wouldn't become trash itself once it was over. That was when a wooden Japanese house emerged as our object of movement.

Receiving the full brunt of bombing attacks during World War II, Japanese cities sustained devastating damage that produced a housing crisis after the war ended. Moreover, the government's economic recovery policy focused on the development of smokestack industries, and the ensuing transformation of Japan's industrial

0: INTRODUCTION

structure affected the entire nation, causing a sudden population flow from the countryside to the cities and sparking a housing construction boom in urban and suburban areas. The first responders to this surge in housing demand were artisans, particularly carpenters, with roots in traditional building crafts. Consequently most houses built after the war were made of wood. After the "oil shock" of 1973, however, Japan's birth rate went into decline, and in the first decade of the 21st century the population itself began to fall. Now there was a surplus of housing, and by 2018 there were nearly 8.5 million vacant units nationwide. Today the country is awash in houses that have outlived their usefulness and simply sit there awaiting dismantling. Why don't we acquire one of those houses, we thought, and move it to Venice?

From an architectural standpoint, the wooden Japanese house is an extremely unique phenomenon characterized by a high degree of flexibility. Additions and renovations are a normal occurrence for traditional wooden houses, which can be modified at will according to circumstances. Hence such structures were eminently suited to the changes in the building production system that occurred after the war. From the mid-1950s on, Japanese architecture became increasingly industrialized, with cement replacing fired clay for roof tiles, aluminum sashes replacing wooden window frames, and plastic drainpipes replacing tin ones. In short, all kinds of building components were transformed into the products of heavy industries, but wooden houses accepted them without complaint. From the 1960s on, by which time building construction had become fully industrialized, wooden housing acquired the look of a bricolage of

handicrafts and heavy industries—or, one might say, a chimera-like composite of industries of disparate eras.

Postwar wooden houses acquired their distinctive characteristics precisely because they underwent dramatic changes of this sort. In that case, we felt, transporting one such house to Venice and reconstructing it in a variety of ways for exhibit should provide insights into that reality. Fortuitously, the exhibition venue is the Japan Pavilion of the Venice Biennale, which has a large garden where we can assemble the structures derived from the house. Venice and its environs have their own culture of wooden architecture, so it may be feasible to have the wood recycled locally after the exhibition is over. Judging by the trial images we drew of the site, it may be hard to tell if the structures that appear there are a product of creation or dismantling, which is part of the fun. In any event we managed to put a proposal together, and emerged victorious from the screening held at the end of May 2019.

Encountering, dismantling, and digitizing Takamizawa House

Once we were selected, we had to hurry to find a wooden house to ship to Venice. Based on our estimates of the time and cost of transport by sea, we would have to acquire a house for free and begin dismantling it in August. But we could hardly expect a house to fall into our laps, so once again we were in a quandary.

Our encounter with Takamizawa House came about quite unexpectedly. I happened to be chatting with the owner of the house across the street from mine, and told him about our troubles finding the right candidate for our project. My neighbor thought hard for a moment, then said, "I'm planning to demolish my house and build a new one. You can have the materials from the old house. Feel free to help yourself." He may have thought it would be a little awkward to go ahead and demolish the house without a word after having heard my story. I was stunned by this stroke of luck. We decided to refer to the house as Takamizawa House in honor of its owner.

Takamizawa House was a wooden house built in 1954 that underwent several expansions and renovations between then and the 1980s. It was exactly what we were looking for. I had actually gazed out on Takamizawa House from my desk while drawing up the proposal for the competition. I had always liked the house, and of all the buildings in the neighborhood it had offered the greatest inspiration when I designed my own home.

The highly skilled building firm TANK accepted the task of dismantling Takamizawa House and reassembling it in Venice. First, however, we had to conduct an exhaustive survey of the house's pre-dismantled state, or it would be impossible to reassemble later. This was a precious opportunity to study a postwar wooden house in detail, so we wanted to approach the task scientifically. While the survey would be conducted by a team led by Norimasa Aoyagi, it was Taichi Sunayama, an architect whose research and practice examines the contemporary relationship between art and technology, who urged us to make optimum use of digital technology to record the survey data. Under Sunayama's guidance, Takamizawa House was digitized via a whole range of methods, from 3D scanning of the entire house and subsequently of its individual elements, to computer modeling based on drawings and measurements.

If we intended to reuse the elements of Takamizawa House, we would have to remove them by hand, one at a time—the house could not simply be demolished with heavy equipment. As soon as we removed the elements we would transport them, in frequent truckloads, to a warehouse where Sunayama and his team had set up a special jig they had devised to carry out a 3D scan of each element as it arrived from the dismantling site. The process did not, however, go smoothly.

A single wooden element might take 30 minutes to scan, but we were limited both in our budget for scanning and in the personnel and time available to carry it out. Scanning a single pillar might yield more than 15 GB of data, but our computer capacity was limited too. As elements were unloaded one after another, the warehouse's capacity rapidly reached its limit as well. Soon we found ourselves having to dispose of some elements at the site. Hampered by constraints of time, budget, personnel, computer data capacity, and warehouse space, we were ultimately able to scan only one-tenth of the total of some 4,000 elements. Nonetheless we managed to compile a list of elements large and small, complete customs clearance procedures, and load the elements into two 30-foot containers. They departed from Japan in January 2020. As I write this introduction in February, Takamizawa House is afloat on the high seas and scheduled to dock in Venice sometime in March.

0: INTRODUCTION

Rebirth in Venice

Our plan is to use Takamizawa House to create an exhibit at the Japan Pavilion on the history of the period the house lived through. Built at the very outset of a long-term economic boom and subject to repeated additions and renovations over the next three decades, Takamizawa House physically embodies the dramatic changes Japanese society underwent during the postwar years. The elements used in the house vary just as dramatically according to the era when they were installed. By exhibiting these elements, we should be able to see how our society and its architecture changed over the years.

We also developed plans to utilize Takamizawa House to exhibit its own history. We will reconstruct some sections of the house, but we will use other parts to build screens, benches, even display panels—in other words, the house itself will become part of the installation. With the reassembly in Venice of a portion of the scattered pieces of Takamizawa House, each of those elements will gain new life. However, the house has lost many more elements in the process of being dismantled and moved; nor were we able to save data about every part. In other words, Takamizawa House has sustained significant losses in both the physical and digital realms. To restore the house we must therefore compensate for the missing elements with new materials or those obtained locally, and for the missing data with new creations. For this purpose our team of architects and artisans plan to leave Japan for Venice. Though the architects will be supervising the reconstruction work, their authority will be anything but absolute. Rather,

they will be sharing ideas with the artisans and with TANK in its role as site manager, and the emphasis will be on improvisation, with decisions made literally on the spot. The end product will be, in effect, a composite of old and new materials, a chimera-like hybrid of the creative efforts of architects, artisans, and other participants.

This hybrid entity should also provide a vivid demonstration that our actions never belong to ourselves alone. The creations of the architects will be a result of the history through which Takamizawa House lived and the fact that it was shipped to Venice; they will also be linked to the actions of the artisans and the experiences of visitors. These mobile elements will showcase not just our actions, but those of countless people linked by the trajectory taken by the elements. That is why we have titled this exhibition "Co-ownership of Action: Trajectories of Elements."

Takamizawa House floats within a vast expanse of time and space. But that is certainly not true of Takamizawa House alone. Every building is nothing more or less than an accumulation of elements that have undergone repeated meetings and partings. Architecture by definition lives within just such a time-space continuum. A work of architecture is not something that one person can lay claim to as their own. It is precisely within the expanse of time and space occupied by a house that we may discover the foundation for coexistence among a diversity of actors.

イントロダクション
門脇耕三
（建築家・構法研究）

本書は、第17回ヴェネチア・ビエンナーレ国際建築展の一環として、会場内の日本館で開催される展覧会「ふるまいの連鎖：エレメントの軌跡」のカタログとして出版されたものである。

ヴェネチア・ビエンナーレは、2年に一度、イタリアの水上都市ヴェネチアにて開催される展覧会であり、西暦が奇数の年には美術展が、偶数の年には建築展が開かれることになっている。ヴェネチア・ビエンナーレはたいへん古い起源をもつ展覧会で、その形式も古式ゆかしい。主要な部分の参加の単位は国で、各国がそれぞれ国を代表する出展作家を選び、独自の展覧会の企画を立てて競演するのだ。万博やオリンピックを思わせるやり方である。実際、第1回のヴェネチア・ビエンナーレは1895年に開催されているが、これは第1回夏季オリンピックがアテネで開催される前年のことであった。

2020年の建築展では、日本館の展覧館のキュレーターを筆者が務めることになった。企画は筆者とともに、建築家の長坂常、岩瀬諒子、木内俊克、砂山太一、元木大輔、デザイナーの長嶋りかこ、編集者の飯尾次郎らと議論を重ねて練り上げたものである。並行して行われたリサーチには、日本建築史を専門とする青柳憲昌、都市史を専門とする樋渡彩、建築構法および木構造を専門とする松本直之、建物の保存・修復を専門とする牧野徹といった研究者が参画している。また展覧会の運営全般に対するアドバイザーとして、建築キュレーターの太田佳代子が加わっている。創造に直接たずさわる表現者ばかりではなく、それを間接的に支援する役回りにある研究者や編集者も加わっていることが、本展に取り組むチームの大きな特徴であるといってよい。この多彩なメンバーが集まって考えたのは、日本のごくありふれた木造住宅を解体してヴェネチアまで運び、展示することだった。

日本の住宅をヴェネチアまで運ぶ。これだけを聞けば、そこにどんな意味があるのかといぶかしまれるかもしれない。それも無理のないことで、正直なところ、われわれ自身さえその意味をきちんとわかっているとはいいがた

い。展覧会の準備の道のりは、この向こう見ずな企画をどうにか前に進ませながら、自問自答を重ねる日々にほかならなかった。

意味が不確かなものを、それでも何とか駆動させようとすることは、主客の感覚に転倒をもたらす。時間が経つにつれて、この企画を自分たちが進めているのか、企画に自分たちが走らされているのか、判然としなくなってくるのだ。とはいえ、この主客の転倒にこそわれわれが可能性を見出していることは間違いない。

移動すること

漠然とした書き出しとなってしまった。しかし、この展覧会について説明するには、その意味を伝えようとするよりも、これまでの経緯を振り返ったほうがうまくいくように思える。

ことのはじまりは2019年の2月末、展覧会の主催者である国際交流基金から一通の封書が届いたことだった。ヴェネチア・ビエンナーレの日本館企画は、キュレーター候補者が競い合うコンペによって選ばれるが、それは筆者がキュレーター候補者に指名されたことを告げる手紙だった。コンペでは出展作家の構成そのものが主要な争点のひとつになるから、とにかくチーミングを急いだ。そういうわけで、企画は白紙のままメンバーだけが決まり、最初のミーティングが行われたのは約1カ月後のことだった。とはいえ、建築展にありがちな模型やドローイングで概念を伝えるような展覧会ではなく、モノと格闘するような展覧会にしたいという思いが筆者にはあった。参加をお願いした建築家やデザイナーは、その思いに賛同してくれたという一点で共通している。

長坂は、モノとの向き合い方の誠実さという点において、筆者がもっとも信頼をおいている建築家のひとりである。彼の作品は、プロジェクトを取りまくモノや人や場所との一回的な対話の結果として結実する。だから長坂の作品には、そこに固有の状況を、作品自体に語らせてし

まうようなところがある。その長坂の口から最初に飛び出したのは、ヴェネチアは遠いから何を持って行くにも費用がかさむはずで、その費用が観客から見えないものになってしまうのだとすると、展覧会としてはもったいないよね、という発言だった。試しに公開されている過去のコンペの提案書を分析してみると、予算全体に対して輸送費と旅費の占める割合がたしかに大きい。この分の予算を展覧会に活かすことができれば面白そうだ。

　また、改めて考えてみると、輸送や移動は現代社会においてますます激しくなっている実感がある。一昔前であれば、家に荷物が届くことはどこか胸が弾む感覚を伴ったが、いまではあらゆる日用品が刻々と宅配され続けていて、荷物の受け取りは日々のルーティンのひとつにすぎない。モノばかりではなく、人の移動もすさまじい。通勤通学はいうに及ばず、海外に出かけることさえ日常の一部である。つまりわれわれは、気づかぬうちに「大移動社会」とでもいうべき状況のなかで暮らし始めている。これを可視化することができれば、現代社会のひとつの明快な表現につながるのではないか。「移動そのものを見せる」という企画のコンセプトのひとつは、このようにして確固たるものになっていった。

木造住宅を扱うこと

　「移動を見せる」ことは決まったが、移動させるべき対象がなかなか決まらない。突破口となったのは、長嶋による「建物は膨大な廃棄物を出す。あなたたち建築家は、そのことをどのように考えているのか」という問いかけだった。展覧会も、もちろん廃棄物を出す。モノと格闘するような展覧会にするのであればなおさらである。この長嶋の言葉に向き合うのであれば、捨てられようとしているものを活かし、会期後もゴミにならない展示とすべきではないか。そのとき「移動するもの」として浮上してきたのが日本の木造住宅だった。

　太平洋戦争で直接の戦場となった日本は、都市部が壊滅的な被害を受け、戦後は住宅の不足が大きな問題となった。また重化学工業が経済復興政策の根幹に位置づけられ、産業構造の転換が全国規模で促されたことから、農山村地域から都市部への急激な人口流入がもたらされた。この結果、都市とその周縁の郊外には、大量の住宅が建設されることになった。この莫大な住宅需要に応えたのは、主に大工をはじめとする伝統に連なる職人たちであり、したがって戦後に建てられた住宅の多くは木造住宅であった。しかし 1973 年のオイルショック以後、出生率は減少を続け、2000 年代の後半からは人口自体も減少を始めている。大量につくられた住宅も余りだしており、全国の空き家の数は 2018 年時点で 850 万戸近い。住宅の老朽化も進んでおり、役目を終えて解体を待つばかりの住宅は日本全国にあまた存在する。そんな住宅を譲り受けて、ヴェネチアへと運んではどうかと考えたのである。

　建築的に見ると、日本の木造住宅はたいへんユニークな存在であり、その特徴は高いフレキシビリティを備えていることである。伝統的な木造住宅では増改築が日常茶飯事であり、状況にあわせて、建物がいかようにも変化することができる。このような特徴をもつ木造住宅は、戦後に起こった建築生産システムの変化もものともしなかった。日本の建築は 1950 年代後半から工業化が進み、焼き物だった瓦はセメントでつくられ、木製の建具はアルミサッシにとって代わられ、ブリキの雨樋はプラスチック製に置き換わるといった具合に、ありとあらゆる建築部品が重化学工業の産物と化したが、木造住宅はそれらも貪欲に飲み込んでいった。建築生産の工業化がすっかり進展した 1960 年代以降の木造住宅は、手工業と重化学工業のブリコラージュ、あるいは来歴の異なる産業のキメラ的複合体の様相を呈している。

　以上のように、戦後の木造住宅は、激しく変化したこととそのものによって特徴づけられている。であれば、そんな住宅をヴェネチアへと運び、さまざまにつくりかえて展示することにもリアリティは見出せるのではないか。幸い展示会場となるヴェネチア・ビエンナーレ日本館に

は、大きな庭があってそこで組み立てることができる。ヴェネチアやその周辺には木造建築の文化もあるから、会期終了後は木材を現地で再利用してもらうことも可能かもしれない。試しにドローイングを描いてみると、壊しているのかつくっているのかわからない状況が出現しそうで、なかなか楽しそうでもある。企画は何とかまとまって、5月末に開催された選考会で勝利することができた。

《高見澤邸》との出会い、解体、デジタル化

　選出後に急がなくてはならなかったのは、ヴェネチアに運ぶ木造住宅の探索であった。海上輸送の期間と予算を考えると、8月頃に解体が始まる住宅を、ただで譲り受けるしか道はない。とはいえそんな住宅が都合よく出てくるはずもなく、またしても途方に暮れることになった。

　出会いは意外なところにあった。イタリアで建築の展覧会を開くことになったこと、しかし肝心の住宅が見つからなくて困っていることを、立ち話で打ち明けた筆者宅の向かいの家のご主人が、思い詰めた顔をして訪ねてこられたのである。曰く、私の家を建て替えることになったから、古い家の資材を使っても構わない。どうぞ自由にしてくださいとのことだった。おそらく話を聞いてしまったからには黙って解体を始めるわけにはいかないと思われたのだろう。この巡りあわせには本当に驚かされた。以後、ご主人のお名前を冠して、この住宅を《高見澤邸》と呼ぶことにする。

　《高見澤邸》は、1954年に新築され、1980年代まで増改築が繰り返されてきた木造住宅で、まさに思い描いていた通りのものだった。実際、コンペ案は仕事場から《高見澤邸》を眺めながら練られたものだったし、そもそも筆者は《高見澤邸》をたいへん気に入っていて、自作である自邸を設計する際に、周辺のコンテクストのなかでも最大の参照源としたのが《高見澤邸》であった。

　《高見澤邸》の解体とヴェネチアでの再組み立ては、腕利きの施工会社のTANKが引き受けてくれることになった。しかし解体に先だって、もとの状態の記録を採っておかないとヴェネチアで組み立てることができない。戦後の木造住宅を詳細に調べられる貴重な機会だから、学術的な調査も行ったほうがよい。調査は青柳が中心となって実施することが決まっていたが、記録はデジタル技術を駆使して採るべきだと主張したのは、芸術と技術の現代的な関係についての実践と研究を積み重ねている砂山であった。そこで《高見澤邸》は、砂山の主導のもと、建物全体の3Dスキャニング、部材のスキャニング、図面と実測にもとづくモデリングなど、あらゆる方法を駆使してデジタル化されることになった。

　《高見澤邸》は部材を再利用するため、重機で一気に解体するわけにはいかず、部材一つひとつを手作業でていねいに取り外す必要がある。取り外された部材は、現場から頻繁に運び出しては倉庫に保管する。この倉庫には砂山たちが独自に考案した3Dスキャニングのための治具が置かれて、運び込まれた部材は一つひとつスキャンされていったのだが、しかし作業は難航した。

　一本の木材をスキャンするのには30分ほどの時間を必要とするが、スキャンにかけられる予算は限られており、投入できる人工も最低限である。木材一本のスキャンによって得られるデータは15GB以上に及ぶが、コンピュータの容量も限られている。部材はどんどん運び込まれて、倉庫の容量はすぐに限界に達したから、現場で廃棄せざるをえない部材も出てくる。時間、予算、人工、コンピュータのデータ容量、倉庫の容量などなどのさまざまな有限性に阻まれて、スキャンできたのは、約4,000の部材のうちの10分の1にすぎなかった。それでも何とか部材や部品をリスト化し、通関手続きを済ませ、30ftコンテナ2本に収められて日本を出発したのは、2020年1月のことだった。この原稿が書かれているのは2月であり、現時点で《高見澤邸》は海上にいる。ヴェネチアに到着するのは3月の予定である。

0: INTRODUCTION

ヴェネチアでの再生へ

　この《高見澤邸》を用いて、日本館では、《高見澤邸》が生きた歴史を展示する予定である。高度経済成長が始まったときに建設され、30年以上にわたって増改築が積み重ねられてきた《高見澤邸》には、戦後の日本社会の変化が深く刻まれている。《高見澤邸》に用いられている部材や部品は、取り付けられた時代ごとに大きく変質しており、こうした部材や部品を展示することで、われわれの社会と建築がいかに変わったかを示すことができるだろう。

　加えて、《高見澤邸》の歴史を展示するために、《高見澤邸》自身が用いられる計画を立てた。《高見澤邸》の一部は再構築されて、ある部分はスクリーンへ、ある部分はベンチへ、ある部分は展示壁へといった具合に、それ自身が展示のための設えとして読み替えられる。バラバラになった《高見澤邸》の一部は、現地で再び組み立てられて、それぞれが新しい生を得ることになるというわけだ。

　しかし《高見澤邸》は、解体と移動の過程で多くの部材を失っている。部材のデータも十分には取得できておらず、《高見澤邸》には、物理的にも情報的にも大きな欠損が生じている。この欠損を新材料や現地の材料で埋めあわせ、あるいは情報的な欠損は新しい創造によって補いながら《高見澤邸》を再生させるために、建築家は日本の職人とともにヴェネチアへと赴く予定である。再構築の作業は建築家が指揮するが、しかし彼らの指示が絶対というわけではない。むしろ職人たちや現場をマネジメントするTANKとアイデアを出し合い、現場ならではの即興的な判断を重視したい。すなわち、われわれがつくるものは、古い材料と新しい材料が混在し、幾人もの建築家や職人の創造性が重層した、キメラ的な混成物である。

　この混成物は、われわれのふるまいが、われわれだけに帰属するものではないことを強く示唆するものになるだろう。建築家による創造は、《高見澤邸》が生きた歴史やヴェネチアまで運ばれてきたことの結果として起きた

ことなのであり、その創造には、職人の手の動きや鑑賞者の体験が連なっていく。移動するエレメントが浮かび上がらせたのは、われわれの行いばかりではなく、その軌跡の上に多くの人々の無数のふるまいが連鎖している様相であった。だからわれわれは、展覧会のタイトルを「ふるまいの連鎖：エレメントの軌跡」と名づけることにした。

　《高見澤邸》の存在は、時間と空間の広大なひろがりのなかを漂っている。しかしこの存在のひろがりは、《高見澤邸》だけに限られるわけではないだろう。あらゆる建物は、離散と集合を繰り返すエレメントの集積にほかならず、建築とはそもそも、そのような時空間的なひろがりのなかに生きるものなのだ。建築は、特定の誰かによって専有できるようなものではなく、その開かれたひろがりのなかにこそ、われわれはさまざまな主体が共存する基盤を見出すことができるのである。

The Japan Pavilion of the Venice Biennale.
Photo by Aya Hiwatashi
ヴェネチア・ビエンナーレ日本館、撮影：樋渡彩

1:
HISTORY
OF
TAKAMIZAWA
HOUSE

《高見澤邸》の
歴史

Designing an Industrial Continuum in Architectural Production:
Takamizawa House as "Industrial Chimera"
Norimasa Aoyagi
(Architectural Historian)

1. The postwar housing industry and the "architect"

Japan's postwar era began in makeshift shacks known as "barracks." At the end of World War II, 20 million Japanese citizens had lost their homes and were struggling to survive amid the bombed-out ruins of the cities. To supply them with shelter required the rapid development of a mass-production system for housing. It would take too long to build houses by traditional methods that depended on carpenters and other manual artisans; what was needed was machine-based factory production that required no such skills. Before the war, modernization of housing for the general Japanese populace had progressed slowly if at all. Now, however, prodded by the urgency of their circumstances in the devastation of post-defeat japan, modernization proceeded apace. The pell-mell modernization of the period following the Meiji Restoration of 1867 was usually described as Westernization, but this was merely a political catchword used to promote modernity. The advanced technology of the West coveted by a backward Japan, expressed as "learning" in the slogan *wakon yosai* ("Japanese spirit with Western learning"), was none other than modernity itself. But did this dualistic distinction between Western "learning" and Japanese "spirit" allow for true modernization? In point of fact, that occurred only after such dualistic conceits were eradicated by defeat in the war and the ensuing national identity crisis. Before the war, Japan had imported the modern technologies of reinforced concrete and steel construction, building high-rise structures in the cities as their populations grew. But only a few intellectuals had their houses designed in modernist architectural styles, with no substantial changes in the housing or lifestyle of the average citizen. Looking back from our present-day vantage point at the surge of modernization (i.e., contemporization) during Japan's postwar economic boom, the prewar version seems like a mere warm-up for what was to come.

1-1. Urbanization as context

In the early 1950s, the government sought to address the need for a dramatic increase in housing by initiating a home ownership promotion policy. This somewhat half-baked strategy of exhorting people to build their own houses was the underlying cause of the unique appearance of the urban neighborhoods that emerged in postwar Japan. With the establishment in 1950 of the Housing Loan Corporation, which provided financing for the construction of small houses with areas of 15 *tsubo* or less (1 *tsubo* = 3.3 m²), members of the middle class began building little "my home" units in the suburbs en masse (the actual work was done by private contractors). Gradually the average citizen came to think of housing as something to be owned, not rented as in prewar days. Land was subdivided into small, affordable plots, dictating that the houses built on them would be extremely compact as well [Fig. 1].

The explosive economic growth of the boom years from the late 1950s to the early 1970s sparked a massive influx of young people from outlying areas into the major cities in search of employment. The ensuing urban population growth and sprawl was accompanied by changes in the social structure as nuclear families be-

建築生産における産業連鎖をデザインする
——「産業キメラ」としての《高見澤邸》
青柳憲昌（建築史）

1. 戦後住宅産業と「建築家」

　日本の戦後は**バラック**からスタートした。住まいを失い、一面の焼け野原に放り出された 2,000 万人の庶民に住宅を供給するため、急いで住宅の**大量生産システム**が構築されなければならなかった。手工業的な大工や職人による伝統の構法では時間がかかるから、職人技術を要しない機械による工場生産が必要とされた。敗戦後の荒廃のなか、戦前には遅々として進まなかった日本庶民住宅の近代化が、逼迫した状況に押されて一気に進められることになったのである。

　明治維新（1867）以降、日本で推し進められてきた「**近代化**」とは「欧化（西洋化）」の謂いであったが、「**欧化**」とは近代化推進の政治理念にすぎない。後進国日本が羨望した西洋の先進技術、当時のいい方で「和魂洋才」の「才」こそが、目指された「近代」そのものであったが、精神（魂）＝「和」と、技術（才）＝「洋」を切り分ける二元論によって、はたして**真の近代化**は可能であったのか。事実、その二元論が太平洋戦争の敗戦と国家的アイデンティティの危機によって打ち砕かれた後、急速にそれが動き出したのである。戦前の日本は、RC 造・S 造といった近代技術を導入し、人口増加とともに都市部に高層建築を建設し、ごく一部の文化人の住宅を**モダニズム建築**でつくったが、結局のところ、庶民の住宅や庶民の生活様式を大きく変えることはなかった。戦後日本の高度成長期に爆発的な勢いで進行した**近代化**（＝**現代化**）をいま改めて振り返れば、戦前は単にその助走期間にすぎなかったともいえる。

1-1. 都市化という文脈

　1950 年代初頭、大量の住宅供給を賄うために政府が打ち出したのは「**持ち家奨励政策**」であった。自分の家は自分で建てよ、という半ば投げやりなこの打開策が、戦後日本に固有の町並みを生み出す遠因となった。15 坪以下の小さな住宅の建設資金を融資する**住宅金融公庫**が

Takamizawa House (2019). Photo by the author
《高見澤邸》(2019)、撮影：筆者

Takamizawa House, exterior view (1954).
Collection of Kazuo Takamizawa
《高見澤邸》外観、高見澤一夫氏蔵 (1954 年撮影)

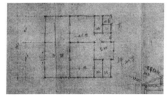

Takamizawa House floor plan
(1954; before design modifications).
Source: "Confirmation Notice (Building)," February 1954
《高見澤邸》(1954) 平面図 (設計変更前)、
「確認通知書（建築物）」(1954 年 2 月)

came the norm, spurring demand for detached housing, which in turn helped sustain economic growth [Fig. 2]. This burgeoning demand for housing construction offered no real work for architects, whose role was largely taken over by the custom home-building companies (known as "housemakers") that appeared in the 1970s.

1-2. Industrialization of housing production

The modernist architecture that emerged in the West in the early 20th century aimed to create a new architectural aesthetic based on an industrialized, universalized production system that would replace traditional manual craftwork. That concept spread around the world. But in Japan, which lagged in the industrialization of its production system, prewar modernist architecture amounted to no more than a cosmetic style; an industrial foundation for modernism was established only after defeat in the war.

Modernist architecture was thus still in its infancy in 1950s Japan. During this period many architects tried their hand at the industrialization of housing production, as evinced by such efforts as Kunio Maekawa's *PREMOS* [Fig. 3], Kenji Hirose's *SH* [Fig. 4], and Kiyoshi Ikebe's *No.* series. Japan's munitions industry, a closed system during the war, had been liberalized, abruptly expanding the range of choices in construction materials and methods available for general housing. Collaborating with the manufacturers who were now springing up like bamboo shoots after a rain, architects led the way in developing technologies that permitted elaborate detail work.[*1]

During periods of revolutionary change in

Mini-development in Setagaya, Tokyo. Photo by the author
東京世田谷のミニ開発、撮影：筆者

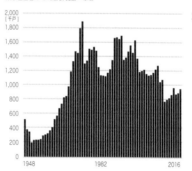

Changes in number of housing starts (from Japanese Government Statistics).
住宅着工戸数の推移（政府統計より）

1950 年に設立され、中流階級が郊外にこぞって小さな「マイホーム」を――**工務店**の請負工事で――建て始める。住宅とは、戦前のように「**借りるもの**」なのではなく「**所有するもの**」なのだという住宅観が、庶民のなかに次第に形成されていく。土地は購入可能な手ごろな大きさに細分化されていき、それに応じて住宅そのものも極度に狭小化していった [図1]。

　1950 年代後半から 70 年代前半の日本の高度経済成長期に、地方から大都市に若者が大量流入し(「集団就職」)、深刻な人口増加と都市膨張を引き起こした。それに併行して**核家族化**が進んだ社会構造の変化が、**戸建て住宅**の需要急増に拍車をかけ、それが日本の経済成長を裏で支えた [図2]。膨大な住宅建設の需要に対して建築家になす術はなく、1970 年代以降、勃興したばかりの**ハウスメーカー**がそれを一手に引き受けることになったのである。

1-2. 住宅生産の工業化

　20 世紀初頭に西欧で生み出された**モダニズム建築**は、工業化され普遍化された生産システムを基盤に、伝統的な手工業にかわる新たな美学と建築を生み出すことを目指したものであり、その理念は世界中に広まった。生産システムの工業化に立ち後れていた日本において、戦前のモダニズム建築は**基盤**のない様式的化粧にすぎず、敗戦後に、ようやくその基盤整備が軌道に乗り始めたのである。

　1950 年代の日本は、それゆえモダニズム建築の揺籃期にあった。**前川國男《プレモス》**[図3] をはじめ、**広瀬鎌二《SH》**[図4]、**池辺陽の《No.》**の各シリーズなど、多くの建築家たちが住宅生産の工業化に取り組んだ。戦時中に閉じていた軍需産業が戦後になって解放され、一般住宅に用いられる建材や構法の選択肢が一気に広がり、建築家たちは、雨後の筍のごとく立ち上がるメーカーと共同しながら、その技術開発を主導して珠玉のディテー

3

Kunio Maekawa, *PREMOS Model 7* (1946).
Courtesy of Mayekawa Associates
前川國男《プレモス7型》(1946)、提供：前川建築設計事務所

4

Kenji Hirose *SH-1* (1953).
Photo by Chuji Hirayama
広瀬鎌二《SH-1》(1953)、撮影：平山忠治

1: HISTORY OF TAKAMIZAWA HOUSE

production technology, architects must lend a guiding, unifying hand. This was as true in postwar Japan as in ancient Greece, when the transition in production technology from wood to stone gave birth to the glorious classical style. In the 1960s, however, Japan's rapid urbanization shifted architects' interest from the house to the city. Architects retreated from the housing industry, and the concepts they had advanced in the 1950s were forgotten as the housemaker firms that took their place scrambled to keep up with the relentless demand for construction.

Urbanization was also accelerating the trend toward large-scale architecture. Height limits on city projects were abolished in 1968, setting the stage for huge buildings far exceeding the scale of what had been permissible before. These projects in turn required the industrialization of every aspect of building construction. The trend of course applied to all industries, not only those associated with architecture, and thus served as an engine for sustained growth across the entire spectrum of society, enabling the government's declared plan to "remodel the Japanese archipelago."[*2] Now that high-quality goods could be mass-produced by machine, without need for skilled artisans, low-cost industrial products were available to the public at large, not just a small elite—making the social ideal of cultural democratization a reality.

1-3. Tradition and modernity in conflict

The drive toward industrialization triggered a reaction in favor of handcrafted, i.e., "traditional" products. The popularity in the 1950s of shin-Nihon-cho ("new Japanese style") homes

[Fig. 5] by such architects as Kiyoshi Seike was a reflection not so much of resurgent nationalism with the signing of the 1951 Peace Treaty that restored Japan's "independence" as it was of the reluctance of most Japanese to slough off the "traditional" customs and habits of the prewar years. In the 1970s, however, when postwar baby-boomers with little attachment to older lifestyles began purchasing houses, "traditional" elements began to disappear from Japanese homes. The history of industrialization in Japan—pretty much a fait accompli by the 1980s—is in part about the process of replacing the "traditional" with the "modern" (i.e., industrial) in daily life.

Plywood ceiling boards printed with wood-grain patterns; cement tiles shaped like traditional Japanese roof tiles; shoji screens covered with plastic instead of easily torn washi paper . . . "Fake" materials like these, so prevalent today, are mass-produced goods made possible by the industrialization of Japanese housing, as well as nostalgic elements born of a revolutionary shift in production. Though such items will be modified or rendered obsolete over time, some will survive—even when their technological foundation does not—as new "traditions" and eventually "styles." Future examples of such elements may be the mesukashi (gapped) ceilings that have replaced traditional saobuchi (board-and-batten) ceilings, and double-sliding aluminum sashes.

2. The evolution of Takamizawa House

1st period: construction (1954)

For Japan, the period from war's end to

ルを生み出したのである（※1）。**揺れ動く生産技術の変革期においては「建築家」の主導理念と統括力が必要とされる**。生産技術が木造から石造へと転換し、見事な古典様式を生み出した古代ギリシアと同様の現象が、ここでも起こっていた。

　しかし、1960年代になると、急速な**都市化**を背景に、建築家たちの関心は「住宅」から「都市」にシフトしていく。建築家は住宅産業から撤退し、それを引き受けたハウスメーカーは膨大な建設に追われ、50年代の建築家たちの打ち立てた理念は忘却されていった。

　一方、都市化は建築の**大規模化**を促した。都市計画の高さ制限が撤廃され（1968）、それまでのスケールをはるかに超える巨大建築が建てられるようになり、その建設には建築に関わる諸産業の**工業化**が必須であった。むろん工業化は、建築関連業に限らず、あらゆる産業に及ぶ。それは高度成長を続ける社会全体の原動力であり、日本列島改造の根拠ともなっていた（※2）。機械さえ操作すれば熟練した職人でなくても高品質のものを量産でき、それゆえ低廉化した工業製品は、限られた社会階層だけではなく、一般庶民も享受できる。**文化の「民主化」**という社会理念が、その根底にはあった。

1-3. 伝統と近代のせめぎ合い

　工業化への強い志向は、反動として**手工業的なもの＝「伝統的なもの」**を呼び起こした。1950年代に**清家清**の作品群［図5］をはじめとする**「新日本調」**の住宅が流行したのは、日本の「独立」が回復した講和条約締結（1951）に伴う**ナショナリズム**の反映であったというよりも、一般庶民にとって戦前までの「伝統」的な生活習慣から脱却するのが容易ではなかったからであろう。しかし、戦後に生まれ、伝統的な生活様式と隔たりのあったベビーブーム世代が住宅を購入するようになる1970年代以降、日本の住宅から「伝統」が次第に姿を消していく。1980年代にほぼ確立される日本の産業工業化の歴史は、日常生

5

Kiyoshi Seike, *House of Professor Saito* (1952).
Photo by Shinkenchiku-sha
清家清《斎藤助教授の家》(1952)、撮影：新建築社写真部

around 1980 was one of transition during which, amid the turmoil brought about by urbanization and industrialization, "traditional" and "modern" (i.e., industrial) blended and contended with one another in the lifestyles of the citizenry. Located in Tokyo's Setagaya Ward, Takamizawa House was built during this period and grew in tandem with Japan's economic growth.

The house Kazuma Takamizawa built in 1954 was a small wooden structure with a residence and two attached shops packed into only 14 tsubo. The shop space was divided in half, with a pharmacy on the south side and a beauty parlor on the north. In a typical example of what is known as "billboard architecture," a wall serving as an advertising billboard was mounted atop the façade, and the exterior walls were covered with Western-style clapboards, a style associated with housing for U.S. Occupation Forces at the time. Although there is no record of the pedigree of the Tamura Architectural Office that designed it, the house's open, modern appearance had a refreshing crispness emblematic of the 1950s. Open to both the west and south, the pharmacy interior had shinkabe-style plastered walls with exposed pillars, while its laminated plywood walls and latticed ceiling were painted emerald green. To secure more space for the beauty parlor, its outer wall was extended out under the eaves enclosing the façade. A row of pivot windows typical of a modern beauty parlor sat atop a waist-high clapboard wall.

The plan of the house called for a mae-domagata ("front doma style") layout with a ground-level unfloored space known as a doma at the front of the house; this was covered with a low floor to serve as a shop. The layout was a traditional one for storefronts in the Kanto region dating back to the Edo period. For some reason or other this space was hastily divided while still under construction into two shops, the pharmacy and beauty parlor. The single-unit living quarters consisted of two connected tatami-floored rooms of 6 and 4.5 mats respectively and a wet area in the rear. Unlike the shops, the residential interior was unpainted. Thus while the public face of the building was given a modern Western look to fit the fashionable image of a rebuilt postwar residential neighborhood, it coexisted with the austere traditional wooden living quarters in the back.

Made of layers of thin plywood, the walls of the tatami-floored rooms were of a low-cost but modern interior design often seen in the 1950s, when materials were still in scarce supply. This was before thicker plywood became available with advances in sawing machinery and broader access to the synthetic resin adhesive developed by the military during the war [Fig. 6].

The brand-new Takamizawa House thus embodied a very natural fusion of "traditional" and "modern" (i.e., industrial). Pillars with itajakuri grooves meticulously cut to hold the laminated plywood, and the tsugite and shiguchi (straight and angle joints) used throughout, testify to the high level of craftsmanship of the carpenters who built it. In this house one can arguably see the zenith of modernization in ordinary homes as it evolved from the Meiji era up to the war.

2nd period: proliferation and subdivision (ca. 1957)

No sooner was it completed than the house began to grow. The shop on the north side was

活のなかの「伝統的なもの」が「近代（工業）的なもの」に
次第に置き換えられていく過程でもあったのである。
　木目を印刷した**プリント合板**の天井板、和瓦の形を模
した**セメント瓦**、和紙のようには破れない**プラスチック
製の障子**……。現代の生活にも溢れているこれら「**偽物**」
の多くは、日本住宅工業化の過程で生まれた量産品であ
り、生産の変革期に生まれた**懐古的エレメント**であった。
それらは淘汰され、時代とともに改変されていくが、技術
的基盤を失ってもなお残るものこそ、新たな「**伝統**」とな
り、いずれ「**様式**」と呼ばれうるものとなるのだろう。既
存の**棹縁天井**を換骨奪胎した**目透かし天井（敷目板パネル
天井）**や、引き違いの**アルミサッシュ**はそのエレメントと
もなりうる。

2.《高見澤邸》の変遷

第1期　〈建設〉（1954）

　戦後から1980年頃までの日本は、都市化と工業化の
渦中で庶民生活のなかに「伝統」と「近代（工業）」が混然
一体となって拮抗しあう過渡的な時代にあった。東京世田
谷に建つ《高見澤邸》は、こうした時代に生まれ、日本経
済の成長とともに成長した家であった。
　1954年に高見澤一馬によって建てられた《高見澤邸》
は、14坪の店舗付き平屋建て木造住宅である。店舗は南
北に仕切られ、南側に薬店（薬舗）、北側に美容室があった。
正面に壁を立ち上げて広告板とする典型的な「**看板建築**」
で、外壁は当時進駐軍住宅によく見られた**洋風下見板張り**
であった。設計者とされる「田村建築事務所」の素性はわ
からないが、開放的でモダンな外観は、**1950年代らしい
清々しさ**に溢れている。薬店は西面・南面とも開放され、
室内は真壁造りで、合板複層の壁や格縁の天井はエメラル
ド・グリーンで**ペンキ塗装**されていた。美容室はスペース
確保のため、正面に廻した小庇の下に外壁面を張り出して
いる。下見板の腰壁の上には、モダンな美容室らしい横長

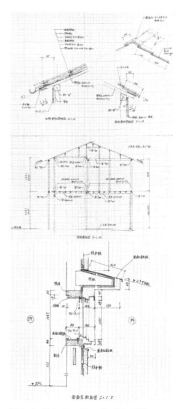

Field notes (Takamizawa House) by Tetsu Makino
《高見澤邸》調査野帳、作成：牧野徹

apparently too small; in any event it was almost immediately extended to the very verge of the facing road by erecting a lean-to structure in front. During this period the 6-*tsubo* section of the house on the north side was sold to a different owner. In 1957 the living quarters were divided by a wall into northern and southern halves, as the shops had been, and the entire ground floor on the north side was converted into a *doma* covered with PVC floor tile. A staircase was built toward the rear and a second floor added to this northern half of the house, which was referred to as the "branch house." (At the same time, the beauty parlor was replaced by a sweets shop.) What was initially a one-story house began to grow, one floor atop another, in a process that resembles the stacking of the portable shrines people carry on their shoulders at Japanese festivals. Already on the verge of splitting in two when it entered this world, by age three the house had expanded both horizontally and vertically, proliferating like a cell undergoing repeated divisions.

The process used to add the second floor is of great interest. Materials were still in short supply in the late 1950s, so roof struts and rafters were reused, new pillars were erected directly above the pillars on the first floor, and the cement roof tiles were replaced with lighter corrugated iron roofing. Low-silled windows were installed in the front wall of the second floor, utilizing the existing billboard-wall structure. Metal-sheet pitched roofs were frequently seen during this period due to the surplus of unused metal recycled as construction material after the war [Fig. 3].

In this tiny house with a frontage of barely 2.7 meters, it comes as a surprise that the new second floor contained a proper-sized *tokonoma* alcove [Fig. 7]. The room boasted mud walls with a plaster finish, *nageshi* tie beams running around the interior, an alcove pillar made of a Kitayama cedar log, sliding-door cabinets at the top and bottom of the *tokowaki* space next to the *tokonoma*, and a window for ventilation and light in the wall of the *tokowaki*. The alcove lintel was finished in the *hakkake* style favored by the architect Isoya Yoshida, suggesting the hand of a skilled carpenter with some exposure to modernism. These touches vividly exemplify a return to tradition in Japanese architectural circles in the mid-1950s, when the prevailing sentiment was that no Japanese house should be without a *tokonoma*.

However, the low-silled windows that had been punched through the original billboard wall on the west side of this room may have been considered a poor match for a Japanese-style space with a *tokonoma*. In any event, some time after the addition of the second floor, a further addition was made to its façade, creating a small sunroom-like space in a triangular layout. Rather than being designed for actual use, this space served as a *tsuke-shoin*-like extension as seen in *shoin-zukuri* architecture. Partitioned with translucent *shoji* screens, it added a note of completion to the traditional Japanese design of the room.

During these renovations, however, various handcrafted elements of this Japanese-style space were replaced by industrial ones. The plastered mud walls were painted over with light blue paint, and the wall separating it from the south-side living quarters was covered with heat insulation, plasterboard and wallpaper. Printed plywood replaced the wood veneer of the

の回転窓を連ねている。

　プランは、前面の土間部分に低い床を張って店舗とするいわゆる「**前土間型**」で、この平面形式は江戸時代関東地方の商家以来の伝統である。何らかの理由あって、建設中に急遽店舗が2分割されて薬店と美容室となったようだが、生活部分は6畳と4畳半の続きの和室と、その奥の水廻りからなるひとつの住まいであった。店舗とは異なり、内装は着色されていなかった。復興住宅地のハイカラ洋風生活に合わせるように、表向きはモダンで洋風の外観をつくり、その裏に伝統木造の質素な生活空間を併存させていたのである。

　薄板の合板を複層にした和室の壁は、戦時中に軍事開発された**合成樹脂**（接着剤）の一般への普及と**製材機械**の発達によって合板が厚板化する以前のもので、資材に乏しい1950年代によく用いられたローコストでモダンな内部意匠であった［図6］。

　誕生したばかりの《高見澤邸》には、「伝統」と「近代（工業）」が違和感なく融合されている。複層合板の**板抉り**がていねいに施された柱や、各所の**継手・仕口**などには、施工した大工の高い**クラフツマンシップ**を見てとれる。明治から戦前までに進められた庶民住宅近代化のひとつの到達点が、この住宅には示されているともいえよう。

第2期　〈増殖と分裂〉（1957頃）

　誕生後のこの家はすぐさま成長し始める。北側の店舗は狭かったのであろう。まもなく正面に下屋をたてて前面道路ぎりぎりまで店舗が拡張された。同じ時期にこの家の北側6坪の所有権が分割されて売却された。1957年、店舗と同様に居住部も南北を壁で隔てて、1階を全面的に**塩ビタイル貼り**の土間とした。裏手には階段を設け、この家の北側部分──高見澤家では「ベツムネ」（別棟）と呼ばれていた──に2階を増築した（同時に店舗は美容室から菓子屋に商売を変えた）。もともと平屋であったこの家は、部分的に、日本の祭りで担がれる神輿のように「**オ**

6

Antonin Raymond, *Cunningham House* (1953).
Photo by the author
A・レーモンド《カニングハム邸》(1953)、撮影：筆者

saobuchi board-and-batten ceiling, plastic foam replaced the straw bed of the *tatami* flooring, and an aluminum sash replaced the wooden frame of the *tokowaki* window. The peculiar juxtaposition of the double-sliding aluminum sash with the *tokowaki* is an especially striking fusion of traditional and modern.

3rd period: reunification (1961)

In 1959, when Takamizawa House was five years old, the Tokai and Kanto regions were devastated by the Ise Bay Typhoon. The Karasuyama River to the northeast of the house overflowed, inundating the ground floor with 10 centimeters of water. In 1961 a second floor was added to the living quarters on the south side (referred to as the "main house"), at least partly for evacuation purposes in event of another such disaster. The outer front (billboard) wall was also rebuilt with a mortar finish for fire protection.

To add the floor, new pillars extending through the second floor were bound to the ground-floor pillars with metal clamps, and angle braces and metal fittings were used to reinforce the joints between the main pillars and the new crossbeams. The roof, which had been divided into north and south sections, was joined together again as a single gable roof. The clapboards on the south side's exterior wall were covered with corrugated sheet iron, transforming the house's woody look to a metallic one. Fiberboard, at this point being manufactured domestically by recycling the massive quantities of sugarcane waste generated by the prewar sugar industry in Taiwan, was used for the interior walls. The rafters were all

replaced with new ones, but the existing cement tiles were retained for the roof. To make a hole in the ceiling for a staircase, thick crossbeams were adroitly inserted through the thinner existing tie beams [Fig. 8].

Kusakabe Komusho, the local construction firm that did the work, says that this method of adding a second floor was standard practice for the day. The image of homeowners throughout the area stacking new floors atop old ones speaks to the frenetic pace of urbanization in suburban neighborhoods in those days.

4th period: renewal and expansion (ca. 1978)

By the 1970s city gas and sewage systems were in place, and public bathhouses began to disappear from the urban landscape. The neighborhood of Takamizawa House was no exception, and in 1978 the structure was extended by about a meter on the east side of the main house (the southern living quarters) to make space to install a "system kitchen" unit, a flush toilet, and a room for the bath. The expansion was accomplished by passing two new beams on either side of the existing pillars, moving the exterior wall back along these beams, and cutting off the old pillars—quite a feat indeed.

Around the same time, the storefront apertures were converted to metal shutters. Their predecessors were four wooden panels (*amado*) covered with sheet metal that had to be slid manually in and out of a storage box on the south side of the building—a fairly arduous daily chore. The installation of shutters that could be mechanically rolled up and down allowed the entire façade to be opened up between the pillars. All the other shops in the neighborhood

Portable shrine (mikoshi) at Tenso Shrine Festival.
Photo by the author
天祖神社祭の御神輿、撮影：筆者

カグラ（御神楽）」されたのである。生まれた時点ですでに分裂しかかっていたこの家は、3歳にして水平・垂直方向に膨張し、早くも細胞分裂を起こしたわけである。

　2階の増築手法も興味深い。50年代後半、いまだ資材が不足するなか、垂木や束などの小屋材を再利用しつつ、1階の既存柱の直上に新設柱を載せ、屋根をセメント瓦から波板鉄板（トタン）に取り替えて軽量化している。正面2階には、当初の「看板」の構造を利用した肘掛け窓が設けられた。当時よく見られた金属板の勾配屋根はそもそもは敗戦で余った大量の金属を建材として利用したものであった［図3］。

　間口がわずか1間半しかない狭小住宅なのに、2階には伝統的で正規の床の間を備えているのは驚きである［図7］。土壁に漆喰塗り、室内に長押を廻して、床柱は北山杉の絞り丸太、床脇に天袋・地袋を備え、床脇の壁には通風・採光用の窓が設けられている。落し掛けは、建築家吉田五十八がよく用いた刃掛けの納まりになっており、その点を見てもモダニズムの洗礼を受けた腕の良い大工の手によるものと推察される。50年代中頃の日本建築界の伝統回帰をよく映しており、"家には床の間がなくてはならない"という当時の日本人の根強い住宅観が感じられる。

　なお、この座敷の西面は既存看板に肘掛け窓を穿ったもので、床をもつ座敷としては不自然に映ったであろう。そのため、2階増築後しばらくしてから、2階の正面も増築してサンルームのような3角平面の小室をつくった。これは使用のためというよりも、書院造りの「付書院」に見立てられたもので、その部屋境に明かり障子をたて、これによりこの座敷が意匠的に完成されたものとなったのである。

　しかし、改修後のこの座敷は、各部が手工業的なものから工業的なものに置換されていった。すなわち、漆喰仕上げの壁は水色ペンキで塗り直され、南側住居との境の壁は断熱材を仕込んでプラスターボード・壁紙貼りに、棹縁天井は突き板からプリント合板に、畳は藁床からスタ

7

Tokonoma alcove in Takamizawa House (branch house).
Photo by the author
《高見澤邸》（ベツムネ）の床の間、撮影：筆者

apparently made the same switch to shutters during this period.

This change coincided with the replacement of the house's wooden fixtures with aluminum sashes, a trend seen in most Japanese housing during this period. The Kaarui-Amado ("Super-light Amado") brand of sash combined a shutter and storage box in a single unit, liberating a happy nation from the daily tedium of sliding heavy *amado* panels open and shut.

In the early 1980s the "branch house" on the north side made room in the back for its own system kitchen, toilet, and bath by building a lean-to extension with corrugated iron roof and walls. Thanks to the installation of a flush toilet, the plumbing no longer needed to face the outer wall as in the days of manually cleaned vault toilets. Not content to cease expanding until it abutted against the lot line on all four sides, this house displayed a remarkable drive to propagate.

5th period: new construction and the end of growth (1982)

In 1982, when Takamizawa House was 29, a new house (known as the "annex") was built on the east side of the lot. Given that the average lifespan of a Japanese house is said to be 26 years, Takamizawa House was already fairly old. Accordingly interior improvements ceased and the house, it would seem, found it easier to propagate outside instead.

After the construction of the annex, however, the house stopped growing altogether; there would be no more expansion or reconstruction to speak of. In the context of the history of modern building methods, this cessation was in-

dicative of the shift from the traditional *shinkabe* method—which facilitated renovations like the lean-to extension, the insertion of large beams, and the stacking of floors by binding new pillars to old ones—to the *zairai* ("conventional") method of employing diagonal braces and *okabe*-style walls with no framework exposed, which did not lend itself to simple extensions and renovations.

By 1980, Japan's industrialization process was basically complete. The remaining half of Takamizawa House's life reflected the stabilization of Japanese society and its production system while the country entered a period of economic stagnation.

Some 40 years passed after the final "cell division" of Takamizawa House. By 2010 both of the shops had closed, but the house itself still stood quietly on its street corner, a surviving anachronism in a neighborhood that had continued to urbanize. In the summer of 2019 it was dismantled, bringing to an end 65 years of existence even as its value was finally being recognized.

3. The architect as a captain of industries

In this way, Takamizawa House gave itself over to the prevailing trend of modernization (i.e., contemporization) in housing—incorporating, one after the other, the industrial products developed and disseminated during Japan's economic boom years. In the process it lost the crispness and unity of the original building, instead acquiring a patina of factory-made elements as a different kind of order rooted in the lifestyle of its residents began to emerge on the inside. By the time Japan's high-growth period

イロ床に、床脇の木製窓は**アルミサッシュ**に段階的に変更されていった。とりわけ引き違いのアルミサッシュを床脇に対峙させた独特の床構えは、「伝統」と「近代」の見事な融合を示している。

第3期　〈再統合〉（1961）

　1959年、《高見澤邸》5歳のとき、東海・関東地方を**伊勢湾台風**が襲った。この家の北東を流れる河川（烏山川）が氾濫し、この家も床上10cmが浸水したという。この被害を受けて南側の住居部分——「オモヤ」（主屋）と呼ばれた——も、水害時の非難場所という**防災目的**もあって2階を増築することになり、1961年にその工事が行われた。正面の外壁（看板）は、このとき都市防火の点からモルタル塗につくり変えられた。

　その増築手法は、新設柱を既存柱に金物（鎹）で抱き合わせて2階までの**通し柱**を立て、主要柱と新設梁の接合部を火打ちや金物で補強するというものであった。南北で分離されていた当初の切妻屋根はこのとき再び統合された。南側の外壁は既存の下見板の上に波板鉄板を覆せて、当初の木質の外観から**金属的な外観**に一新された。内壁には、戦前の台湾製糖業で排出される大量のバガスを再利用して国内生産されるようになった**繊維ボード**の一種が用いられている。垂木はすべて新材に取り替えられたが、屋根瓦には既存のセメント瓦が再利用され、階段をつくり込むために既存の細い小屋梁に太い梁が**アクロバチック**に挿入された［図8］。

　この施工を行った地元の日下部工務所は、こうした2階増築の手法が当時一般的であったと話す。住宅が次々と「オカグラ」されていった周辺地域の、沸き立つような都市化の熱気が感じられる。

第4期　〈設備更新と増築〉（1978頃）

　1970年代になると**都市ガス**や**下水道**が整備されてい

8

Staircase beams in Takamizawa House (main house).
Photo by Naoyuki Matsumoto
《高見澤邸》(オモヤ) の階段梁、撮影：松本直之

1: HISTORY OF TAKAMIZAWA HOUSE

came to an end, Takamizawa House had made
the transition from a handicraft-based tradition-
al-modern home to a contemporary one emblematic of an industrialized society. It is, in fact,
a rare example of a house that provides a real,
not virtual, image of the vicissitudes of postwar
Japanese society. It merits the appellation "real
image" precisely because housing is like a mirror
that accurately reflects the lifestyles of ordinary
citizens—and because buildings are, in essence,
a composite of the various industries operating
in a society.

Takamizawa House epitomizes the vernac-
ular architecture of an industrialized society.
None of the changes it underwent involved
the participation of "architects." In the sense
of being "architectless" it may resemble the
"architecture without architects" written of
by Bernard Rudofsky,[*3] though not in the
sense of exhibiting residential forms and details
born of the collective wisdom of an indigenous
culture. Nonetheless it went through repeated
cycles of proliferation and renewal like a living
organism, expanding until it reached its limit.
In effect it metabolized in a manner not seen
in any of the works of "predetermined harmo-
ny" envisioned by the Metabolist architects of
the 1960s. Moreover, substructural elements
were added, in ad-hoc bricolage fashion, to the
surface of the original handcrafted house. This
metamorphosis, in which traditional and modern
(industrial) elements were cobbled together into
one entity, recalls the chimera of Greek mythol-
ogy, a hybrid creature composed of the parts
of several animals. If, in this building, we sense
something sublimely architectural, or perhaps
something exuding the vitality of a monstrous
creature, that is without doubt because there

Takamizawa House, 1955, 1966
(Photos from the collection of Kazuo Takamizawa)
《高見澤邸》1955年、1966年、高見澤一夫氏蔵

き、都市部から次第に公衆浴場が消えていった。周辺地域のそうした趨勢を反映し、《高見澤邸》は 1978 年にオモヤの東側を半間ほど増築しつつ、**システムキッチン**、**水洗便所**などの水廻りを更新し、**浴室**をつくった。増築手法は、既存柱に新設梁 2 材を挟み、外壁を外側に持ち送って既存柱を切断するという、やはりアクロバチックなものであった。

それと前後して、商店の開口部を**シャッター**に取り替えた。それまでの雨戸は鉄板貼り板戸 4 枚立てで、開け閉めの際には人力で南面に設置された戸袋に移動していたから、毎日の作業が大変であったという。その点、巻き上げ式のシャッターは機械仕掛けで手軽に柱間を全開放できる。周辺の商店も同じ頃に軒並みシャッターに変更していったという。

木製建具を**アルミサッシュ**に変えたのもこの頃で、日本の一般住宅にアルミサッシュが普及した時期とちょうど重なる。「**カールイ雨戸**」という商品名のサッシは雨戸・戸袋が一体化された製品で、重たい雨戸の日常的な開閉作業から解放された日本人の喜びに共感できる。

1980 年代になるとベツムネ（北側住居）にもシステムキッチンや浴室が導入され、その際に裏手にトタン屋根・トタン壁の下屋を出して増築した。水洗式便所に更新されたため、旧来の汲み取り式のように便所を外壁に面して配する必要がなくなったのである。四周の敷地境界ぎりぎりまで床面積の拡張を止めていない。この家の貪欲な**増殖意欲**に感心させられる。

第 5 期　〈新築と成長停止〉(1982)

1982 年、《高見澤邸》29 歳のとき、敷地の東側に「シンタク」（新宅）が新築された。設計・施工はオモヤの増築と同じ工務店である。日本の一般住宅の平均寿命は 26 年といわれているから、このとき《高見澤邸》はすでに相当な老年で、それゆえ内部での増殖を止めて、外に飛び出して増殖したわけである。

しかし、このシンタクの建設後は、増改築がほとんど行われず、成長が停止してしまった。それは、近代構法史の観点からみると、下屋の設置、大梁の挿入、柱抱合わせの「オカグラ」など、増改築が自在な真壁造りの「**伝統軸組構法**」が、大壁化しながら耐震の観点で筋かいの設置を進め、結果的に増改築が容易ではなくなった「**近代軸組構法**」に変化したことを意味している。

日本の産業工業化は 1980 年頃までにほぼ完了していた。それ以降のこの家の後半生には、**低成長時代**を迎えた日本社会と**生産システムの安定化**が反映しているようである。

《高見澤邸》が最後の細胞分裂を終えてから、およそ 40 年の歳月が流れた。2010 年頃までに商店はいずれも廃業し、周辺地域の都市的変化から取り残されながらも、街角にひっそりとたち続けていたが、2019 年夏にその価値が発見されるとともに解体され、長いようで短い 65 年の生涯を終えた。

3. 諸産業の統率者としての建築家

こうして庶民住宅の近代化（現代化）という大きな流れに身を委ねた《高見澤邸》には、建設以来、高度成長期に開発され普及した工業製品が次々と取り込まれていった。その過程で、オリジナルの建物がもっていた爽やかさや統一感を失いながら、その一方で住み手の生活に根ざした別の秩序を内部に生み出しつつ、高度成長が終焉する頃には、手工業にもとづく**伝統的な近代民家**から工場生産品で塗り固められた**工業化社会の現代民家**に変容していた。この家は、戦後日本の激動の社会を、虚像ではなく**実像**として映し出す稀有な住宅であろう。それがまさしく「実像」たりえる所以は、**住宅**が一般庶民の生活様式を如実に反映する鏡のような存在だからであり、建築がそもそも社会の諸産業の複合体だからである。

《高見澤邸》は、工業化社会の**バナキュラー建築**である。この家の変遷のなかには、どこにも「建築家」が関与

is no "architect" involved, however paradoxical that may sound.

A fresh look back at the history of architecture in Japan reveals that when new industries were introduced to ancient Japan from the Asian continent, a compromise was effected between them and indigenous traditional industries, giving birth to a new kind of architecture that no one had seen before. Even with artisans from the continent supervising the development of these new architecture-related industries, architectural production itself was a hybrid of new and old,[*4] and the actual manufacture was handled by indigenous artisans. The inevitable result was a style of architecture that differed from the continental architecture on which it was modeled (just as the "Western-style" architecture of the Meiji era was not identical to actual Western architecture). Moreover, architectural elements ranging from roof materials and designs to floors, ceilings, fittings, and fixtures all underwent modifications over the next several centuries. Though a second influx of new architectural styles during Japan's medieval period also had some impact, a uniquely simple, subdued domestic style known as *chusei wayo* ("medieval Japanese style"—early-modern artisans simply called it *Nihonyo*, "Japanese style") had already coalesced.

Indeed, we might say that "Japanese style" was defined by this process: acceptance of a chimera-like hybrid of disparate industries, followed by digestion and modification over time that ultimately yielded something completely different. What was "Japanese-style" if not the ingenuity of the artisans who refined diverse architectural elements, not to mention the sensibility of the bureaucrats, architects, and commoners who did not merely accept but applauded, without quibbling, the industrial chimera of the Asuka period (ca. 593–710), with its mix of disparate industries of varying national origins? Takamizawa House is proof that this same sensibility survives today.

Indeed, architecture could in this sense be said to derive from the reorganization, by architects, of an intermingling of industries from both within and without the architectural sector. If Japan had not already had its own Sue-ware pottery firing techniques when new roof tile technology was imported from the continent during the Asuka period, great temples would not have sprung up as they did throughout Japan's ancient cities. Likewise, if *washi* paper-making techniques had not been developed in the Heian period (794–1185), the *shoin-zukuri* style of residential architecture, to which *shoji* and *fusuma* sliding doors made with *washi* are central, would surely not have appeared a few centuries later at the beginning of the early-modern period. Nor should we forget the passion and tenacity of the architects of the 1950s, who created a new architecture utilizing technologies developed by the modern munitions industry. Throughout history, whenever a paradigm shift has occurred in the production system, architects have always invited diverse industries into the architectural fold, exercising both the principles and authority required of leaders in turbulent circumstances as they gave birth to a new era of architecture. Built without architects during the final phase of modernization, when industries became fully industrialized, Takamizawa House represents the reversal of that phenomenon, challenging us to contemplate what architecture is, and what an architect is.

The Chimera (CC BY-SA 3.0)
キメラ (CC BY-SA 3.0)

Kondo (main hall) of Horyuji temple (7th century).
Publish: Horyuji / Print: Benrido
《法隆寺金堂》(7世紀)
発行：法隆寺／印刷：便利堂

Tokuma Katayama, Akasaka Detached Palace (1909).
Source: State Guest Houses of Japan website
(https://www.geihinkan.go.jp/akasaka/about/)
片山東熊《赤坂離宮》(1909)
出典：内閣府迎賓館ウェブサイト
(https://www.geihinkan.go.jp/akasaka/about/)

していない。**建築家不在**という点では、バーナード・ルドフスキーの**「建築家なしの建築」**（※3）に近いが、土着文化が内包する民族学的叡智に裏打ちされた住居の形式や細部（ディテール）を表出しているわけでもない。しかし、まるで生命体のように絶えず**「増殖」**と**「更新」**を繰り返して限界まで膨れ上がり、結果としてみれば、1960年代の**メタボリズム**（メタボリ）の建築家たちによる（予定調和的な）どの作品よりも新陳代謝している。そして、オリジナルの手工業的民家の表面に、**二次部材**として更新されたエレメントが、場当たり感覚でこの家にブリコラージュされている。「伝統」と「近代（工業）」が異質同体化したその変身の様態は、ギリシア神話に登場する怪物**キメラ**をわれわれに連想させる。もしもこの建物に優れて建築的なもの、あるいは何か怪物じみた生命力のようなものを感じるとすれば、それは、逆説的ではあるが、「建築家」が不在であったからに相違ない。

　しかし、改めて日本の建築史を振り返ってみれば、古代日本では、大陸から導入された新規産業と既存の伝統的な産業が折衷されて、それまで誰も見たことがなかった新たな建築が生み出されていた。大陸より渡来した工人たちが建築関連の新規産業を指導していたとしても、建築生産は旧産業との混成体であったし（※4）、モノの生産自体は土着の職人の手によって行われたのだから、モデルとされた大陸の建築とは必然的に異質のものになっていたはずである（明治時代の**洋風建築**が西洋のそれとまったく同じではないように）。しかも、その後、数百年をかけて、屋根の素材や形状、床、天井、建具など、建物のさまざまな部分に改変が重ねられていき、中世になると再度流入した新様式にも間接的に影響されながら、穏やかで軽快な日本固有の様式（**中世和様**）――近世の工匠は「日本様」と呼んだ――が成立したのである。

　とすれば、産業が折衷されたキメラ的状態を一旦受け入れ、時間をかけてそれを咀嚼しながら改変し、最終的には別のものに昇華させてしまうのが「日本的」であったとはいえないか。各部に洗練を加えていった工匠たちの創

What will a new generation of architects—standard bearers of the architecture of the future—make of Takamizawa House? How will they incorporate the industrial continuum into their own designs?

Notes

*1 *Detail Special Issue: New Perspectives on Famous Postwar Houses*, issue no. 217, Shokokusha, July 2018

*2 Kakuei Tanaka, *Building a New Japan: A Plan for Remodeling the Japanese Archipelago*, Nikkan Kogyo Shimbun, Ltd., 1972

*3 Bernard Rudofsky, *Architecture Without Architects: A Short Introduction to Non-Pedigreed Architecture*, 1964 (Japanese translation published by Kajima Institute Publishing Co., Ltd., 1984)

*4 Yasutada Watanabe, *Research on the Organization of Japanese Architectural Production, 1959*, Meigensha, 2004

Note: The preceding discussion reflects the ideas of exhibition curator Kozo Kadowaki as well as the consensus of the research team that conducted the survey of the dismantled Takamizawa House. The team consists of the author and team leader (Ritsumeikan University), Naoyuki Matsumoto (University of Tokyo), and Tetsu Makino (Kenbun Co., Ltd.), assisted by Kimihito Ito (Master's Program, Meiji University). We also wish to express our immense gratitude to Kazuo Takamizawa and Eichi Kusakabe for their invaluable cooperation with the survey.

• Changes in the Urban Environment of Takamizawa House (pp. 36-37)
Aya Hiwatashi, text; Aya Hiwatashi, Kohei Tanaka (Hosei University), illustrations
• Changes in the Layout of Takamizawa House (pp. 38-39)
Norimasa Aoyagi, text; Makoto Isono and Kimihito Ito (Kozo Kadowaki Laboratory, Meiji University), Tetsu Makino, illustrations
• Changes in the Framework of Takamizawa House (pp. 40-41)
Norimasa Aoyagi, text; Firas Najah Hawasly and Go Nanzaki (Mikio Koshihara Laboratory, Tokyo University), Kimihito Ito, illustrations
• Changes in the Elements of Takamizawa House (pp. 42-45)
Naoyuki Matsumoto, text; Kimihito Ito, Firas Najah Hawasly, Go Nanzaki, illustrations

意もさることながら、出自の異なる異質の産業が混成されてできた**飛鳥時代の産業キメラ**を、違和感なく受け入れて拍手喝采できるような人々——官僚にせよ、庶民にせよ、建築家にせよ——の感覚がそもそも「日本的」なのであり、《高見澤邸》を見れば、それと同じ感覚が現代にも繋がっていることがよくわかる。

　建築とは、その一面において、**建築内外の多くの産業**が絡み合い、それらが「**建築家**」によって**再編成**されてはじめて成立するものであるといえるだろう。飛鳥時代に大陸から屋根瓦の新技術が輸入されたとき、日本に既存の須恵器焼成技術がなかったら、古代都市に大寺が林立することはなかったし、書くためのモノとして和紙の製造技術が平安時代に確立されていなかったら、障子や襖を前提とする書院造りは近世初期に成立しなかったはずである。同様に、近代の軍需産業で開発された技術を駆使して新しい建築を生み出した1950年代の建築家たちの情熱と執念を忘れるべきではない。歴史上の生産システム変革期において「**建築家**」は、いつも諸産業を建築界に招き入れつつ、混迷の状況下で**指導理念**と**統率力**を発揮し、新時代の建築を生み出してきたのである。産業が一気に工業化していった近代化の最終局面において、「建築家」が終始不在であった《高見澤邸》は、その逆像として、われわれに「建築」とは何か、「建築家」とは何者かを考えさせてくれる。

　さて、未来の新建築の担い手たる建築家たちは、この《高見澤邸》をどのように解釈し、自らの創作のうちに産業の連鎖をどのようにデザインしようとしているのであろうか。

註
※1——『ディテール　特集＝戦後名住宅の新しい見方』217号（彰国社、2018年7月）
※2——田中角栄『日本列島改造論』（日刊工業新聞社、1972）
※3——バーナード・ルドフスキー『建築家なしの建築』（鹿島出版会、1984／原著＝1964）
※4——渡邊保忠『日本建築生産組織に関する研究 1959』（明現社、2004）

付記
本稿の主旨は、本展キュレーター門脇耕三氏の着想、およびリサーチ・チームの総意にもとづくものである。《高見澤邸》解体調査を行ったリサーチ・チームのメンバーは、青柳憲昌（立命館大学、統括）、松本直之（東京大学）、牧野徹（建文・建築文化研究所）であり、伊藤公人（明治大学修士課程）がそれを補佐した。また、本調査への多大な協力を賜った高見澤一夫氏、日下部栄一氏には心より謝意を表したい。

・《高見澤邸》の周辺都市の変遷（36−37項）
　テキスト：樋渡彩
　作図：樋渡彩＋田中航平（法政大学）
・《高見澤邸》の間取りの変遷（38−39項）
　テキスト：青柳憲昌
　作図：牧野徹＋磯野信（明治大学門脇耕三研究室）＋伊藤公人（同）
・《高見澤邸》の軸組の変遷（40−41項）
　テキスト：青柳憲昌
　作図：伊藤公人＋フィラース・ナジャーフ・ハワースリー（東京大学腰原幹雄研究室）＋呉南崎（同）
・《高見澤邸》のエレメントの変遷（42−45項）
　テキスト：松本直之
　作図：伊藤公人＋フィラース・ナジャーフ・ハワースリー＋呉南崎

Changes in the Urban Environment of Takamizawa House
《高見澤邸》の周辺都市の変遷

During the Edo period (1603-1867) this area flourished as a suburban farming village. Housing began to proliferate here after the Odakyu Line opened in 1927 with two stations in the area, Kyodo and Chitose-Funabashi. The neighborhood of Takamizawa House is located midway between these stations, so it was still relatively pastoral in the 1930s [Fig. 2-a]. The Karasuyama Canal flowed through it from west to east, and rice paddies filled the low-lying areas, interspersed with woodlands. A Shinto shrine dating back to the 16th century stood on the high ground.

Residential construction took off in Tokyo after World War II, and this was true in Kyodo as well [Fig. 1-b]. A north-south road was built in front of the shrine, and the farmlands became factories and public housing. Lining the street near the shrine were a public bathhouse, a barber shop, a tofu shop, a soba shop, and a drugstore (in Takamizawa House), forming a small but thriving commercial district in the 1960s [Fig. 2-b].

As the center of commercial activity gradually shifted from the shrine to the area around Kyodo station, the shops were converted one by one into residences. This trend was already underway in the 1980s. Today single-family dwellings are joined by growing numbers of apartment houses and hybrid office-residence units [Fig. 2-c], and many are being replaced by apartments for singles.

江戸時代からこの地域は近郊農村として農業が発展していた。1927年、小田急線開通により経堂駅と千歳船橋駅が置かれると、その周辺の住宅開発が進められる。《高見澤邸》周辺は両駅の中間点にあることから、1930年代はまだのどかな風景の広がる一帯であった[図2-a]。烏山用水が西から東に流れ、低地部分には水田が広がり、雑木林が点在していた。高台には16世紀起源の神社が立地している。第二次世界大戦後、本格的な住宅開発に乗り出し、経堂も開発が進められた[図1-b]。ここでは神社の前面に南北に貫く道が敷かれ、農地は工場、都営住宅に変貌した。神社周辺には、銭湯、散髪屋、豆腐屋、そば屋、薬屋《高見澤邸》などが建ち並び、1960年代には商店街になるほど賑わいのある通りとなった[図2-b]。
次第に賑わいの中心が神社から駅前に移るようになると、店舗は徐々に専用住宅へと切り替わっていった。その兆しはすでに1980年代には始まり、現在では、戸建ての専用住宅から、集合住宅、そして事務所を併設した住宅も増えている[図2-c]。また、単身者向けアパートへの建て替えも進んでいる。

1930s

Fig. 1   Transition of Tokyo's urbanization
図1   東京の市街地化の変遷

a

■■ Densely inhabited area / 人口集中地区

Fig. 2   Changes in land and building use around Takamizawa House
図2   《高見澤邸》周辺の土地利用および建物用途変遷

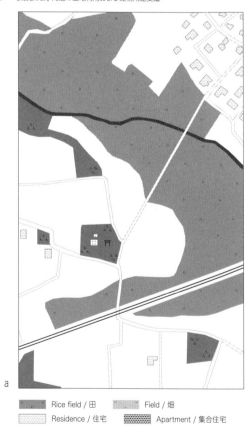

a

Rice field / 田   Field / 畑
Residence / 住宅   Apartment / 集合住宅

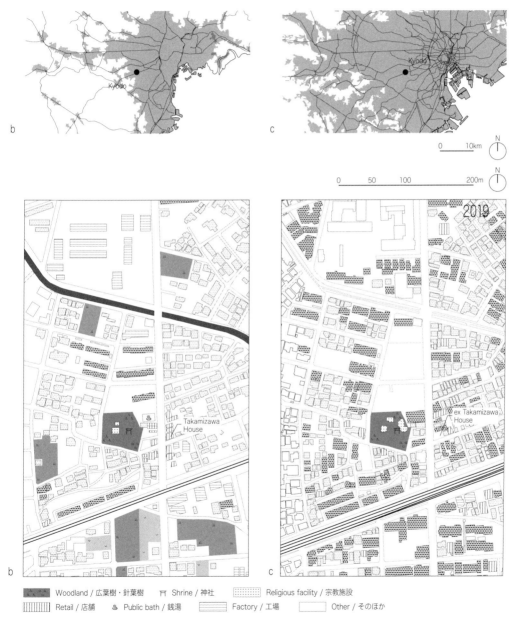

1960   2015

2019

Woodland / 広葉樹・針葉樹   卄 Shrine / 神社   Religious facility / 宗教施設
Retail / 店舗   ♨ Public bath / 銭湯   Factory / 工場   Other / そのほか

Takamizawa House

ex Takamizawa House

Kyodo

1: HISTORY OF TAKAMIZAWA HOUSE

Changes in the Layout of Takamizawa House
《高見澤邸》の間取りの変遷

1st Period: A wooden, single-story example of "billboard architecture" with space for a shop in front. The shop area was divided in two, north and south, during construction. The single-unit living quarters had two tatami-floored rooms and a wet area in back.

2nd Period: The north-side shop was extended in front, and its ownership changed. In 1957 the living quarters were also divided, with the north side (branch house) ground floor covered in PVC tile and a second floor added with a staircase in back. Low-silled windows were installed in the billboard-wall façade, which was soon extended to form a sunroom partitioned by *shoji* screens.

3rd Period: After ground-floor flooding in a 1959 typhoon, a second floor was also added to the main house in 1961, with the roofs of the two halves of the house restored to a single gable roof. The billboard wall was given a mortar finish and the south wall clapboards were covered with corrugated iron.

4th Period: The main house was extended in back in 1978 for a new wet area with bath. Metal shutters were installed over the storefronts, and aluminum sashes were inserted in the wooden window frames. In the 1980s a corrugated-iron lean-to was added to the back of the branch house to hold a new wet area.

5th Period: An annex was built on the east side in 1982, after which there was no further significant growth. The second-floor overhang of the annex nearly touched the main house, forming an outdoor corridor below.

第1期: 木造平屋建ての「看板建築」。前面土間部分を店舗とする「前土間型」の平面である。建設中に店舗が2分割され、店舗部分は南北に仕切られていた(回り縁痕跡などより考察)。生活部分は6畳・4畳半の続きの和室と、その奥の水廻りからなるひとつの住まいであった(南北境の旧鴨居や6畳天井上の旧棹縁天井などより)。

第2期: 北側店舗の正面が下屋で拡張された(張出し側面に引違い窓が残存)。同時期に所有権が分割・売却され、1957年に居住部にも南北境の壁がたてられた。ベツムネ1階は塩ビタイル貼りの土間であった(初期のPタイルが床下に残置)。また、裏手に階段を設けて2階が増築された。2階座敷西面には既存の「看板」に肘掛け窓を設けたが、まもなく2階正面を増築してサンルームをつくり明かり障子がたてられた(柱の痕跡や風蝕などより)。

第3期: 伊勢湾台風(1959)の水害を受けて、1961年にオモヤも2階を増築することになった。この時までオモヤの当初屋根をそのまま延ばしてベツムネ2階の外壁と納めてあったが(垂木掛けの痕跡より)、この増築によって切妻屋根が再び一体化された。「看板」をモルタル塗に変え、南側外壁は既存の下見板の上に波板鉄板が覆せられた(当初下見板が部分的に残置)。

第4期: 1978年にオモヤの東側を増築し、水廻りを更新して浴室がつくられた。同時期に商店の開口部はシャッターに取り替えられた。既存の木製窓の敷鴨居にアルミサッシが挿入された。1980年代にはベツムネ裏手にトタン貼り屋根・壁の下見を出して水廻りが更新された(トイレ外部木製ドアが残置)。

第5期: 1982年、シンタクが新築された。その後は増改築がほとんど行われず、成長が停止してしまった。シンタクは2階をオーバーハングさせて外部通路を取りつつ、南棟の外壁にぎりぎりまで近接している。

1954

1st period
<Construction>

第1期
〈建設〉

ca.1957

2nd period
<Proliferation and subdivision>

第2期
〈増殖と分裂〉

2F PLAN 1:300

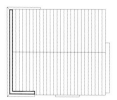

1. Tatami room 2. *Tokonoma*
3. *Tana* 4. Sunroom
1. 和室 2. 床の間 3. 棚
4. サンルーム

1F PLAN 1:300

Addition/renovation
増築部

オモヤ / Main house
ベツムネ / Branch house

オモヤ / Main house

1. Pharmacy 2. Beauty parlor
3. Tatami room 4. Kitchen
5. Toilet 6. Entrance
7. Closet 8. Storeroom
1. 薬店 2. 美容室 3. 和室 4. 台所
5. トイレ 6. 玄関 7. 押入 8. 納戸

1. Pharmacy 2. Sweets shop
3. Tatami room 4. Kitchen
5. Toilet 6. Entrance
7. Closet
1. 薬店 2. 菓子店 3. 和室 4. 台所
5. トイレ 6. 玄関 7. 押入

038

3rd period
<Reunification>

第 3 期
〈再統合〉

4th period
<Renewal and expansion>

第 4 期
〈設備更新と増築〉

5th period
<New construction and the end of growth>

第 5 期
〈新築と成長停止〉

1. Tatami room 2. *Tokonoma*
3. *Tana* 4. Sunroom 5. Closet
6. Storeroom

1. 和室 2. 床の間 3. 棚 4. サンルーム 5. 押入
6. 納戸

1. Tatami room 2. *Tokonoma*
3. *Tana* 4. Sunroom
5. Closet 6. Storeroom 7. Terrace

1. 和室 2. 床の間 3. 棚 4. サンルーム 5. 押入
6. 納戸 7. テラス

1. Tatami room 2. *Tokonoma*
3. *Tana* 4. Sunroom 5. Closet
6. Storeroom 7. Terrace 8. Western-style room

1. 和室 2. 床の間 3. 棚 4. サンルーム 5. 押入
6. 納戸 7. テラス 8. 洋室

シンタク / Annex

1. Pharmacy 2. Sweets shop
3. Tatami room 4. Kitchen
5. Toilet 6. Entrance
7. Closet 8. Storeroom

1. 薬店 2. 菓子店 3. 和室 4. 台所 5. トイレ
6. 玄関 7. 押入

1. Pharmacy 2. Sweets shop
3. Tatami room 4. Kitchen
5. Toilet 6. Entrance
7. Closet 8. Bath

1. 薬店 2. 菓子店 3. 和室 4. 台所 5. トイレ
6. 玄関 7. 押入 8. 浴室

1. Pharmacy 2. Sweets shop 3. Tatami room
4. Kitchen 5. Toilet 6. Entrance
7. Closet 8. Storeroom 9. Bath
10. Western-style room

1. 薬店 2. 菓子店 3. 和室 4. 台所 5. トイレ
6. 玄関 7. 押入 8. 浴室 9. 洋室

1: HISTORY OF TAKAMIZAWA HOUSE

Changes in the Framework
of Takamizawa House
《高見澤邸》の軸組の変遷

1954

1982-2019

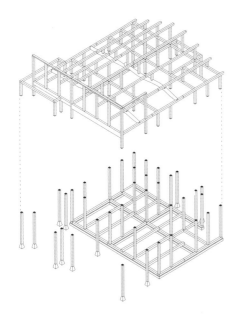

1st period: <Modern house>
Craftsmanship-based building production

第 1 期：〈近代民家〉
クラフツマンシップに支えられた建築生産

5th period and later: <Contemporary house>
Industrialized, component-based building production

第 5 期以降：〈現代民家〉
工業化・部品化が進展した建築生産

Japanese houses were once built using a "traditional framework" composed of wooden pillars, beams, and roof trusses. The walls were no more than secondary members, allowing for the decorative *shinkabe* style of plastered walls with exposed pillars between which lightweight, mobile fittings could be inserted. This design added flexibility to the overall structure. One could freely extend the original frame simply by adding on to the pillars and beams, which were also easy to replace since their connecting joints were not rigid.

On the other hand, more walls naturally enhanced resistance to earthquakes. In the modern era the frequency of earthquakes in Japan was addressed by making walls thicker and inserting diagonal braces. The addition of bracing became increasingly standardized as structural technology improved, and its design gradually changed as well, partly as a consequence of the Great Kanto Earthquake of 1923. With the end of the postwar economic boom, the *shinkabe* style gave way to the *okabe* style of plastering over the wood frame. The less flexible walls deprived structures of their previous adaptability to extension and renovation, transforming the "traditional framework" system into the more rigid "modern framework" system.

Built in 1954, Takamizawa House was subjected over time to a remarkable number of additions, replacements, and alterations that eminently demonstrate the inherent flexibility of "traditional framework" construction. First, the facade of the branch house was extended, and in 1957 it was given a second floor by raising the entire roof frame atop new pillars erected directly above the old ones. The original house had lacked bracing, but now braces were added, in incomplete fashion, to the remodeled sections. Then, in 1961, tall pillars were raised alongside the pillars of the main house and new beams laid across them to support a second floor, with extra-thick beams inserted where the greatest load was concentrated. Later, in 1978, beams were passed through the pillars at the back of the house and the pillars relocated outward to form an extension. Virtually no further expansion or renovation took place after an annex was built in 1982 by the *zairai* ("conventional") method of modern framework construction exemplified by the *okabe* style.

日本の住宅は、柱・梁・小屋組（屋根）で構成される「伝統軸組構法」という軸組システムでつくられていた。壁は二次的要素にすぎず、意匠的には柱が現れる真壁造りとなり、柱と柱のあいだには、軽量で動かしやすい建具が入れられる。「壁」の簡便さはシステムの柔軟性を生み、梁と柱を継ぎ足せば、既存の軸組を自由自在に増築できるし、接合部も固定的なものではないから、既存の柱や梁を交換して改築することも難しくない。

　一方で、「壁」が多いほうが耐震上有利であることも当然である。日本には地震が多いため、近代になるとその点が意識され、壁を厚くしてその中に筋かいを入れるようになる。筋かいの入れ方は、構造技術の発達に伴って次第に合理化されるとともに、意匠的にも緩やかに変容し、関東大震災（1923）をひとつの契機として意匠的にも緩やかに変容し、戦後の高度経済成長後の日本住宅は真壁造りから大壁造りに変化した。それは、増改築が自在であった軸組システムが、堅い壁の増加とともに柔軟性を失い、「近代軸組構法」という固定的な軸組システムに変化したことを意味している。

　《高見澤邸》（1954）の軸組には、じつに多くの部材の継ぎ足し、交換、移動が行われており、「伝統軸組構法」が本来もっていた柔軟性がよく発揮されている。まず、ベツムネの正面が増築されて、柱の直上に新しい柱が継ぎ足され、既存の小屋組はその上に持ち上げられた（1957頃）。当初は筋かいがなかったが、この時の改造部には、未成熟なかたちで筋かいが入れられた。次いで、オモヤの柱の脇に背の高い柱を添え、新しい梁を架けて、荷重が集中する部分に太い梁を挿入した（1961）。さらに、住宅裏手の既存柱を梁で挟んで固定し、柱の位置を外側に移動した（1978）。その後、大壁が卓越する「近代軸組在来構法」でつくられたシンタク（1982）には、増改築がほとんど見られない。

041 1: HISTORY OF TAKAMIZAWA HOUSE

Changes in the Elements
of Takamizawa House
《高見澤邸》の軸組の変遷

1954

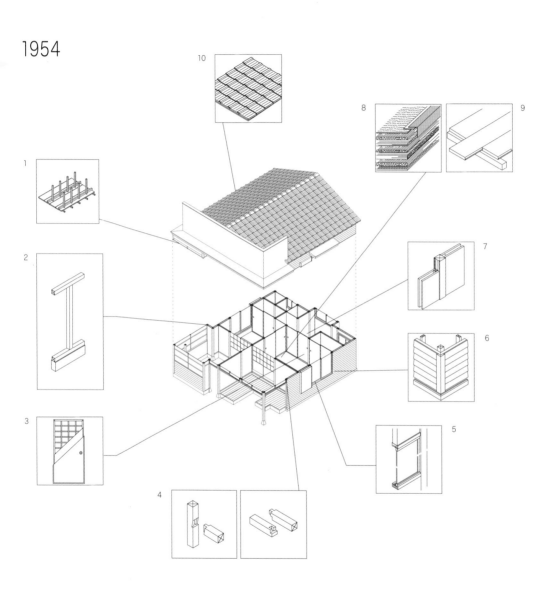

1st period: <Modern house>
Craftsmanship-based building production

第 1 期：〈近代民家〉
クラフツマンシップに支えられた建築生産

1. Board and batten ceiling
Type of ceiling used in Japanese-style rooms, with thin ceiling boards laid over narrow crosspieces.

2. Wood frame construction
Traditional structure of wooden columns and beams connected by hand-cut joints. In modern structures braces are added to improve earthquake resistance.

3. *Fusuma* (sliding screen)
Sliding doors made of a wooden lattice covered with thick paper.

4. *Tsugite · Shiguchi*
(Japanese joinery)
Straight and angled joints used to connect members in wood-frame structures, traditionally hand-made by highly skilled artisans.

5. Wooden sash
Wooden sashes holding glass panes became common in Japanese houses with the increased use of glass in the early 1900s.

6. *Shitami-itabari* (wood siding)
Exterior siding made of long overlapping wooden clapboards.

7. Plywood
Plywood was used in prewar construction, but only became widespread after the war with the availability of improved veneer adhesives.

8. *Enko-ita* (strip wood flooring)
Long, thick boards came into popular use for flooring with the proliferation of machining before the war.

9. Traditional tatami matting
Traditional mat-style flooring with woven rush-grass facing atop a bed of rice straw.

10. Cement roof tile
Roof tiles made of cement replaced traditional fired-clay tiles, sometimes with asbestos added for reinforcement.

1. 竿縁天井
細い横木をならべ、その上に薄い天井板を載せた、和室に一般的に用いられる天井形式。

2. 木造軸組
手刻みの接合部によって柱梁を組み合わせてつくる伝統的な建築構造。近代以降は、筋かいなどにより耐震化が図られた。

3. 襖
木製格子の骨組に和紙を貼ってつくった引き戸。

4. 継手・仕口
木造建築の部材同士のジョイント。伝統的には手刻みでつくられ、細工的な工夫が凝らされる。

5. 木製サッシュ
ガラスをはめた木製のサッシュは、大正時代にガラスの普及とともに日本の住宅に広まった。

6. 下見板張り
木製の横長の板を下から互いに重なるように固定した外壁構造。

7. 合板
合板は戦前から建築に使われていたが、ベニヤを貼り合わせる接着剤の進歩によって戦後に本格的に普及した。

8. 縁甲板
厚手で長尺の床用の板材。機械加工の普及に伴って、板床構法として戦前から広く普及した。

9. 畳（藁床）
稲藁を縫い重ねた畳床に、藺草でできた畳表を被せてつくる伝統的なマット状の床材。

10. セメント瓦（厚形スレート）
伝統的な焼き物の瓦をセメント材料で置換したもの。石綿を混入して補強することもあった。

pp. 42, 44
Illustration sources/references:
Yoshichika Uchida, ed.,Takashi Ono + Takuro Yoshida + Seiichi Fukao + Yasuhide Segawa, Building *Construction Methods* (5th edition), Ichigaya Publishing, 2007
Illustrated Building Construction Dictionary Editorial Committee, *Illustrated Dictionary of Building Construction*, Shokokusha Publishing, 2001

42、44項
図版引用・参考：
内田祥哉編著、大野隆司＋吉田倬郎＋深尾精一＋瀬川康秀著『建築構法（第五版）』（市ヶ谷出版社、2007）
建築図解事典編集委員会編『図解事典 建築のしくみ』（彰国社、2001）

1: HISTORY OF TAKAMIZAWA HOUSE

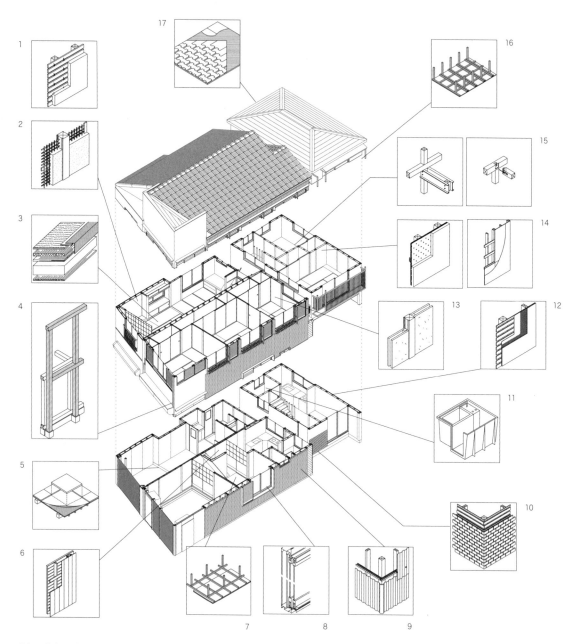

5th period and later: <Contemporary house>
Industrialized, component-based building production

第 5 期以降：〈現代民家〉
工業化・部品化が進展した建築生産

1. Lath and plaster
Construction method of laying plaster atop thin wooden boards spaced slightly apart. Imported from the West, it became common in postwar Japanese housing.

2. Mud wall
Traditional wall construction method of coating a woven-bamboo lath with mud, no longer used in standard housing once board substrates came into use after the war.

3. Industrialized tatami matting
Tatami manufacture became industrialized after the war, replacing traditional materials with plastic foam padding and PVC facing.

4. Extension of wood frame
Frequent extensions and renovations are the norm for Japanese wooden houses; the frame of Takamizawa House underwent several extensions.

5. Plastic floor tile
Floor covering of PVC tile, production of which soared in response to high demand from postwar occupation forces, leading to its use in Japanese houses.

6. Printed plywood
Plywood printed with wood-grain patterns became popular after the war as a finish for walls and ceilings.

7. Insulation fiberboard
Board made of glued wood fibers was manufactured after the war using waste materials.

8. Aluminum sash
Aluminum sashes for residential use went on the market in 1961, becoming a standard feature of housing construction in the 1960s.

9. Corrugated galvanized iron
Iron sheeting for residential roofs and exterior walls became common as a result of its use in temporary housing after the Great Kanto Earthquake of 1923.

10. Exterior wall tile
First popular on the exteriors of reinforced-concrete buildings, ceramic tiles began to appear on wooden houses in the 1960s.

11. Unit bath
Prefabricated bath units made of plastic

12. Metal lath and wall cement
Exterior wall construction method of covering a metal-mesh lath with cement, favored as a way to fireproof wooden houses.

13. Fiberboard
Board made of waste plant fiber was first produced domestically before the war, but remained popular in the postwar era.

14. Plasterboard
Plasterboard (drywall) was used as backing for plaster-finished walls in the 1960s, but as plastering fell out of favor, drywall coated with vinyl wallpaper became the norm.

15. Steel woodwork joint
After the war, joints in wood-frame structures were reinforced by steel members to improve aseismic performance.

16. Unitized panel ceiling
Ceilings made in wooden-panel units that retained the look of traditional ceilings proliferated with the mass production of housing in the 1960s.

17. Artificial slate
Made of cement, this flat roofing material became common in the 1960s after the technology was introduced from the United States.

1. 木摺漆喰
隙間をあけて並べた小幅の板に漆喰を塗りつける構法。もともとは欧米の構法だが、戦後は一般の住宅にも普及した。

2. 土壁
竹を編んだ下地に土を塗りつけた伝統的な壁の構法。戦後にボード下地が普及すると一般の住宅からは姿を消した。

3. 畳（化学畳床）
戦後には畳の工業化が進んだ。発泡プラスチック製の畳床や、塩化ビニル製の畳表など、化学製品への置き換えが試みられ、普及した。

4. 軸組の増築
日本の木造住宅では増改築は日常茶飯事で、《髙見澤邸》の軸組もさまざまに増築された。

5. 塩ビタイル（P タイル）
塩化ビニル樹脂製の床仕上げ材。戦後、進駐軍からの大量受注を機に本格的な製造が開始され、その後広く普及した。

6. プリント合板
木目が印刷された合板。天井や壁の仕上げとして戦後に広く普及した。

7. インシュレーションボード
木の繊維を接着剤で固めてつくったボード。戦後、廃材を原料として生産が開始された。

8. アルミサッシ
1961 年に住宅用アルミサッシが発売され、1960 年代に一般に定着した。

9. 波形鉄板
住宅の屋根や外壁に使用される。関東震災後のバラック建設で用いられ、その後一般の建物にも普及した。

10. タイル張り
もともとは RC 造の建築外装として普及したが、1960 年代以降、木造住宅にも使用されるようになった。

11. ユニット浴室
浴室をプレファブ化したプラスチック製品。

12. ラスモルタル
金属製の網（ラス）にセメントを塗って仕上げる外壁構法。木造住宅の防火のために普及した。

13. 繊維板
廃植物の繊維を原料とするボード。戦前に国産化に成功し、戦後も大量に生産された。

14. ラスボード＋左官、石膏ボード＋壁紙
1960 年代に左官壁の下地として普及したが、手間がかかる左官壁も少なくなり、その後は石膏ボードにビニルクロスを貼る仕上げが一般化した。

15. 鋼製挟み梁、羽子板金物
耐震性能を高めるため、戦後になると軸組の接合部は鋼製の部材で補強されるようになった。

16. 敷目板パネル天井
伝統的な天井の雰囲気を残しながら、パネルを用いたユニット化した天井。住宅が大量に建設されるようになった 1960 年代以降、急速に広まった。

17. 人工（化粧）スレート
セメント製のフラットな屋根葺材。戦後、アメリカから技術導入され、1960 年代に定着した。

1: HISTORY OF TAKAMIZAWA HOUSE

Planning Meeting Dialogues
企画会議的対話

確固たるコンセプトがまずあって、何をなすべきかを明確にしていく。展覧会は、一般的にはこのように計画される。しかし本展で先立っていたのは、日本の住宅をヴェネチアまで移動することであり、展覧会の主題は、開催までのアドホックなプロセスそのものにある。だとするならば、ここで行われることの意味は、むしろだんだんと、事後的に明らかになってくるのだろうし、展覧会のコンセプトを鍛え上げるプロセスも、もっと開くことができるのではないか。そのように考えて、外部からの識者をお招きした企画会議を実施することにした。

企画会議に参加してくださったのは、土居義岳、千葉雅也、大黒岳彦、國分功一郎の各氏であり、このカタログには、和文で約1万字の記事と、それを半分に抄訳した英文を対話の記録として収録した。結果的に、ここで交わされた膨大な対話は、展覧会のコンセプトばかりではなく、展示計画にも反映されることになったが、その結末は、展覧会開幕後に、ぜひ読者自身の目で確かめていただきたい。

Exhibitions are typically planned by starting with a firmly established concept, then figuring out how to bring it to fruition. This exhibition, on the other hand, was predicated on the transport of a Japanese house to Venice, and its theme is none other than the ad hoc process that will have transpired between that event and the show's opening. Consequently the meaning of the undertaking seems likely to reveal itself over time, and not in full until after the fact. In that case, we thought, we should make the process of refining the exhibition concept an open-ended one as well. It was with this in mind that we invited a number of eminent thinkers outside our team to join in our planning meetings.

Our guest participants were Yoshitake Doi, Masaya Chiba, Takehiko Daikoku, and Koichiro Kokubun. In this catalog, our dialogues with them take up some 10,000 characters of Japanese text, with the English translation abridged to about half that length. Those wide-ranging discussions ultimately had an impact that extended beyond the concept of the exhibition to its actual planning. We hope readers will judge the results with their own eyes when the show opens.

Eclecticism, the Ordinary, Authenticity
Yoshitake Doi (Architectural historian)

With: Kozo Kadowaki (Architect and construction studies)
+ Ryoko Iwase (Architecture and landscape)+ Toshikatsu Kiuchi (Architect)
+ Daisuke Motogi (Architect)

Layers of time in Japanese houses

Kozo Kadowaki: Takamizawa House, the structure we dismantled for this project, was built in Tokyo in 1954 as a single-story residence, but it underwent repeated extensions and additions into the early 1980s. This period happened to coincide with revolutionary changes in construction methods in Japan, as well as changes in the city of Tokyo itself.

There are two topics we would like to discuss with you, Professor Doi. One is "Japanese-style eclecticism." There are many examples of eclecticism throughout Japan's history—the Japanese are said to be relatively receptive to influences from other cultures. It's my feeling that this tendency is not unrelated to the circumstances of Takamizawa House, in the sense that the house seems to have very naturally absorbed the grafting of industrial products onto a traditional wooden structure. I would hypothesize that this phenomenon is emblematic of the "Japanese-style eclecticism" of postwar housing. The second topic is the meaning of this process of dismantling a building and rebuilding it in different configurations. From a Western viewpoint that prizes authenticity, this action of ours—pulling apart an actual house, shipping it elsewhere and reassembling it into entirely different structures—may well appear quite provocative. I would like to hear your views on how we can find positive meaning in this action.

Yoshitake Doi: Homes in advanced nations are mostly rented, but Japan's postwar housing policy promoted home ownership as a goal for the average citizen. The establishment of the Housing Loan Corporation in 1950 to further this goal effectively defined the structure of Japan's construction industry. Land was subdivided, becoming a salable product, and the industry was subdivided into specialties as well, creating a huge market.

The concept of public housing, or "social housing," emerged in Western Europe before the Russian Revolution. Up through the 19th century housing construction—for detached homes as well as apartments—was a private industry. But early in the 20th century, a housing crisis triggered by failed rent policies and population growth led to the establishment of public corporations and direct financing by governments. That was the beginning of public housing, which is linked to the advent of modern architecture. A supply model for Western-style housing was created in Japan with the formation of the Japan Housing Corporation in 1955. This public housing was expected to provide what was later called the "civil minimum"—gas, electricity, water, and basic sanitary facilities, i.e. a shower and flush toilet. The inexpensive, efficient construction and production methods that made this possible originated with the social-welfare policies of the period after World War I.

1: HISTORY OF TAKAMIZAWA HOUSE

Based on this reading of the history of Japanese housing, we may first analyze Takamizawa House in terms of developments in the construction industry. As it underwent repeated extensions and renovations, the house reflected the rational methods and materials of the time. Simultaneously, it represents the cumulative history of the era, the neighborhood, the city at large, and the family living there. In other words, this one structure contains multiple layers of time imprinted with the greater part of the history of housing production in postwar Japan. Generally speaking, buildings in other countries are built just once, so a single house could be said to embody one particular era or spirit. By contrast, even the most ordinary single-unit dwellings in Japan contain multiple layers, and I think it's fascinating that we can actually study the cause-and-effect relationships among these layers.

In pondering the meaning of "dismantling a building and rebuilding it in a different configuration," it occurs to me that, first of all, Takamizawa House strikes a happy balance between "ordinary" and "peculiar." In this respect the house is the perfect starting point for a discussion of Japanese materiality. We could say, for example, something like "You may think that Japanese materiality consists of wood—but in fact, there are many different interpretations of what constitutes 'wood'."

Kadowaki: For the purposes of this exhibition we're using the word "elements" to describe objects that are neither "materials" that can be worked into any kind of shape, nor "parts" that are themselves finished products. We decided to use "elements" to describe those in-between objects that come with various kinds of information attached.

Doi: That raises an issue I'd like to consider. Modern architecture is said to have begun with Joseph Paxton's iron-and-glass Crystal Palace in 1851. That's only partly an exaggeration, one that contains a truth: from the prevailing perspective, the history of modern architecture originates with materials. We cannot ignore the fact that it is the potential in materials that gave birth to technology and its aesthetics. To alter this geometry, we must adopt a different perspective through which we reinterpret how the materiality we call "wood" has been defined in Japan. Insofar as conventional interpretations of objects have been extremely simplistic and are ripe for reassessment, I think that offering the perspective of "elements" is of great value as our next step.

A non-European model with multiple time axes

Doi: I should add that modern architecture tends to be based on a technological determinism. The idea that materials like concrete and steel gave birth to functionalist designs in which technology trumps art is a simplistic perspective that treats materials as mere specifications. When objects become complex and layered, they acquire a logic of their own and are no longer simply layers of objects. Emile Durkheim declared that while people create society, a society is not formed by adding one person at a time. In other words, he believed that sociology must analyze human groups not as the sum of their parts, but as a new, different order. The same can surely be said of architecture. What I find intriguing about this project is the potential this process of reassembling dismantled elements offers to reveal ideas and plans for new configurations and to enable the creation of entirely different structures from the same elements. I would like to see what sort of new order architecture might acquire through iterations of the process of breaking a structure down into elements and reassembling them.

Kadowaki: My thoughts exactly. Takamizawa House, too, represents an accumulation of objects that acquired its own order, but underwent repeated changes because it lacked the underlying unity that a human actor like an architect might impose on it. Lack of a unifying actor is a characteristic of pre-modern architecture as well. One of the themes of this exhibition is the question of what to make of changes of this sort.

Ryoko Iwase: Professor Doi, what is your thinking about the point of divergence between "materials" and "elements"? I am interested in the crossover capacity of materials at the stage before they become elements.

Doi: Do you mean in the sense that steel can become a building or an automobile? Such distinctions don't exist at the blast-furnace stage, but emerge in the process of turning the steel into a product. We could say that a building is already emerging when that turning point is reached. According to the 19th-century German architect Gottfried Semper, human encounters with materials like wood and iron gave birth to crafts appropriate to the properties of those materials, and these developed into technologies. This was part of Semper's theorization of the British construction industry following the Industrial Revolution, in which he systematically analyzed the correlation between various crafts and industrial fields.

Before the reconfiguration process begins, you will have all sorts of elements laid out in the warehouse at the Venice site, and I expect those will metamorphose into pre-construction materials. How will you handle them?

Kadowaki: Though we will be breaking the building down into its elements, we wish to avoid returning them to the state of raw materials. For example, we don't intend to turn a floorboard back into a mere piece of lumber to be used for an entirely different component.

Toshikatsu Kiuchi: We will not be using Takamizawa House just as a source of materials. Rather, the reconfiguration process will be based on the sorting out of information at various levels associated with architecture. For instance, if we notice that the house mixes unpainted materials with painted materials in a certain ratio, we may take that as information giving visible form to the daily life-history of Takamizawa House, and attempt to achieve approximately the same overall ratio in the finished reconfigurations at the Venice site. In this way we may be able to create environmental textures that would not emerge were it not for the information embedded in Takamizawa House.

Kadowaki: Another intriguing aspect of Takamizawa House is the way in which its elements are worked. For example, we can observe the care that went into making the joints and fittings in the original sections that utilized traditional techniques, but the sections added later exhibit a somewhat more haphazard approach. They do not achieve a smooth fit with the older sections. On the other hand they appear to employ newer, more complex configurations.

Doi: In the 1950s there were carpenters in every neighborhood, and their traditional techniques dated back to before the war. By the 1980s, though, those techniques had been lost, replaced by new technologies that have a certain refinement, but they cut themselves off from any tradition of techniques.

In the European countryside you can find many houses containing layers on different temporal axes. There are two models used in Europe for unifying these disparate strata, the organic model and the mechanical model. With the organic model you seamlessly connect different layers together. The iron structures of the 19th century and the high-tech structures of a century later are remarkably compatible. With the mechanical model, you have stone structures and iron structures in contrastive configurations. But in Japan you find a layering approach that follows neither of these models. It would be interesting to clarify the logic of that approach.

Is architecture relying on transport ordinary for Venice?

Iwase: Our planning for this exhibition began with the question, "In an era when we can obtain any kind of information anytime, anywhere, what is the meaning of intentionally holding an exhibition in Venice?" I hope we can create an exhibition of the entire system of actions associated with "making" something along a temporal axis, including the acts of dismantling, transporting, and building. However, we are still at the stage of searching for that meaning.

Doi: The act of "sending" itself is a strategic approach vis-à-vis the Venice Biennale. Because it is surrounded by the sea, Venice has historically been a place with few construction materials of its own, bringing them in from elsewhere as well as recycling old materials. In all the world, Venice stands out in this regard. In John Ruskin's *The Stones of Venice* [1851–53] the protagonist is stone, around which he builds his discussion of Venice's buildings. It's quite fascinating that he contemplates architectural history across space and time around the axis of materials. This exhibition seems like it will resonate with this "Venetian style." Here's a somewhat ironic question: Will the results of creative endeavors that rely on the transport of building materials turn out to be very ordinary by Venetian standards?

Daisuke Motogi: That's certainly an intriguing observation. We live today in a mass-transport society in which things move around at a remarkable speed and scale. For its part, Venice set up the transport system that made it a trade center because it lacked the ability to produce things on its own. Without that production capacity, it had to build with only the things that were shipped there. The result was the ultimate in bricolage—a very contemporary phenomenon.

Doi: It's my view that in addition to differences in materials and construction methods, another factor in architectural bricolage is the industrial structure of a country. In contemplating the meaning of shipping dismantled elements to Venice and rebuilding them in different forms, it might be interesting to consider the option of using construction materials, wooden elements and so on that are part of Venice itself. If someone challenges the authenticity of that approach, I think we can respond with the argument that authenticity can only be found in what emerges when elements are reassembled in creative new configurations through the meaningful use of a "Venetian-style" format.

Kadowaki: I would certainly like this project to address the question of authenticity from a perspective that departs from the typical ones. One key to achieving that perspective may be a consideration of what place the transformation of structures via this "ship and build" process occupies in the history of architecture.

1: HISTORY OF TAKAMIZAWA HOUSE

折衷、オーディナリー、オーセンティシティ
土居義岳（建築史）

聞き手：門脇耕三（建築家・構法研究）＋岩瀬諒子（建築・ランドスケープ）
＋木内俊克（建築家）＋元木大輔（建築家）

日本の住宅に積層する複数の時間

門脇耕三： 今回解体した《高見澤邸》は 1954 年に環状 8 号線のやや内側に平屋として建てられ、80 年代の初頭まで増築と増棟が繰り返された住宅です。この時期はちょうど建築構法の変革期にあたりますが、それに加えて、東京という都市の変化の状況にも左右された住宅でした。今日は土居先生と議論したいテーマが 2 つあります。ひとつは「日本的な折衷性」です。日本には歴史的に数々の折衷事例があり、日本人は海外からの文化流入に比較的抵抗感がないといわれています。このことと、《高見澤邸》の状況には関係があるような気がしています。つまり、伝統的な木造住宅に工業製品が継ぎはぎされていくような状況を、《高見澤邸》はごく自然に受け入れているわけですが、これは「日本的な折衷」の戦後住宅におけるひとつの発露ではないかという仮説です。もうひとつが「建物を解体し、別の形に再構築する」ことの意味です。オーセンティシティを重視する西洋的な観点からすれば、今回の私たちの展示主旨である、実在した建築をばらばらに解体して移送し、別の形に組み立てるという行為は非常に挑発的と受け取られる可能性もあります。こうした行為にどのような積極的な意味を見出していけるのか。土居先生のご意見を伺いたいと思います。

土居義岳： 日本の戦後の住宅政策の方針は、持ち家、戸建住宅です。先進国では家は借りるのが一般的ですが、日本はかつて住宅の購入を平均的市民の目標に仕立てました。それが可能になるよう、終戦後間もない 1950 年に住宅金融公庫を設立し、建設産業の構造を整えました。土地が細分化されて商品となり、産業も細分化して巨大なマーケットができました。

門脇：《高見澤邸》周辺には同時期に団地も建てられています。団地は社会主義的で、大学教育を受けた西洋型の建築家が設計する RC 造の建物です。一方、戸建住宅は市場主義的で、日本の伝統技術を受け継ぐ大工が在来構法で建てている。資格制度的には、前者は 1 級建築士、後者は 2 級建築士に対応するわけですが、日本の戦後住宅史において、相反する 2 つのシステムが並存していたという事実は興味深いと思います。

土居： 公共住宅でいえば、1917 年のロシア革命よりも前に、西ヨーロッパで「社会住宅」あるいは「公共住宅」という概念が登場しました。19 世紀までは戸建も集合住宅も民業でした。しかし 20 世紀初頭、家賃政策の失敗や人口増加により住宅問題が深刻化したため、公社をつくり国庫から直接融資をするようになった。それがいわゆる公共住宅の始まりで、近代建築の始まりにもリンクしています。日本では 1955 年に日本住宅公団が発足し、こうした西洋型住宅の供給モデルをつくりました。日本では建築家は民業ですが、西欧では建築家は伝統的に行政と深く関わり、しばしば地方官僚でもありました。

こうした公共住宅に求められたのは、後にシビル・ミニマム（最低限の生活環境）と呼ばれる考え方です。つまりガス、電気、水道のインフラ、そしてシャワーや水洗トイレなど最低限のサニタリーを備える。安くて合理的な構法や生産方法は、こうした第一次世界大戦後の社会主義的な政策に由来しています。

このような住宅の形成史をおさえたうえで、まずは《高見澤邸》を建築産業から捉えることができるでしょう。増改築を繰り返すなかで、《高見澤邸》にはその時々の合理的な材料や構法が反映され、同時に時代や地域性、都市性、住んでいる家族の歴史も積層した。つまり、ひとつの建物のなかに複数の時間のレイヤーが存在し、そこに第二次世界大戦後の住宅生産史の大部分がプリントされている。一般的に、外国の建物は一気につくられ、ひとつの建物にはひとつの時代や精神しか投影されていないと考えられます。しかし日本の平均的市民の戸建住宅にはこれだけのレイヤーがあり、それらのレイヤー同士の因果関係をリサーチができること自体がとても面白いのではないでしょうか。

「マテリアル」か「エレメント」か

元木大輔： われわれにはまだ《高見澤邸》をどのような ものとして読解すべきなのか、統一的な戦略が見出せて いません。例えば「オーディナリーなもの」と見るのか、 あるいは「奇妙なもの」と見るのか。「日本ではこういう ものは意外と日常的に存在する」と、「日本人が見ても不 思議なブリコラージュだ」では、全体の話が大きく変わっ てしまいます。都内でも古い街にはこういう住宅があり ますが、少し郊外に行くと見られません。そういう住宅を オーディナリーと呼べるのか。また「オーディナリー」に ギリギリ属しているから、あえて「奇妙」と呼んで創作の 契機にしているところもある。片方の見方に舵を切れば フレーミングしやすいのでしょうが、それでは何かしっ くりきません。これが日本の住宅の表象だといい換える ようなことをせず、ある種の東京のスペシフィシティに 自然に向き合うほうが、現在の気分に忠実だと思います。

土居： 私はそのとき、オーディナリーかどうか以上に「そ れを日本的なものとしてアピールしたいのか」という疑 問を抱きます。例えば、日本の文化喧伝のうち、海外で広 くウケたのは「間（ま）」という概念でした。それが成功し たのは、哲学的で、いろいろな解釈や意味を込めやすかっ たためでしょう。どういった展示であれ「国際文化のなか で日本をどう位置づけているのか」という問いは向けら れますね。

門脇： 工業化部品も採用しながら、無頓着にメンテナン スとブリコラージュを繰り返してきたのが《高見澤邸》の 特徴で、それが当時のオーディナリーだというのであれ ば、現在ではそれは失われていることも事実です。《高見 澤邸》のシンタク（1982）がまったく改修されていない のはまさにその証左で、1980年代頃から在来構法が非常に 静的なものになってしまったためでしょう。こうした自 然な経緯をさらけ出すというか、あっけらかんと見せる ほうがいいかなと考えています。

今回の展示に「間（ま）」のようなコンセプチュアルなタイ

トルをつけるのは、主旨とは違う気がしています。例えば 2016年の日本館のテーマ「縁（えん）」は日本独自の概念 ですし、「間（ま）」の次の空間概念として展開できる可能 性を感じて感心しましたが、今回はそういういい方で名 指すのは何か違うように思うのです。もう少し複層的な、 物事が折り重なって複雑になっていくさまをちゃんと展 示したい。

土居： 《高見澤邸》は「オーディナリー」と「奇妙」のバラ ンス感覚がいいですよね。ここから「日本のマテリアリ ティ」という話はストレートにできるでしょう。「日本の マテリアリティって、木だと思っていますよね。でも、木 の解釈はじつにいろいろあるんですよ」という主張はあ りえる。

門脇： それをこの展示では仮に「エレメント」と呼んで います。「マテリアル」のような何にでも加工できる素材 ではなく、「部品」のような製品でもない。その中間の、さ まざまな情報が紐づいたモノを「エレメント」と呼びたい と考えています。

土居： そこは考えたい問題です。近代建築史は、鉄と ガラスでつくられた《水晶宮》（ジョセフ・パクストン、 1851）を出発点にしてしまっていますよね。このよく知 られたストーリーは、半分は脚色ですが、半分は真実で もある。この視点から見たとき、歴史の根源はやはりマテ リアルにあるのです。マテリアルの可能性が技術を生み、 美学を形成してきたことは事実なので、無碍にはできま せん。

1: HISTORY OF TAKAMIZAWA HOUSE

したがってそのジオメトリを変えていくためには別の視点、つまり日本に割り当てられた「木」というマテリアリティの配分を、解釈によって変えていく。そのなかで、次のステップとしてエレメントという見方があるということを提示していけば、これまでのモノの解釈が非常に単純だった、見直す価値が大いにあるということがいえるのではないでしょうか。

部分の総和を超えた複雑なシステムとしての建築

土居： とはいえ近代建築は、どうしても技術決定論になってしまいがちです。コンクリートや鉄といったマテリアルによって機能主義的なデザインが生まれた、技術が芸術を決定論的に支配した、というのは、マテリアルを非常に単純なスペックとして見ている、とても短絡した考え方です。むしろ、モノが複雑化して積層すると、それは独自の論理を持ち、単純なモノの積層ではなくなる。社会学者エミール・デュルケームは、社会とは何かを考えました。社会をつくっているのは人間だが、人間を一人ひとり足しても社会にはならない。要するに、人間の集合を扱うには、単純な総和ではなく別物と捉えなければ、社会学は成り立たないと考えたわけです。建築もまさにそういうもので、柱、壁、床などをただ組み立てても成り立ちません。そこに別の新たな秩序を考えなければ、建築にはなりえないということです。

今回のプロジェクトが面白いのも、一度分解した部材を組み立て直すことで、新たな構築の意志やプランなど何かが現れるかもしれないし、同じ材なのにまったく違う形の建築ができる可能性があるということです。部材にばらしては組み立て直すという反復によって、建築がどのような秩序を獲得し、それとともにどう変容していくのかということには興味があります。

門脇： モノが集まり、総和を超えた複雑なシステムやある種の超越性が生まれる。建築とはまさにそういうものです。《高見澤邸》もそうしたモノの集積ですが、しかし建築家のような人格的な主体が与える全体性や首尾一貫性が欠落しているがゆえに、あれだけの変化を繰り返してきました。物事を統合する主体の欠落は近代以前の建築の特徴でもあり、今回の展示のひとつのテーマは「この変化をどう考える？」という問いなのです。

そしてその裏返しとして、分解した一つひとつのエレメントの来歴は言語化できるけれど、それを組み立て直したときに現れるであろう複雑な系をうまくいいあてることができず、まだもやもやしているところがあるのです。

岩瀬諒子： 土居先生はこのプロジェクトに関して、部材を組み立て直すことと言われていましたが、「マテリアル」と「部材」の分岐点についてはどのようにお考えになりますか。私は「部材」になる以前の「マテリアル」のもつ越境性に興味をもっています。例えばイグサを「マテリアル」と想定したとき、織り上げれば畳という住宅を構成する部材になり、練り混ぜれば塗り壁として様態が変化していくように、畳や壁材としてパッケージされたものが「部材」というような感覚があります。

土居： 私にも近い感覚はあります。例えば、鉄は建築にも自動車にもなりえますね。マテリアルとしての鉄そのものはどの産業にも特化しないし、それが溶鉱炉にある段階では区別がないけれど、製品化するプロセスで建材部品になったり自動車部品になったりします。この分岐点ですでに建築が発生しているとも考えられる。19世紀に活動したゴットフリート・ゼンパーは、人間と木や鉄などの出会いから、それらの特性に適合した工芸が生まれ、それが技術に発展するという図式で考えた。この考え方は、産業革命後のイギリスの建築産業を理論化したものだったのです。ゼンパーは、諸工芸（諸技術）と産業諸分野の相関性をシステマティックに考えたわけです。ただゼンパーはそもそも建築の人であり、部品としての鉄はあまり評価しなかったという欠点はありましたが。

だからご指摘のとおり「マテリアル」から「部品」が分岐するプロセスはとても重要です。イギリスでは、工業規格が19世紀末や20世紀初頭に確立されたそうです。そし

てその規格にもとづいて I 型鋼を大量に製造し、アジアな
どに売りつける。この鉄製品のような建材の国際マーケッ
トがあった。ここでもイギリスの鉄産業のなかで、鉄は建
材にも戦艦にもなりうるけど、どこかで分岐して異なる
部品になる。もし建材になれば建築はそこで始まる。施主
がいようがいまいが、H 型鋼や I 型鋼がストックされ、そ
れが建材になりうる時点で建築は始まっているともいえ
るわけです。部材がつくられた時点で、すでに建築のあり
ようが投影されているわけです。

新旧技術による日本的な折衷

土居： ヴェネチアの会場で再構成をする前に、線材や面
材、その他のいろいろな部材を資材庫に並べるわけです
ね。それは建材になる前のマテリアルと化すと思います
が、それらはどのように扱うのですか。

門脇： 建物をエレメントに解体しても、マテリアルにま
では戻さないようにしたいと考えています。つまり、根太
だったものをただの木材（マテリアル）に戻して違う部位
に使用するようなことはせず、それが根太だったという
情報は保持すべきなのではないかと思っています。

木内俊克： わざわざ《高見澤邸》という既存の建物を解
体して再利用するのだから、それを単にマテリアルとし
て用いるのではなく、建築に紐づくさまざまなレベルの
情報を取捨選択して再構成ができたらよいと考えていま
す。もちろん、モノの文化的価値など大文字の歴史として
綴られるような意味にまで遡及し、ヴェネチアのコンテ
クストにそれを織り込んでいくことはなかなか難しいか
もしれません。しかし、例えば素地のまま使われていた材
と、着色されて使われていた材がある割合で混在してい
ることに気がついたとして、それを《高見澤邸》が生きて
きた日常の履歴が顕在化した情報だと捉えれば、それら
の材が運び込まれるヴェネチアの会場全体でも仕上げの
混在を同じような割合に近づけてみるなど、意味として
は薄い、けれども《高見澤邸》に刻み込まれた情報がなけ

れば生成されなかった環境のテクスチャーのようなもの
はつくれるかもしれない。

現時点では、エレメントの来歴からどのレベルの情報を
切り出し、どう取り扱っていけばよいのかはまだはっき
りしていません。そしてだからこそ、解体した材を清掃し、
整理し、梱包し、移し、現地で受け取り、またそれらの記
録を管理するといった、設計の前準備のような作業まで
含め、それがエレメントを構成する重要な情報につながっ
ていくかもしれないという予感を抱きながら、必要な手
続きを一つひとつていねいに組み立てていくことが重要
だと考えています。また、わざわざ集団で再構築すること
や、移動の履歴の見せ方さえも展示に仕込むなど、一連の
営みそのものを見せていくことによって、深く来歴に言
及したり、設計の対象として特別に取り扱わなくても、そ
れ自体が建築の問題だということを見せるチャレンジな
んだという感覚があります。

《高見澤邸》は、年代ごとにエレメントのもつ物性や価格
にその瞬間に必要に応じて反応し、アド・ホックにつくり
続けられてきました。もしかしたらこうした議論に「建築
家なしの建築」（バーナード・ルドフスキー）的な側面を読
んでみることも可能かもしれません。

門脇： もうひとつ《高見澤邸》の面白いところは、部材の
加工がわりといい加減で、工芸的な性格が希薄なところ
だと思います。伝統技術が色濃いオリジナルの部分には、
継手仕口などにていねいな仕事が見られますが、その後
の増築はもう少し場当たり的になっていく。工業化され
た部品を使い始めているからか、既存部分との接続が滑
らかではないのです。しかし一方で、ルールが定まってい
ない、何か新しい複雑な系を取りまとめているようにも
見える。

元木： 私も《高見澤邸》にはマテリアルの来歴は積層さ
れているけれど、マテリアル間の接合部には、意志やデザ
イン、哲学のようなものがないように感じます。先につく
られたものと、新しくつくられたものの関係性はとても
ドライですよね。

土居： それには技術の変化が関係しているのでしょうね。1950 年代は町中に大工がいて、彼らの使う伝統技術は戦前のそれとつながることができました。しかし 80 年代にはそうした技術は失われ、新しい技術に置き換えられるようになった。新しい技術には繊細さはあるけれど、技術体系を自ら切断してしまうのです。

ヨーロッパの田舎には異なる時間軸が積層している住宅も多いのですが、ヨーロッパの場合ばらばらなレイヤーを統合する際に 2 つのモデルがあります。有機体的モデルと機械的モデルです。有機体的モデルでは異なるものがシームレスに繋がってゆく。19 世紀の鉄構造と 100 年後のハイテクがけっこう相性がいいのはそんな感じです。他方、機械的モデルでは石構造と鉄構造が対比的に構成されていたりする。しかし、日本は有機体的でも機械的でもないレイヤーの重ね方をしていて、それが論理として引き出せれば、冒頭でおっしゃっていた工業製品の折衷という見方としても、面白いかもしれませんよね。

輸送に頼った建築はヴェネチアのオーディナリーとなるのか？

岩瀬： 今回のプロジェクトの大きな特徴に、ヴェネチアという遠く不便な場所に長い時間と多くのコストをかけて部材を移送し、展示する点が挙げられるかと思います。私たちの企画会議は「いつどこにいても自由に情報が手に入る時代に、わざわざヴェネチアで展示をする意味とは何か」を考えることから始まりました。解体や移送、施工も含め、時間軸を含んだつくることに関わる行為全体を系として展示したいと考えていますが、そのことのもたらす意味を探している段階にいます。《高見澤邸》を定点とした日本の建築部材や産業の歴史を展示するのか。施主の人生や建築のつくられ方のアドリブ性など《高見澤邸》に付随する情報はたくさんあるけれど、結局何を「送る」のか。

門脇： そもそも「送る」という行為によっていろいろなものが失われます。輸送の過程で部材が物理的になくなってしまうこともあるでしょうし、どこにくっついていたのかわからなくなってしまうこともあるはずです。しかし、その欠損は新たな参加を促すのではないかとも思います。建築を新しく一からつくるわけではないし、その場所にあったものを再生するわけでもない。でも「送る」という操作によって、新しくつくるのでも、自動生成でもない、「第 3 の方法」が見つかるのではないか。つまりここでは「つくる」行為の根源が変質することを期待しているのです。それはおそらく、われわれが日常的に行っているファイルを共同編集するような行為にも通底する、新しい「つくる」感覚です。いずれせよ「送る」ことによって作動する連鎖の感覚から生まれる「つくる」という行為を考えたいのですね。

土居： たしかに「東京の世田谷のこんな物件を復元しました」だけでストーリーになるかどうか。私は「送る」行為それ自体がヴェネチア・ビエンナーレ国際建築展に対する戦略的手法だと思います。ヴェネチアは海に囲まれた立地のため歴史的にも建材が少なく、ほかの場所から運び入れてきたのだし、古材の再生利用もされます。世界中をみてもヴェネチアは特に顕著です。ジョン・ラスキンの『ヴェネツィアの石』（井上義夫編訳、みすず書房、2019 ／原著＝1851-53）は建築史の本ですが、ひとつの建築の作品性については無頓着で解説がない。代わりに石が主人公で、この建築に使用されている大理石は中東ではこの彫刻に使われていて……と、石の話が建物を横断していく。つまり、マテリアルを軸にして時空を駆け巡る建築史を考えているところがとても面白いのです。今回の展示も、こうした「ヴェネチア性」を示唆していることになるのではないか。「輸送された建築部材に頼った創造の産物はヴェネチアのオーディナリーとなるのか？」というある種のアイロニカルな問題です。

元木： 移動が困難なヴェネチアにわざわざモノを持って行くことが展覧会として有効に機能しなければならない。

参加する個々の作家性の前に、まずこの大きな命題があるのです。日々このアイロニーと奮闘しているのですが、それを「ヴェネチア性」におけるアイロニーと捉えることで少し整理がつきそうな気もしますね。われわれは現在、モノがこれほどのスピードとスケールで移動する大量輸送社会に暮らしている。一方、生産力をもたないがゆえに移動のシステムを先取りしていたのが、交易都市ヴェネチアです。そして生産力がなく、移動して流れ着いたモノだけで何かを構築するということは、究極のブリコラージュであって、それも非常に現代的な現象です。こうした意味で「ヴェネチア性」は今回の展示にとってとても示唆的ですね。

門脇： なるほど、面白いですね。1980 年代初頭に《高見澤邸》自体のつくり方が変わり、成長が止まる。時代が流れて社会システムも複雑化し、家族も変容した。《高見澤邸》が建っていた周囲は住宅地化し、《高見澤邸》を産んだ商店街も役目を終えた。こうした状況のなかにあった住宅を「送る」ことで、止まってしまったものにもう一度生命力を吹き込む。そうした象徴的な意味合いも生み出したいと思います。

岩瀬： そもそも建築の立地はなかなか変わりません。『ヴェネツィアの石』が石を主人公にして語られたように、都内某所に建てられ、増改築を繰り返した住宅が突然ヴェネチアで再構築され、そのコンテクストがまったく変わってしまうことによって住宅も変容する。重なるはずのなかった 2 都市の地図を重ねる。実際、図面を重ねると《高見澤邸》がそのまま日本館の敷地に入るという発見もありました。

木内： しかし家を擬人化してストーリーをつくるより、再起動のさせ方でいまの日本のリアリティを伝えるほうがよいと思います。現にわれわれはそうやって価値を再生産することの豊かさを見せようとしているし、そのことを楽しんでいます。

オーセンティシティを再定義する

門脇： 展示が終わった後、送った部材をどうするかについても検討する余地があります。木材は現地でも需要があるようなので、もちろん使ってもらいたいと思っています。展示が話題になれば、ヨーロッパの大学や関係者に話をもっていくことも可能かもしれません。

博物館的な陳列方式になるのは避けたいけれど、送った部材を並べるというふるまいも面白い行為です。例えばランドスケープアーキテクトの石川初さんが、徳島県神山町の山間の民家で農業を続けながら周辺の既成品や廃材を採集してストックし、それらをブリコラージュして日用品として使っている人々を「FAB-G（ファブじい）」と呼んで紹介しています。石川さんによれば、「FAB-G」たちはブリコラージュに取りかかる前に、廃材を素材・形状・大きさなどに従って分類し、一定期間寝かせておくそうです。つまり収集とブリコラージュのあいだに、廃材からもともとの用途を忘却させるようなプロセスが必要になる。われわれが部材を並べることにも、同じような意味合いが見出せそうです。

また、部材の再利用はオーセンティシティという話にも関わってきます。冒頭で、そもそも解体して別の形に組み立てる行為が西洋の「ヘリテージ」の概念に対する問題提起だといいましたが、他方で部材の再利用にはある程度の「記憶喪失」が必要です。しかし完全な「記憶喪失」が起こると、部材はただのユニバーサルなマテリアルになってしまいます。完全な「記憶喪失」はすべてをマテリアルと見なす現代社会の暴力に与する感じがして、それはしたくない。われわれはほどよいところで「記憶喪失」を止めなければいけないと感じているのです。

土居： 「日本は木の文化、西洋は石の文化」という表現が文明開化以降定着しましたが、私の実感としては、そこまでではないように思います。石だって、木ほどの代謝性はなくてもばらばらにすることはできます。19 世紀における教会建築の保存も、かなりの部材がリプレイスされて

いますし、過度な修復もしています。では修復において石の総量の30％がリプレイスされた建築の「オーセンティシティ」とは何か。19世紀時点での修復はその程度のものでしたが、その時点ではまだ「修復」という考え方も存在していなかったのです。ヨーロッパでオーセンティシティが問題になるのは、そういう背景からなのです。だから、ヨーロッパで中世の教会を見るときは、これは中世の教会であるとともに、19世紀に再解釈された教会でもあり、2つの時代を表象しているのだ、という目で見なければならない。

また、修復には技術が関与します。中世は石の切り出しも原始的で、各部材の寸法が異なるけれど、近代になると機械により石をほぼ同じ大きさで切り出すことが可能になる。それは材の太さや目地の間隔に現れます。いまでは日本の建築用素材は鉄とガラス産業に多くを頼っています。一方ヨーロッパは技術のバラエティが豊富に残っており、製造業者や小売店の層も多種多様ではないでしょうか。

坂茂さんも「日本は工業化が進んでいるから選択肢が多いように見えるけれど、じつはとても少ない。蛇口ひとつ探すにも、全世界のメーカーから探さなければいけないのです」と話していました。こうした視点に立てば、建築は究極のブリコラージュともいえますし、古くから建築のブリコラージュ性は大切だといわれてきました。素材や工法の違いに加え、各国の産業構造もそこに重ねうるというのが私の考えです。

解体した部材をヴェネチアに移送して「別の形に再構築する」ことの意味を考えるうえでも、ヴェネチアならではの建材や木材を使うという選択肢を組み込んでも面白いかもしれません。このときオーセンティシティはどうなるのかと問われれば、「ヴェネチア性」のフォーマットを有意味に使い、部材が別の次元に組み上がったときに現れるものにしかオーセンティシティは現れない、という論理を立ち上げればいいと思いますよ。

門脇：以前、長坂常さんと「木造と組積造のどちらがフレキシブルか」という議論をしたことがあります。一般的には木造のほうがフレキシブルだと考えられているものの、長坂さんは、石やレンガ一個から置き換えられる組積造のほうがフレキシブルではないかという。これは非常に刺激的なアイデアでしたが、今回のプロジェクトでも、一般的にいわれているような次元ではないところからオーセンティシティについて考えてみたい。そのためには、この一連の行為による変態を、建築の歴史性の発露としてどうやって位置づけるかが鍵になりそうです。

今日のお話からいただいた主な議論のフックは、マテリアルの可能性が技術と美学を駆動するという、これまでの技術決定論的な話とは違った別のストーリーを示すことができそうだということです。もうひとつは超越性。つまり、構成要素が所属していた系とは違う複雑な系に転化してしまうことです。分解した部材の一つひとつを博物学的に並べて見せることにはもちろん学術的な意義がありますが、展示全体としては、そうした意義をさらに超越した面白さを表現できればいいと思います。

2:

TRAJECTORY
OF
TAKAMIZAWA
HOUSE

《高見澤邸》の
軌跡

1954

1955

1964

1965

1966

2019

Talk: Fusion and Collaboration by Designers and Builders

Naritake Fukumoto (Design and construction) + Jo Nagasaka (Architect) + Kozo Kadowaki (Architect and construction studies)

"It can be done, let's do it"

Jo Nagasaka: In June and July 2020 four teams of architects will be taking turns preparing exhibits at the Japan Pavilion in Venice. Fukumoto-san, I hope your construction firm TANK will be advising us not only on process management but also on design coordination and the actual exhibits. I also hope you will use the knowhow you have acquired to devise solutions to the various problems the architects will encounter. Most problems can be solved by the architects as long as we have drawings, models, and structural calculations to work from. But under these unique working conditions—using old materials that don't meet consistent standards of size, strength, and so on—we are all bound to make a few miscalculations. In such cases, on-site advice from TANK will be invaluable.

Although the improvisational aspect of the project on-site has been reduced from that of the idea we proposed in the national competition, it will still require the help of TANK. Designs alone might be enough to produce a superficially attractive exhibition, but the architects themselves have to understand that the design process is of a piece with the construction process, both inside and outside. That, I think, is the challenge of this project—but actually, it's the norm for handicrafts, isn't it? Architecture inevitably entails design and execution competing with each other to achieve their respective aims, and the competition creates a wall between them. In this project we intend to remove that wall and have both practices collaborate to achieve a common goal. After all, the problems of design and those of construction merge into one.

Naritake Fukumoto: I agree that that's our role here. All the conditions in play—time, budget, tools—are tougher than those we are accustomed to. When unexpected problems occur at the site, we need to be able to say, "It can be done. Let's do it." If the architects participating in this project were to all bring in their own builders, those differences would become very pronounced. It's a lot of responsibility for TANK to try to pull everything together, but I think we can create an environment where the designers and builders work as a team.

A fusion of design and construction

Nagasaka: I'm sometimes in the position of putting in a word about TANK's process management, construction estimates, and the like. Most contractors won't let you participate in such decisions. But because TANK and I share the same philosophy of merging design and construction, we can divide up processes and estimates and still assemble a project together, as well as agree on the various conditions that apply. In the current project we will use that process to figure out a construction method and develop it with all the participating architects, weaning out redundancies and waste. It should be an interesting experience, and part of the concept is, I think, to continue the process as long as it is interesting, without aiming for a peak.

Kozo Kadowaki: In a European context, the architect is expected to be an autonomous force, so the mutual independence of the design and construction processes is considered a given. However, the two fields have different business models: architects do not procure materials, while contractors do. For an architect, the ideal contractor is one who will purchase expensive materials and sell them cheap. Meanwhile, contractors want to buy materials at a bargain and sell them to the architect for a premium. Due to this conflict, the common wisdom is that neither party can trust the other. But it seems odd, doesn't it, that they should treat each other as adversaries when they share the same basic goal of doing quality work.

Fukumoto: So you make some money off materials, then what? I think builders should only expect to be evaluated by the originality of their construction work.

Kadowaki: A while back it was considered "architectural" to use expensive-looking materials, like covering surfaces with stones. But that's not so much the case anymore. Values have changed, and so has the model followed by contractors. When TANK began doing construction work, wasn't that when everything was being covered with lauan veneer? [laughs]

Nagasaka: We've been told that the materials we use look cheap but are surprisingly expensive! [laughs]

Kadowaki: Besides, if clients want to, they can always check prices on the Internet. So never mind the procurement of materials, what contractors can do is accumulate knowhow, apply it to their construction, and collaborate with architects toward the shared objective of building a good work of architecture.

Fukumoto: That's what we aim for, certainly. Building things in a three-way collaboration of client, designer, and builder is actually a lot of fun.

Kadowaki: Still, it's true that builders don't

perform the same function as architects. You seem to be doing something that departs from the conventional builder model, but is that really feasible?

Fukumoto: I think about that all the time. You tell me! [laughs] I don't know if you can call this one of our strong points, but take, for example, building methods that are extremely common-place these days, like using LGS ceiling boards. We are always asking ourselves if there are alternative methods we could use, and we talk about it with the architect. That is where my greatest interest lies.

If you dismantle it and toss it in a warehouse, watch out

Fukumoto: Thinking back to the dismantling of Takamizawa House this past summer, there was a shift in our outlook at some point or other. Initially we thought we could pick up any and all elements we found interesting. But as the architects developed and shared their design proposals, we began to realize that this approach wasn't called for. As soon as we came to a collective understanding that it would be extremely difficult to build all these things in Venice without careful advance planning, we gave up on the idea of treating everything and anything as a candidate for selection. That was an interesting moment, when everyone at the site realized that at the same time.

At first, all the architects were marking anything they thought might be usable—bathtubs, toilet paper holders, wallpaper, old window glass. But none of those things appeared in the sketches for their proposals.

Nagasaka: Why not, I wonder?

Kadowaki: Toilet paper holders and wallpaper definitely have some kind of appeal when they are part of a house, but the instant they are removed or peeled away, they morph into trash and acquire a kind of barbarity that renders them unmanageable. What initially seemed to be a cute, docile residence can go rogue when it's dismantled and tossed in a warehouse. I think it's extremely important that everyone experienced that transformation. Usually it's the opposite. I touched on this in one of our dialogues, but 20th-century fine art can be said to have entailed isolating everyday objects from their context and sticking them in the white cube of a museum. This time, however, we found ourselves in an untenable situation—whether because there was no white cube, or because there were just too many objects to deal with.

Fukumoto: That change in thinking occurred midway through the dismantling process. By the end, everything began to look like trash. Very few items remained cute to the very end.

Where creators and participants can play together

Kadowaki: From that point on, the interest of the architects shifted to the frame of the house. The principle is much like that of reno-vation architecture in Japan today, where you strip away surface elements and reconstruct the house around the frame.

Fukumoto: Then, when the frame had been exposed and they began dismantling it from the second floor, we were amazed that such thin linear elements had kept the house standing for so long. But even though the joints had been

put together well, you could see some terrible damage in cross-section.

Kadowaki: Frames in the 1950s weren't much more than stacks of lumber. Japanese archi-tecture was basically like that. It wasn't until the 1970s that you began to get more rigid forms of construction. The Takamizawa House annex [1982] fit that description, but the other sections didn't seem very solid at all, did they.

Nagasaka: You could say the house survived on the strength of its surface elements, so there is potential in our use of those elements. If all we do is reconstruct the frame, we lose some opportunities for improvisation, and it will look very bare-bones, not particular expressive. So I think it's fine if we take the attitude that we'll work out some things at the site, including structures involving the frame. That's as long as our designs allow, from the outset, for the possibility of interesting developments occur-ring on-site.

Kadowaki: We're not just talking about surface elements. The structure is a major factor in securing authorization for the exhibits, so we certainly can't ignore it. But we need some kind of scheme for attracting participation. Once again it comes down to how TANK will respond to the circumstances at hand, doesn't it.

Fukumoto: Yes, and that's a big reason why we look forward to this on-site building project.

Nagasaka: The piloti space is where the archi-tects and carpenters will do their work. There will be work tables and some kind of conduit for lowering materials down from the warehouse. We're not just going to be playing around like Sunday carpenters, but neither will my firm Schemata be drawing plans of everything in ad-vance. I'd like to see the architects and builders

設計者と施工者の融合と協働

福元成武（建築施工）＋長坂常（建築家）＋門脇耕三（建築家・構法研究）

work together on a program that will encourage the subsequent creation of interesting designs. If the workplace just runs according to plan, that will take all the fun out of the work and design that emerge from it

Kadowaki: In that case, it sounds like a good idea to create an environment that puts a little pressure on successive architect-builder teams by installing a 24-hour camera on one of the pilotis and sharing real-time information from the site via Japanese satellite relay. That should be the next phase of communication once a basic design is decided on in Japan. If we want to design a site that creators and participants can enjoy together, we need TANK's participation from start to finish. Sounds like TANK's responsibility is only going to get bigger! [laughs]

やれます。やってみよう

長坂常： 2020年6-7月にヴェネチアの日本館で4組の建築家が交代しながら展示をつくっていくわけですが、福元さん率いる施工組織TANKにはその工程管理だけでなく、デザイン的な連携、さらに展示全体も見てもらいたい。そして建築家たちのさまざまな迷いを、蓄積したノウハウで解決してもらいたい。図面と模型と構造計算があればたいていのことは設計者の力で解けますが、サイズ、強度などに一定の基準のない古材を使用する今回の特殊な状況下では、だれしも少し読みがずれることがあるだろうと思っています。それがTANKに現場施工的なアドバイスをお願いする理由です。

　国内コンペ時のアイデアと比べると現場での即興性は減っていますが、それでもTANKでなければフィットしない仕事になるでしょう。張りボテの展示でよければデザインだけで建っちゃうけれど、表も裏もつくり方とともにある設計のプロセスを建築家自身が理解していないといけない。今回はそれが問われるプロジェクトだろうと思います。でもそれはものづくりにとって本来普通のことですよね。建築はどうしても意匠と施工の互いの目的を全うするために競争になる側面があって、その競争が壁をつくっています。今回はその壁を取り払って、目的に向かって一緒につくる。設計の問題とつくり方の問題は融合しているのですから。

福元成武： 私もそういう役割だと思っています。時間も予算もわれわれの道具も、いつもより厳しい条件になります。現地で予測しなかったことが起こりえるなかでも、「やれます。やってみよう」といえることが重要です。今回の参加建築家がそれぞれ独自の施工者と組むことになったら、その違いが大きくでただろうと感じます。そこでTANKが一手にまとめることの責任も大きいですが、設計者と施工者が一緒にものづくりができる状況をつくれるのではないかと思います。

設計とつくり方を融合する思考

長坂： 僕は普段たまに、TANK の工程管理や施工見積もりにも口を出します。工務店は普通そのメカニズムを共有させてくれません。しかし TANK とは設計とつくり方を融合する思考が共有されているので、工程も見積もりも分解して、各種条件とともに一緒にプロジェクトを組み立てていきます。今回は建築家全員とそのような仕方でつくり方を発見し、無駄を見つけ、プロセスを積み上げていく。それが面白いし、ピークを設けず面白がり続けるのがコンセプトでもあると思っています。

門脇耕三： ヨーロッパ的な文脈において、建築家は自律的でなければならないので、設計と施工が独立していることは大原則ですが、そもそも 2 つはビジネス・モデルが違うのです。建築家は材料の仕入れをせず、施工者は仕入れをします。建築家からすれば、高い材料を仕入れて安く売ってくれる工務店がいい。一方工務店は安く仕入れて建築家に高く売りたい。この相反があるからお互いに信頼してはならないとされている。しかしこれでは、本来どちらもいいものをつくろうとしているのに敵対的関係が深まっておかしいじゃないか、という話ですよね。

福元： いま仕入れで儲けてどうするのかと思っちゃいますが。施工のオリジナリティを評価してもらうしか選んでもらえる道はないと思ってます。

門脇： 昔前なら例えば石を貼るとか、高そうな材料を使うことが「建築的」と思われていましたが、いまはそういう感覚が薄らいで評価軸も変わり、工務店のモデルも変わってきているのでしょうね。TANK が施工を始めた頃はもうそこらじゅうラワンだらけだったんじゃないですか？（笑）

長坂： われわれなんか「安そうな素材使ってるのに、意外と高いのね」とかいわれますよ（笑）。

門脇： 施主もその気になればネットで価格を調べられますし。だから仕入れでどうこうするのではなく、施工に知恵を使い、ノウハウを蓄積し、そしていい建築をつくることを共通の目的にして建築家と協働していく。

福元： 僕らはそうですね。施主―設計者―施工者の 3 者合意でものをつくっていくのが、やっぱり気持ちがいいし楽しいですね。

門脇： ところがそうはいっても、建築家と同じことをしているわけではないですよね。これまでの施工者のモデルと違うことをやっているとしたらそれは何なのか。

福元： それをずっと考えているんですけどね。教えてくれませんか（笑）。ただ、強みかどうかはわかりませんが、例えば軽天ボードの工事など、いまではまったくありふれた施工を、それを最善と思わずに疑ってみて、これに代わる施工手段はないかとつねに考え、建築家と話し合うようにはしています。そこに一番関心がありますね。

解体して倉庫に突っ込むと、もうやばい

福元： 夏の《高見澤邸》の解体現場の話をすると、われわれのなかで何段階かの心境の変化がありました。最初は、面白そうな部材は全部きちんと採取しようと考えていたのですが、建築家のデザイン案や進捗を共有するにつれて、いや、そういうていねいさじゃないなと思い始めました。ある程度事前にきちんとプランニングしなければヴェネチアで全部つくるのは大変だぞという空気が共有された瞬間、僕らは何もかもを採取対象と見込むのをやめました。全職人がそのことに気づいた面白い瞬間でした。
最初、建築家の皆さんがバスタブやトイレットペーパーのホルダーや壁紙や古い窓ガラスなど、使えそうなものにマーキングをしていったのですが、それらが一向にスケッチのなかに出てこないわけです。

長坂： どうして出てこなかったんでしょうね。

門脇： トイレットペーパーのホルダーや壁紙は家の一部としてあるときはたしかに可愛らしいのですが、取り外したり剥がした瞬間に一気にゴミになり、ちょっとやそっとでは取り扱えない凶暴性をもって向かってくる。最初はおとなしくて可愛い佇まいの住宅だったのに、解体し

て倉庫に突っ込むと、もうやばいのね。みんながあの変化を体験したのはすごく重要だと思います。普通は逆なのです。企画会議的対話でも話したことですが、20世紀のファインアートは日用品をその文脈から切断して美術館のホワイトキューブに突っ込んで成り立たせていた、という側面があります。しかし今回は、ホワイトキューブがないからなのか量がすごいからなのか、とんでもないことになった。

福元： その意識の変化は解体作業の中盤に起きて、終盤はもうすべてゴミのように見えてくる。最後まで可愛かったものは少なかったですね。

つくる者と参加する者が一緒に楽しむ舞台

門脇： そのときから建築家の関心は軸組に移っていったわけです。面材を引き剥がして軸組だけを頼りに再構成している日本の昨今のリノベーション建築とも共通する原理ではないでしょうか。

福元： それから、いよいよ軸組が露わになり、2階から解体していく段階で、こんなに細い線材でよく長年建ってたなと思いましたね。それでもちゃんと継手・仕口がつくられていましたが、断面欠損がひどかった。

門脇： 1950年代の軸組はほとんど積み木ですよね。むしろ日本の建築は元来そうで、ガチガチに固め始めたのは70年代くらいからといえます。《高見澤邸》ではシンタク（1982）がそうで、シンタク以外はあまり固めてる感じはなかったのではないですか？

長坂： 面材の強度でもっていたともいえるので、われわれが面材を使っていく可能性もありますね。軸組を再構成するだけだと即興性が少なくなりますし、スカスカで、表現に見えにくいかもしれない。だから、こことここは軸組の構造も含めて現地で考えるという姿勢でもいいんじゃないですか。現場で何か面白いことが起きるよう、あらかじめ設計に組み込んでおければ。

門脇： 面材だけの話でもないし、構造は展示認可に繋がる

からほっとくわけにもいかないけれど、何か仕掛けを考えないといけませんね。あらためてTANKがこういう状況にどうコミットしていくかという話になりますね。

福元： はい、現地施工の楽しみはそこにあると思っています。

長坂： ピロティは建築家や大工が作業をする場所で、作業台や、資材庫から資材をピロティへ降ろすパラシュートなども、単に日曜大工を楽しむのでも、スキーマが図面を全部書いてしまうのでもない、次に連なる作業を引き出し、面白いデザインをつくるきっかけとなるようなプログラムとして、建築家たちや施工者と一緒に考えるのがいいと思っています。そこが計画通りの作業場だと、続く作業もデザインも楽しいものにならないでしょう。

門脇： そうすると、現場のリアルタイムの情報を、例えばピロティ壁面に設置する24時間接続カメラで日本のサテライトと共有し、続く建築家や作業者にプレッシャーをかけるくらいの環境をつくるのがいいんでしょうね。日本でだいたいの設計が決まると次はそういうフェーズになるはずです。つくる者と参加する者が一緒に楽しむ舞台をどう設計するか、そのことにTANKはとことん付き合いますよと。TANKの責任がますます大きくなりますね（笑）。

20190823.00_03_52_23.still026.jpg

20190823.00_46_31_22.still074.jpg

20190823.00_11_16_18.still036.jpg

20190823.00_47_12_07.still076.jpg

20190823.00_12_30_14.still038.jpg

20190823.00_48_38_08.still089.jpg

20190823.00_11_53_06.still044.jpg

20190823.00_45_12_07.still081.jpg

2: TRAJECTORY OF TAKAMIZAWA HOUSE

20190823.00_54_27_25.still088.jpg

20190823.01_31_00_04.still160.jpg

20190823.00_59_18_10.still093.jpg

20190823.01_36_05_28.still165.jpg

20190823.01_04_49_12.still104.jpg

20190823.01_39_32_18.still171.jpg

20190823.01_26_47_21.still155.jpg

20190823.01_40_30_11.still172.jpg

20190823.01_41_42_11.still175.jpg

20190826.01_45_25_17.still199.jpg

20190823.02_16_25_12.still223.jpg

20190826.01_45_54_06.still200.jpg

20190823.02_21_27_21.still235.jpg

20190826.01_58_38_02.still210.jpg

20190826.01_31_09_26.still180.jpg

20190823.00_04_24.still027.jpg

2: TRAJECTORY OF TAKAMIZAWA HOUSE

20190928.00_04_10_28.still031.jpg

20190928.00_16_57_28.still054.jpg

20190928.00_06_11_06.still037.jpg

20190928.00_20_38_05.still059.jpg

20190928.00_10_54_19.still042.jpg

20190928.00_23_27_28.still063.jpg

20190928.00_14_06_14.still048.jpg

20190928.00_27_06_05.still069.jpg

20190928.00_31_46_03.still081.jpg

20190928.01_49_44_18.still182.jpg

20190928.00_45_48_29.still106.jpg

20190928.02_09_18_03.still190.jpg

20190928.01_27_28_10.still157.jpg

20190928.02_11_44_28.still200.jpg

20190928.01_39_32_27.still167.jpg

20190928.02_23_19_06.still234.jpg

2: TRAJECTORY OF TAKAMIZAWA HOUSE

Et Tu, Object?!
Masaya Chiba (Philosopher and writer)

With: Kozo Kadowaki (Architect and construction studies) + Daisuke Motogi (Architect) + Toshikatsu Kiuchi (Architect)

Architecture as an aggregate of objects

Masaya Chiba: This is a fascinating project that links a variety of themes together. The approach of contemplating how to connect parts that are different in nature is itself linked, I believe, to an approach in Japan that focuses on parts and fragments in all of the arts as well as in the construction of space. The theme of focusing on the handcrafted creations of artisans, instead of on the dominant position of the architect at the apex of a hierarchy, also evokes what I think is a distinctively Japanese relationship with objects. In this respect it serves as a critique of the Western privileging of the subject—which has, granted, been subject to such internal critiques as deconstructivism and fragmentation.

This project has a considerable affinity, for example, with the object-oriented ontology of Graham Harman and others that has attracted attention in recent years. Harman's philosophy takes it as an ontological premise that individual objects—animate and inanimate, even a single nut or bolt—are fundamentally autonomous and dwell contentedly in their own utterly unrelated, closed realities.

The latter half of the 20th century saw a proliferation of thought postulating that the world is composed of dynamic relations among objects. Harman described that philosophy as "correlationism" and criticized it through a revival of substantialist thought. My own thinking is that introducing the approach of isolation or disconnection facilitates creativity, but so does a correlationist approach; neither one is exclusively valid.

Harman has some association with architec-tural circles, and is currently a distinguished professor at the Southern California Institute of Architecture (SCI-Arc). Advocates like the architect David Ruy who have been influenced by Harman discuss how to apply object-oriented ontology to architecture in practice. In general terms, they are trying to figure out how to treat architecture as an aggregate of objects, rather than as a single conceptual entity.

Mediating with incompleteness and finitude

Kozo Kadowaki: Of the parts making up the dismantled Takamizawa House, we are shipping some 1,200 to Venice, but if you count those we were forced to abandon, the total number of parts comes to over 4,000. That quantity far exceeds the limits of human perception, nor can it possibly be handled as data. In the realm of architecture, we customarily deal with such huge amounts of data by drawing plans. A plan is a medium that makes it possible to manipulate objects by reducing the world of actual objects to two dimensions. When we confront objects themselves, we run up against the reality of a quantity of information too massive to access, let alone manipulate or manage. That poses a serious dilemma for us.

In the course of addressing this dilemma, we came to the realization that our plan to bring an incomplete object to Venice and rebuild it, missing parts and all, serves as a metaphor for the world as we perceive it. The main point of this project is how to deal with the missing elements that cannot be compensated for in this incomplete thing we have brought to Venice. Those absences serve as blank slates where creativity will manifest itself, places where something—not you or I, but *something*—will stealthily enter.

Chiba: Human perception has always been rendered finite by a variety of constraints. The reduction of the house's materials to a quantity that can be brought to Venice expresses the extent of the limitations humans endure due to physical, social and economic constraints when we attempt to perceive objects. On top of that, the process of reconfiguring the house is a metaphor for the process of human perception, and also demonstrates the social nature of that perception.

Toshikatsu Kiuchi: This reconfiguration of objects is a visible manifestation of mediating with finitude. We might say that all manner of things are temporarily fixed in a certain place while retaining their respective fundamental capacities. Your comments reminded me of the High Line (2009–) in New York. This is a park that is operated under a system known as railbanking, according to which it may in theory be returned anytime the railroad wants to use it again. The railbed is maintained to allow for future reuse while it functions as a temporary park.

Chiba: So it manifests a different capacity while its original capacity is held in reserve?

Kiuchi: Exactly. I think this exhibition can show us that architecture is the temporary fixing of diverse objects while they are in a state of being held in reserve.

Chiba: Think of a washing machine, which normally washes our clothes without complaint, but could "go rogue" at any time [laughter]. A short circuit could release a tremendous burst of power. This analogy relates to labor issues as well. A salaryman may docilely commute to work every day, but under certain trying circumstances, who knows what he might do? Nowadays objections to the status quo are being raised in every part of society. Whether we're talking about women's issues or economic inequality, we hear angry voices telling us that they've been silent until now, but they aren't going to take it any more. In that sense, I think it would be great if this exhibition gives rise to cries of "Et tu, object?!" "And you, pillar?!" [laughter]

Kadowaki: We architects have long been accustomed to leading very expensive projects under our own names, but that is an extremely rare position to be in in contemporary society. It would be unthinkable to hear a statement like "Kengo Kuma is building the New National Stadium" applied to any other industry or product. What I mean to say is that the world is increasingly run by systems—in spite of which architects continue to work as individual actors, but that position is starting to feel oppressive. The most rational attitude for architects today might well be to support an uprising of "objects" against the system.

Is it architecture, or carpentry?

Kadowaki: From the outset, we thought about this project in terms of a narrative of forgetting that these individual elements were once part of a whole. One fascinating phenomenon is that objects that had an endearing quality when viewed as part of the house suddenly take on a savage aspect when broken up. Wallpaper that looked quite lovely when it covered the walls turns into something like rubbish when it's peeled off, and you no longer want to touch it [laughs].

Daisuke Motogi: When it was decided that Takamizawa House would be our raw material, it reminded me of the degree to which we have taken pre-finished materials as a given until now. In previous designs we worked with finished objects to which we added some variables. But when everything is a variable, it's out of control.

Kadowaki: Takamizawa House has been renovated many times over, but from around the 1970s precut wooden materials came into use, and the house suddenly became domesticated, didn't it. What I mean is, carpenters before then had the skills to work with "noise." That handicraft-like approach functions as a sort of critique of our method of drawing plans at a desk. And yet, if everything were handcrafted, it would just be a regression to the old days. Our challenge is to achieve a healthy tension between techniques that accommodate noise and the plan-drawing approach.

Chiba: I agree. Incidentally, the subtitle of Harman's second book, *Guerrilla Metaphysics* [Open Court, 2005], is *Phenomenology and the Carpentry of Things*. Not architecture, but carpentry. When we think about the component-like nature of objects, you could say that our approach is more like carpentry than architecture. That seems pertinent to our discussion today.

Kiuchi: After I finished graduate school I spent some time working in studios in New York and Paris, where computer-aided digital design had completely taken over. Nowadays there seems to be a degree of exhaustion with the technology, and one way people are trying to alleviate that fatigue is to adopt a more carpenter-like approach to making things. It isn't simply a regression, because digital technology is part of what makes it possible. Through digitization anyone can design complex or irregular objects that only skilled artisans could handle in the past. Now that this is a worldwide trend, though, one begins to wonder what awaits us down the road if everyone heads in the same direction.

A project with an aesthetic ethics

Kadowaki: Before I think of it in terms of architecture vs. carpentry, the component-like or fragmentary aspect of this project suggests to me an image of structures surviving in incomplete form as fragments, an image that corresponds to industrialized parts. Because industrialized parts have complex designs, it is probably impossible to handle them in a carpenter-like way. If anything, it may become necessary to handle fragmented structures in an architect-like way.

Kiuchi: Handling industrialized parts in an architect-like manner would mean taking into consideration the properties, context, and industrial history of those parts, would it not? If so, are we then returning to the stance of locating objects within the relations among objects?

Chiba: What I find most intriguing is the aspect of directly manipulating structures at the mid-scale level by contemplating the potential of fragments.

Kadowaki: Digital designers in Europe consistently treat objects as having plasticity that can be sculpted. They are fond of processes that create shapes from scratch, using concrete squeezed from a tube or huge chunks

of synthetic wood from which anything can be carved. But I don't think that works for architecture. I identify with a lazier attitude of closely observing what's already there and working it as little as possible. Something like wanting to be a carpenter, but stopping just short of becoming one.

Still, I'm not sure what to make of this attitude. A desire to stop just short, to be rendered impotent—we certainly have something of that in us. Right at the beginning, Chiba-san, you cited "Japanese" as a keyword, and come to think of it, this attitude may be a very Japanese one.

Kiuchi: Don't people in the object-oriented ontology camp talk about things like the relationship between missing objects and impotent humans?

Chiba: I doubt it. After all, they talk about the infinite power concealed in objects. I have some misgivings about that notion myself. If anything, I'd rather think about encounters between finite objects from which something is missing.

Kadowaki: I feel exactly the same. I would like to treat things, be they objects or people, as having something missing from the outset. I think that is precisely what forms our ethical perspective.

オブジェクト、お前もか?!
千葉雅也（哲学者・作家）

聞き手：門脇耕三（建築家・構法研究）＋元木大輔（建築家）
＋木内俊克（建築家）＋長嶋りかこ（グラフィックデザイナー）

モノの無限性とオブジェクトの集合体としての建築を考える

千葉雅也： さまざまなテーマを繋ぎ合わせたとても面白いプロジェクトですね。グランドプランのなかで理念的なものを表現するというよりも、異質な部分同士をどう連合させるかと考えるアプローチは、部分性や断片性に着目する日本の諸芸術や空間のつくり方にもつながるものだと思います。建築家という支配的な立場をヒエラルキーの頂点とするのではなく、職人の手仕事による制作にフォーカスを当てるテーマも日本的なモノとの関わり方を感じさせるもので、西洋的な主体性に対する批評になっている。もちろん西洋の文脈のなかでも、そうした主体性に対する脱構築や断片性への着目などはある種の内部批判としてあって、東アジア的な手仕事への意識のもち方と通底するところもあるわけです。

例えばこのプロジェクトは、少し前に話題になったグレアム・ハーマンらのオブジェクト指向存在論と親和性が高い。オブジェクト指向存在論では、モノを一定の秩序のなかで一定の機能性や目的性に収まっている状態から解放し、自由化することが考えられている。ハーマンの哲学のベースにあるのは、一つひとつのオブジェクトは根本的に独立していて、それぞれがまったく無関係に自閉的なあり方をしているという存在論的前提です。生物も無生物も、ボルトやナットひとつとっても、それぞれが固有の自閉的な享楽を生きている。ハーマンの哲学には、そういうある種、汎神論的な、アルフレッド・N・ホワイトヘッド的なビジョンがあります。そこでは、モノとモノとの関係性は二次的であると考えられている。

20世紀後半にはしばしば、オブジェクトの自律性よりも、それらが構成するダイナミックな関係性こそが世界のあり方だとする思想が見られました。とりわけ1970年代から80年代には、モノの実体性を関係性のほうに解消してしまうことこそが最先端の思想だという風潮が強かった。しかし、ハーマンはそうした考え方を「関係主義」と呼び

批判します。そういうタイプの思考をとると、この世界のすべてのものごとは多かれ少なかれ関係し合っているとするホーリズム（全体論）になる。大乗仏教の縁起思想からニューエイジまで、そういう発想が広くあります。この時期に活躍したインテリは現在もこの種の思考をとることが多く、例えば中沢新一さんが最近提唱されているレンマ学というのは、縁起、関係主義のひとつの徹底といえるでしょう。断っておくと、僕は別にハーマンが正しいといっているわけではなく、関係主義は関係主義でひとつの捉え方だと思うんですね。関係主義的な見方をとったほうがクリエイティブになれる局面もあるし、分離や隔離や切断という視点を導入したほうがクリエイティブになれる局面もあって、どちらか一方が正しいわけではない。僕の切断論にしても、見えない関係性が複雑に構築されていることを前提にしたうえで、それだけでは不十分だからいっているのであって、切断だけが重要だといっているわけではありません。

ともあれハーマンの哲学は、一時期の関係主義ブームからすると完全に過去のものとなったかのような実体論を復活させて注目を集めたわけです。そのハーマンは建築業界とも接点があって、現在はSCI-Arc（南カリフォルニア建築大学）のディスティングイッシュトプロフェッサーを務めています。SCI-Arcでは、彼の影響下にある建築家のデイヴィッド・ルイをはじめとした論者たちによって、オブジェクト指向存在論を建築の現場にどう実装するかという議論がいろいろと展開されています。大まかにいえば、建築を一個の理念的統一体としてではなく、オブジェクトの集合体としてどう取り扱うかということが検討されているといっていいでしょう。今回のプロジェクトは、まさにそういう議論の延長線上で考えることができると思います。

「全体は部分の総和以上のものである」というのがホーリズムの考え方ですよね。彼は逆に、「部分こそが全体がなしうること以上の無限のポテンシャルをもっている」と考える。例えば、風車を例にしてみると、風車というひとつのシステムのなかに歯車が収められているときには、歯車は

本当にやりたいことを我慢していることになる。これは擬人的ないい方ですが。もし歯車を一定の目的性から解放し、自由化してやったら、歯車にできることはもっとたくさんある。ハーマンの議論はそういう方向性なんですね。

門脇耕三： 建築界では意匠を抽象的に表現するモードと具象的に表現するモードが交互にやってきて、しばらく前は抽象ブームでした。いまはその揺り戻しとして具象を考えようというタイミングで、そこでハーマンが参照されているふしがあると思います。

千葉： ハーマンの理論というのは、見ようによっては1970−80年代に席巻したポストモダン思想の重要な部分をひっくり返しているだけともいえるわけですよ。そう考えると現代思想ゲームの単純な逆張りのように見えなくもないのだけれど、今回のプロジェクトにおけるモノの無限性のきわめてリアルな話を伺っていると、むしろそこからハーマンの哲学が逆照射されて説得性が増した感じがしますね。

不完全性と有限性の調停を可視化する

門脇： 今回のプロジェクトではハーマンの哲学はそれほど意識していなかったのですが、実際にモノと向き合っていくと、素朴なレベルでその無限性にぶち当たるんです。例えば、1本の古い柱を3Dスキャンしてみるとデータ量が15GBもある。しかもスキャンできるのは表面だけで、内部の組成まではわからない。解体した《高見澤邸》の部材数はヴェネチアへ輸送するものだけで約1,200で、破棄せざるをえなかったものを含めると4,000を越えます。この数は人間の認知限界をはるかに超えるもので、データとしてもとうてい扱えるものではない。この膨大なデータを扱うために、建築の世界では慣習として図面を引きます。つまり図面は、現実のモノの世界を2次元に縮約することで、対象を操作可能にするメディアであるというわけですね。モノそれ自体に向き合おうとすると、そのあまりに膨大な情報量とアクセスできない実在性にぶち当たって、

制御もマネジメントももとより不可能となり、大変な思いをさせられる。今回はあらためてそのことに気づかされました。

その過程で、欠損した不完全なモノをヴェネチアに持って行って不完全なまま建てるという今回のやり方は、われわれの認識世界の比喩になっていると思うに至りました。不完全なモノを持って行って、そのどうしても埋め合わせられない部分をどう考えるかというのがこのプロジェクトの胆で、そこはクリエイティビティが発露する余白でもあるし、私でもあなたでもない何かが忍び込んでしまう場所でもある。

千葉： そもそも人間が対象を科学的観察のように中立的に認識する場面などはなく、認識はさまざまな制約によってつねに有限化されているわけですね。資材をヴェネチアに持って行けるだけの量に縮約することが、人間がオブジェクトを認識するときに身体的・社会的・経済的な制約によってどれほどの有限化を蒙っているかということを表現している。加えて、それを再構築する作業は人間の認識過程そのものの暗喩であり、認識の社会性を表しているともとれます。

木内俊克： モノの再構築は有限性の調停の可視化であって、そこで取り扱われるモノが、全体のシステムの一部分として収まることが最良の状態ではないかもしれない。いってみれば、あらゆるものはそれが本来もっている力能を保持したまま、ある場所に仮固定されているわけですよね。お話を伺っていてニューヨークの《ハイライン》(2009−)を思い出しました。高架鉄道の廃線跡を利用した公園です。公園はレール・バンキングというシステムによって運用されていて、将来、鉄道として再利用したいときにいつでも戻せるように、線路としての利用が可能な状態を保持したまま、一時的に公園として使っているのです。

千葉： もとの力能を留保状態にしたまま、別の力能を発揮させているわけですね。

木内： そうです。《ハイライン》は最初からそういうものとして取り扱われ記録もされているのでわかりやすいです

が、そもそもあらゆるものが留保状態にありながら仮固定されているのが建築だということを今回の展示で見せられたら、前向きな建築のビジョンの提示になると思います。

千葉： 洗濯機ひとつとっても、普段はおとなしく洗濯してくれているけれど、いつキレるかわからないところがあるじゃないですか（笑）。漏電でもすれば、とんでもない力が解放されるわけでしょう。この話は労働の問題にもつながるもので、おとなしく会社に通っているサラリーマンでもいざという時にはどうなるかわからない。いまの世の中はいたるところで異議申し立てが起こっていて、フェミニズムの問題にしても経済的格差の問題にしても、「いままではおとなしくしていたけれど、これからはどうなるかわからないぞ」というピリピリした気配が蔓延しているわけですよ。革命の予感ですね。そんななか、今回の展示で「オブジェクト、お前もか？！」とか「柱もか？！」となれば（笑）、面白いと思うんです。

門脇： われわれ建築家のふだんの仕事では、それとはまったく逆にオブジェクトを制御可能なものとして扱うので、今回のプロジェクトにはどこか居心地の悪さを感じるのも事実です。

ボトムアップとトップダウンをシェイクする

千葉： それは経営者の目線ですよね。建築家というのは経営者であって、アーキテクトという言葉に示されているように、ひとつのアルケー（原理）のなかにすべてを従属させていく職能なわけでしょう。そこで従属的な役割を担わされているのが職人さんで、だからこそ時には反旗を翻して暴れたりする。昔、うちの実家を建てたときも、白いコンクリートのモダンな家なのに、職人さんがどこからか銘木的なものを持ってきて勝手に玄関の小上がりにくっつけ始めるわけですよ（笑）。それはひとつの反乱であり、従属的に労働させられている立場の人たちがもつバロキズム──ヤンキーイズムにもつながるような──であって、まさに装飾というべきものです。装飾というのはアルケーに

抵抗するものですから。そういう意味では、今回アーキテクチャーをすべて部材のレベルにバラすというのは、装飾的ないかがわしさを建築のいたるところに見出していくことだともいえる。バラすとすべてが装飾として立ち上がり直してしまって、収拾がつかなくなるわけですよ。

門脇： バラすことで装飾化するわけですね。なるほど。ただそこで気になるのは、これまでの建築家は支配的な立場に立つ計画主体だったわけですが、いまはその役割も変わってきています。建築家はいまなぜ、モノの暴動や反逆に加担するようになったのか。それこそが問われるべきではないでしょうか。

千葉： たしかにそうですよね。建築家としてそこはどうなんですか？

門脇： ひとつ思い当たるのは、支配の対象が人間から人間ではないものに移っているということでしょうか。われわれ建築家は個人の名前で巨額のプロジェクトを統率してきましたが、そういう立場は現代社会では非常に珍しい。「隈研吾が《新国立競技場》をつくる」というような話は、ほかの産業やプロダクトではまず考えられない。普通は法人が主体になります。ようするに、世の中はどんどんシステムが動かすようになってきている。そのなかで建築家はいまだに個人主体でやっているのだけれど、それもだいぶ息苦しくなっていて、反−システムとしてのモノの暴動に加担したい気持ちになっているのではないか。その意味で、暴動側に加担するということは、いまの建築家にとって合理的な態度なのかもしれません。

千葉： ただ、それでも建築家の固有名性というのは完全になくなるわけではないと思うし、部分から意図しない秩序が生成していくことと、部分たちの暴動を統率しようとすることの、その拮抗の場において何かが成り立てばいいのではないかという気もするんですね。
思い返してみれば、僕がテキストを書くやり方もそうで、一時期からアウトラインプロセッサや Twitter を使ってアイデア出しをすることがルーティンになっているんですね。例えば、Twitter で思いついたことをつらつらとツイー

トして、それをそのままアウトラインプロセッサにコピペする。そこに別の箇条書きを書き加えたり、並べ替えたりする。そうすると、それだけでちょっとしたエッセイができてしまうわけです。さらに、それぞれのパーツはまったく別の展開可能性をもっていて、違う文脈に移すことで新たな連想が生まれ、そこから別の原稿が書けたりする。僕はいま、そういうルーティンがいいと思っていて、小説も部分的にはそういうふうに書いているんです。

門脇： テキストの iPS 細胞（人工多能性幹細胞）という感じですね。

千葉： そうかもしれません。パーツの多能性というのはテキストや言語のレベルでも活用できる。僕の原稿の書き方は、オーサーとして、あるいはアーキテクトとしてつくるというよりも、部分や装飾のレベルから立ち上げていって、結果としてアーキテクチャーができるという感じなんですね。ただ、絶対にボトムアップでやらなければいけないという「主義」にもしないところがポイントで、トップダウンのところがあってもいい。僕はアウトラインプロセッサの自由な使い方を Tak. さんという方から学んだのですが、彼はトップダウンとボトムアップを繰り返しながら自在にライティングすることを「シェイク」と呼んでいます。シェイク的なアウトラインプロセッサの使い方が、僕のなかでワークフローを劇的に変えてくれたのです。

元木大輔： パーツの多能性をどんどん別様の展開可能性に変えていくというのは、今回のプロジェクトにとっても示唆に富んでいますね。それで思い出したのですが、アルヴァ・アアルトがデザインした有名なスツール「Stool 60」があります。彼はもともとフィンランドバーチの無垢材を曲げる技術を開発して、最初はレリーフなどをつくっていたんですね。そこからシンプルなスツールをつくり、椅子やテーブルなどの家具をつくり、その家具を売るための会社をつくった。「L-Leg」というスツールに使われた脚について、アアルトは 4 パターンのモジュールを考案するのですが、家具だけでなく量産住宅のあらゆるパーツに対応できるような計画があったそうです。最初はただ曲げていた

だけのものが、モダニズムにつながるものになっていったわけです。ただ、おそらくハウスメーカーのほうが安かったからでしょう、量産住宅には至りませんでしたが。

最近僕は「Stool 60」のパチモノを集めていて、オリジナルは 2 万円くらいするのですが、コピーは 1,000 円くらいで買えるんですね。スツール 1 脚につき 3–4 本の脚がついているので、「L-Leg」を装飾、もしくはあらゆる可能性を秘めたパーツと考えると、1 本 200–300 円で手に入れることができる。ただ、パーツとしては売っていないので分解する必要があります。スツールという機能から開放されることで部分の暴動が起きるかもしれない。

それは建築か、大工仕事か

門脇： それぞれのパーツがいったん全体の一部であることを忘れるというストーリーは、今回のプロジェクトで当初から考えてきたことですね。面白いのは、住宅として見ているときは可愛らしい佇まいだったものが、バラすと途端に凶暴になるという点です。壁には可愛らしい壁紙が張ってあったのですが、剥がすとゴミのように見えて、触りたくなくなってくる(笑)。

千葉： それは面白いですね。僕はオブジェクト指向存在論によくわかっていないところがあったのですが、今日お話を伺って、「そうか、ハーマンってこういうことを考えていたのか」とすごく腑に落ちた感じがします。

門脇： 解体現場でモノたちがもっている圧倒的なリアリティに向き合ってしまうと、デザインが考えられなくなるどころか、凶暴さに心が砕けそうになりました。図面とはそうしたリアリティを忘れさせてくれるメディアだということをあらためて思い知らされました。

元木： 今回《高見澤邸》を素材にすることが決まってから思ったのは、いままででいかに製材されたモノを前提にしていたかということです。これまでの設計は、まず整ったモノがあって、そこに変数を絡めていくという手法でしたが、全部変数だととうてい扱いきれない。これまでの自分たち

はわりとノイズを受け入れて設計しているほうだという自負が吹っ飛んでしまうくらいのインパクトがありました。

門脇：《高見澤邸》は何度も改修されていますが、1970年代くらいから製材した木材が使われ始めて、急に飼い慣らされるんですよね。それまでは製材されていない曲がった材も使われていた。つまり当時の大工さんには、ノイズと付き合える技術があったわけです。そうした手仕事的なものが、われわれがやっている机上で図面を引くやり方に対して、批判的に機能することはたしかです。しかし、だからといってすべてが手仕事になってしまうと、単純な回帰になってしまう。われわれに求められているのは、ノイズと付き合う技術と図面的な思考とをどう緊張させるかということなのかもしれませんね。

千葉： そういうことだと思います。ところで、ハーマンの2冊めの著作である『Guerrilla Metaphysics（ゲリラ形而上学）』（Open Court, 2005）のサブタイトルは「Phenomenology and the Carpentry of Things」というんです。「Architecture（建築）」ではなく「Carpentry（大工仕事）」というところがポイントで、オブジェクトの部分性を考えることは、建築的というより大工仕事的な思考をとるといえる。それは今日のお話にすごく通じますね。

長嶋りかこ： 情報を圧縮して操作するグラフィックは建築の図面を描く行為に近いかもしれませんが、扱っている情報量もパーツも建築よりずっと少ない。なのでモノのリアリティに戸惑う経験は建築家ほど多くないように思います。自分の場合だと例えば印刷機のエラーやそれによる損紙など、普段廃棄となるノイズ的なものを素材として扱う場合、特性を知るために最初は大工仕事的な思考が必要となりますが、そのままだとマテリアルの開発で留まるため最終的には情報を整理しどう見せるかを考え組立てる必要があり、その際に図面的思考を用いているかなと思います。

木内： 僕は大学院を出た後しばらくニューヨークとパリのアトリエで働いていたのですが、国際的なコンテクストではコンピュータを使ったデジタルデザインが席巻していて、いまは若干疲弊しているところもあるんですね。その疲弊を解消しようとみんなが向かった方向のひとつに、大工的なつくり方があると思います。それは単純な回帰ではなく、むしろデジタル技術がそれをアップデートするという考え方です。それまで熟練した職人にしか扱うことのできなかった複雑なモノやイレギュラーなモノでも、データ化することで誰でも取り扱えるようになる、ないしはさらに複雑化できるというシナリオです。そうした流れが世界中にある一方で、大工的なふるまいさえあればモノの暴走を乗りこなしていけるし、それが調停のすべてだと短絡することには疑問を感じる部分もあります。

千葉： そのことは、オブジェクト指向存在論的なものや断片主義のその先は何かという話にもつながってくるので、僕も考えたいところなんですよね。僕のテキストも断片的といわれることがあって、たしかに断片的なものや部分性を意識することはあるのだけれど、それは構造的な操作をするためにいったん断片の次元まで降りていくということであって、細かい手仕事をしていればそれでいいと自己目的化してもしょうがない。それは今日のお話に結びつけていえば、大工的なものから建築的なものへもう一度戻るということになるのかな。

門脇： もう少しいうと、僕のなかでは建築的か大工仕事的かという文節以前に、今回のプロジェクトにおける断片性や部分性には、構造が不完全なかたちで残っている断片のイメージがあって、そのイメージに合致するのが工業化部品です。工業化部品はそれ自体が複雑に設計されているために大工的に取り扱うことはたぶん不可能で、むしろ断片化した構造を建築家的に取り扱うということが必要になってくるのだと思います。

元木： ゴミ問題にヒントを与えるということも、断片性や部分性がフォーカスされることによる効果だと思います。つまり、新しくつくらなくても、もとからあった何かの部分で代用しようという動きが広まることが期待できる。そしてもうひとつ、部分性への着目は多様性を考えるうえでもヒントになるかもしれません。これまでダサく見えてい

たモノの個性を認め、その個性をどういう文脈で発揮すれ
ば魅力的になるのか。そういうまなざしに価値が生まれる
ことへの期待もあります。

プロジェクトに宿す美学的な倫理

木内：門脇さんのお話を受けると、工業化部品を建築家的
に取り扱うということは、その部品の属性や文脈、産業的
来歴を考慮するということなんですよね。そうすると、も
う一度、モノとモノの関係性のなかにモノを位置づけると
いうところに戻っていくのでしょうか。

千葉：むしろ、断片のポテンシャルを考えることによって
中規模なレベルの構造を直接的に操作するというところが
面白いんでしょうね。

門脇：ヨーロッパのデジタルデザインの人たちは、一貫し
てモノを可塑的なものとして彫刻的に扱うんですよね。彼
らはチューブから練り出したコンクリートや何でも削り出
せる巨大な合成木材を使って、かたちを一から生み出すよ
うなやり方を好みますが、僕はあれはちょっと違うかなと
思っている。僕はどちらかというと元木さんの感覚に近い
のですが、もとからあったものをよく観察し、なるべく手
を動かさないでサボるような態度に共感する。大工になり
たいのだけれど、その手前で大工になることを寸止めする、
といったらいいでしょうか。

千葉：大事なのは、それが属している文脈や自分のコント
ロールから離れた、他者としての素材を寄せ集めてきて、
他者と他者のあいだにどういう関係性を設定するかという
ことだと思うんですね。僕がテキストを書くとき、僕がゼ
ロからつくり出しているわけではない。テキストを書くと
いうことはすでに他者が使っている言葉を借りてくるとい
うことで、言語表現のオリジナリティも、他者としての言
語やフレーズをどう関係づけるかという点にこそある。僕
はそういう態度でテキストを書いているんですね。

門脇：しかし、この態度は何なんでしょうね。寸止めした
い欲望というか、去勢されたい欲望というか、そういうも

のがわれわれには明らかにある。これはきわめて日本的な
もので、西洋の人にはなかなか理解されない感覚ではない
でしょうか。

千葉： 明らかにわれわれの倫理、しかも美学的な倫理です
よね。

木内： 千葉さんの言葉を借りれば「動きすぎてはいけな
い」ということでしょうか。有限性にぶち当たってどこか
で止まる。そのことをどう受け入れていくかが問われてい
ると。

門脇： 長嶋さんがこの去勢された日本男児たちの議論を
どう聞いたか気になるところですが(笑)。

長嶋： 都市を見渡せばいたるところで大地を掘削してビ
ルが建てられていて、あまりいい風景ではないなと思っ
て見ているのですが、そんななか自省的に緩やかに立ち
上がろうとする「オラオラ」ではない美学的な倫理は、私
はとても好ましいと思っています。

門脇： 最初に千葉さんが「日本的」というキーワードを
語ってくれましたが、われわれはあまりそのことを意識し
ていなかったんですね。しかし、いわれてみればたしかに
すごく日本的なものなのかもしれない。

木内： 欠損したオブジェクトと不能な人間の関係性のよ
うな話は、オブジェクト指向存在論界隈の人たちはしてい
ないんですか？

千葉： していないと思います。彼らはむしろ、オブジェ
クトには無限の力が秘められているといういい方をしてい
ますからね。その点に僕も一抹の違和感を覚えるんです。オ
ブジェクト同士は無関係に自閉的なあり方をしているとい
うのが彼らの考え方で、結局は関係主義をひっくり返した
だけのように見える。僕は、欠損を抱えた有限性のオブジェ
クト同士の出会いみたいなことを考えたいのです。

門脇： まったく同感です。モノであろうと人であろうと、
あらかじめ欠損を抱えたものとして向き合いたい。それこ
そがまさにわれわれの倫理観なのだと思います。

3:
ON
DIGITAL
DESIGN

デジタル・デザインの
建築論

Data and Loss
Taichi Sunayama
(Architecture and art studies)

Technology has made it possible to peel away the information that once adhered so firmly to objects, and give it autonomy. When we buy things from Amazon, we receive information first and the goods later. The items we stick in our cart won't arrive until the next morning. Meanwhile, the information stripped from those items takes on a life of its own. Information begets new information, leading on the one hand to the conveniences offered by digital twin environments, and on the other to an information dystopia of surveillance and fakery. In a world where both aspects coexist, creativity must develop a point of view that goes beyond judgments of right or wrong.

In this essay I would like to report on two projects we have implemented for *Co-ownership of Action: Trajectories of Elements*, the Japan Pavilion exhibition at the 17th International Architecture Exhibition of the Venice Biennale. One is the construction of a database of structural elements, and the other is a demonstration experiment in 3D scanning.

Our subject is a house very typical of those built in Tokyo in the 1950s, which we have dismantled for reassembly in Venice. The house had undergone repeated extensions and renovations that cut up, added on, or otherwise altered its constituent elements over time, transforming the house into a unique structure. How should we go about determining the value of these changes? And, by dismantling, transporting, and reassembling this structure on a new site in new configurations that incorporate the various kinds of "loss" that have occurred along the trajectories traced by its elements, what opportunities for creativity will we find in those very losses?

The house

As the research section of this book (1: History of Takamizawa House) makes clear, the elements that were patched, recombined, and replaced during the many extensions and renovations of the house that is the subject of the exhibition gave it a form that embodied a unique set of trajectories. Having survived the upheavals of postwar Japan up to the present day in a suburban Tokyo neighborhood, Takamizawa House was in its final days before dismantling when August 2019 arrived.

That was the month—nine months before the opening of the Venice Biennale—that Takamizawa House was chosen as the subject of the Japan Pavilion exhibition. We picked it as the most convenient of several candidates in terms of access and post-dismantling transport in the Tokyo area, where most of the people designing and working on this exhibition are located. To paraphrase the words of curator Kozo Kadowaki, the objective of the exhibition is not to simply treat the elements of the house as materials to be recycled. By painstakingly deciphering this one house, we can glean from the scars and inscriptions on its pillars an image not only of the lives of its residents, but of the history of postwar Japanese industrial technology that sustained those lives. Our task, then, is to carefully lift off the information that has been deposited on these elements. A higher level of theory and practice are demanded of us if this exhibition is not to devolve into a mere exercise in recycling materials.

データと欠損
砂山太一
（建築・芸術学研究）

　技術は、それまで物にピッタリと貼り付いて存在していた情報を、引き剥がし独立させることを可能にした。Amazonで買い物をするとき、私たちは情報を先取りしていて、物は後から到来する。カートに入れた商品は明日にならないと手元には届かない。そして物から引き剥がされた情報は、独り歩きもする。情報が新たな情報を生産し、一方ではデジタルツインと呼ばれる利便性追求による希望的な風景、他方では監視とフェイクが瀰漫する情報的なディストピア、それらが同居する今日的状況において、創造性は正邪を超えた観点を描き出すことが必要と考える。

　本稿は、第17回ヴェネチア・ビエンナーレ国際建築展日本館展示「ふるまいの連鎖：エレメントの軌跡」のために実施された「部材データベース構築」および「3Dスキャニングの実証実験」についてのレポートである。

　昭和期の日本・東京に建てられたありふれた住宅。それを解体し、イタリア・ヴェネチアで組み直す。対象住宅は増築と改築を繰り返し、建物を構成する部材は切り刻み継ぎ足され、時間をかけて独自な形態へと変貌していた。その変化をいかに価値あるものとして認めていくことができるか。解体・移動・再構築を経て、物が辿る軌跡のなかで起こるさまざまな「欠損」を取り込みながら別の土地で新たに組み上げることで、その欠損自体にわれわれはいかなる創造性の契機をみるのだろうか。

対象住宅

　本書の「1:《高見澤邸》の歴史」でも明らかにされているように、本展で対象としている住宅は増築・改築を繰り返してきた。継ぎ接ぎ、組み換え、交換されてきた部材は、その形状に独特の軌跡を抱えている。東京の周辺で、激動の昭和から平成・令和元年まで生きた《高見澤邸》は、2019年8月、解体直前の最後の時間を過ごしていた。

　《高見澤邸》が対象住宅に決定したのは、展覧会オープン9カ月前の2019年8月。いくつかの候補物件のなかから、本展の設計・作業者が集中している東京圏を中心に、場所へのアクセス、解体後の移動など、もっとも利便性が高い物件が選ばれた。「Co-ownership of Action: Trajectories of Elements」と題する本展は、キュレーターの門脇耕三の言葉にもあるように、単に住宅の構成材を、資源として再利用することを目的としていない。住宅ひとつをていねいに紐解いてみることによって明らかになってくるのは、細かな柱の傷や印から浮かび上がる生活の姿はもちろんのこと、その生活を下支えしてきた戦後日本の産業技術の来歴そのものである。このような、物に蒸着した情報をていねいに汲み上げること。本展を単なる資材リサイクル活用の展示に陥らせないためにも、より高度な思索と実践が要求される。

3Dスキャニング

　3Dスキャニングは、レーザー照射による測距や写真画像からの類推などの情報技術を用いて、立体物の形状を点の集まりやポリゴン面の集まりとしてコンピュータ内に取り込む技術である。建築領域においては、近年、既存建築物の保存修復や土木における測量分野など、3Dスキャニングの応用が一般化しつつある。建築遺産の改修プロジェクトなどでは、ファサードから内部に至るすべてが立体的にデータ化され、長年の時間経過のなかで変化した特殊な形状を微細に記録し、より高度な修復作業に役立てる技術として広く使われている。ほかには杉林をスキャンデータ化し、杉林の森林管理や木材流通の市場管理など、建築木材のロジスティクス・システム構築の根幹的な役割を果たす事例が見られる。

　従来、専門家の経験則的な知見に委ねられていたものを、可視的な情報としてデータ化することによって建築のあらゆるフェーズにおいて共有可能なものとし、設計から施工、資材管理に至るまでをシームレスに把握可能にしつつあるといえる。

3: ON DIGITAL DESIGN

3D scanning

3D scanning utilizes such technologies as laser ranging and photograph-based reconstruction to store data about the shapes of solid objects on computers as collections of points (known as point clouds) or polygon surfaces. In the field of architecture, 3D scanning has become common in recent years in such architecture-related applications as the preservation and restoration of structures or surveying for public works projects. It enjoys widespread use as a technology that enables more sophisticated repair work on historic buildings and the like by permitting 3D digitization of the entire structure, from façade to interior, thus providing a detailed record of changes in the structure's shape over its lifetime. In an example of a different application, scan data of cedar plantations plays a pivotal role in the development of logistics systems for the management of lumber at all points from plantations to markets.

Information that once depended on the empirical knowledge of specialists can now be digitized into visible data and shared across all phases of the building process, giving us seamless access to that information at every step from design to construction to materials management.

Point clouds

One of a number of 3D scanning technologies, laser scanning measures the distance to objects in millimeter units by irradiating them with a laser beam, then compiles a three-dimensional image of the object from this data. With recent improvements in portability through the development of simpler, more compact equipment, laser scanners have begun to enjoy widespread use. Unlike past surveying techniques that required measurement of each dimension and conversion of these numerical values into lines, arcs and other visual information, laser scanning makes it possible to store data on an entire building as a point cloud.

One day in the summer of 2019, when the highest recorded temperatures in history were measured at 396 spots in the northern hemisphere, we placed a laser scanner on the street in front of Takamizawa House. Mounted on a tripod, the 30-centimeter-square device could scan its surroundings up to a distance of 350 meters. We went on to place the scanner at a total of 12 different surveying points with views of the perimeter of the house, the outer walls, and rooms inside the main house, branch house, and annex. We began scanning at 10 in the morning and continued until the sun had gotten so low that the shadows of buildings covered the street. The cracked and peeling red rust-proofing paint on the corrugated iron sheet covering the south side . . . the thick layers of wallpaper, a new layer added by each new tenant in the home-and-shop units . . . the extension walls, leaning at precarious angles yet somehow still standing . . . staircases that sometimes served as benches, sometimes as bookshelves, their function changing at the whim of the residents . . . posters of steam locomotives pasted over rips in the paper of the *fusuma* sliding doors . . . the pattern of marks left by table legs on the PVC flooring . . . the color of the Western-style wallpaper varying from room to room depending on the amount

点群

　3D スキャニング技術のひとつであるレーザースキャナは、大量のレーザー光を照射することによって対象物までの距離を mm 単位で取得し、そのデータから立体形状をつくりだす測量術である。近年、小型化・簡易化による携行性が向上していることから、多くの導入事例がみられる。寸法をひとつずつ数値で取り、線や円弧などの図形情報として置き換える従来の測量と違い、一体的に建築物を点の集まりとして保存することができる。

　2019 年、北半球の 396 カ所で観測史上最高気温を記録した夏、対象物件である《高見澤邸》の正面道路にレーザースキャナが設置された。三脚の上で 30cm ほどの筐体を鎮座させ、町並みを 350 m 先まで見渡す。周辺環境、外壁、オモヤ、ベツムネ、シンタクの各部屋にていねいにスキャナが置かれていく。測量地点は合計 12 ポイントを数える。午前 10 時から始まったスキャニング作業は、日が傾き正面道路が建物の影で満たされる夕方まで続いた。南面波板のひび割れ剥がれかけた赤い錆止め塗装、住居兼店舗だったためテナントが変わるたびに上書きされてきた壁紙の積層する厚み、不安定な傾きによじれながらもなんとなく成立してきた増築壁、生活者のふるまいに応じてときには腰掛け、ときには本棚に役割を変えてきた階段、ふすまの破れに貼られた SL のポスター、テーブルの脚の跡が細かく残る塩ビ床、喫煙量に応じて部屋ごとに色の変化をみせる欧風の壁紙。スキャナは場の空気そのものを別の世界に絡めとっていくように、レーザー照射の鏡板をくるくると回転させる。

　はたして《高見澤邸》はいったいいくつの分子から成っているのだろう。そんなことを考えるのは途方を失うが、レーザースキャンによって取得された《高見澤邸》の最後の一日の立ち姿は合計 10 億粒の点データに変換された。点一つひとつが空間的な位置情報と、色情報を携えている。そこにあるのは、粗い分子の集まりのような状態で、柱も畳も床の間もバナナのかたちをした壁掛けフックも、すべて淡々とコンピュータの空間内に並ぶ色の粒で、記号的な分節はない。

ラベリング

　レーザースキャナが、分節なく、すべてに平等な眼差しで《高見澤邸》を見つめている頃、デジタル記録チームは並行してまた別の作業を進めていた。

　《高見澤邸》は解体される。解体されるとそれまで結託し建物の形をとどめていた物たちは、部材へと還元される。そうすると各部材が担っていた役目や機能は、部材同士の空間的な関係性が紐解かれたと同時に霧散する。柱だったものが、ただの資材と化す。解体された家の部材を使用してヴェネチアで再構成するために、その部材がもともと《高見澤邸》のどの位置にあり、何の役割を担っていたのかを番札として記録しておくことが必要となる。

　番札は 5 つの情報を組み合わせてつくられた。「場所」「方角」「分類」「要素」「番号」。「場所」は、《高見澤邸》のオモヤ、ベツムネ、シンタクの 3 つの棟を 1、2 階に分けて合計 6 個のパターンで表記した。「方角」は、その部材が「場所」内部でどの方角の箇所についているかを表す。「分類」は内装天井、外壁、屋根など建築の部位が当てられた。「要素」は「分類」よりもさらに細かい区分としてトタンや羽目板など構成部材名で分けられた。「番号」は一連の同様の構成部材のなかの各材に対して割り振られた。これらの名前は、表計算ソフトなどに見られるテーブル形式のデータ表にまとめて管理される。また一つひとつの部材には、データリストに対応したバーコード付きのラベルが、新品の規格材の値札のように貼られた。

部材スキャニング

　10 月、解体されラベルを貼られた部材たちは、まだ暑さの残るなかで東京新宿区の高田馬場に位置するビルに移動された。もともと印刷所が入り、新たにオフィスとし

of cigarette smoke. As if carrying the very air off to another world, the scanner spun its laser mirror round and round.

How many molecules make up Takamizawa House? If that seems like a ridiculous question, consider that a single day toward the end of the life of the house, as recorded by laser scanning, yielded one billion points of data. Each point carries with it not only spatial coordinates but color information as well. Like a collection of very rough-hewn molecules, everything in the house—the pillars, the tatami flooring, the *tokonoma*, the banana-shaped wall hooks—have become colored particles arrayed in the computer's space, devoid of any identifying characteristics.

Labeling

While the laser scanner scrutinized Takamizawa House with a gaze that treated all objects equally, without discrimination, the digital recording team had its own tasks to carry out.

Takamizawa House would be dismantled, and all the objects that had collaborated to maintain the form of the building would revert to their status as elements. When that happened, the role or function performed by each element would vanish from view with the unraveling of its spatial relationships to other elements. What was once a pillar would morph into a mere piece of lumber. If we intended to use the elements of the dismantled house in our reconstructions in Venice we needed to record, on numbered labels, information about the location and function of each element when it was part of Takamizawa House.

We created labels with five types of information on them: location, direction, category, member, and number. There were six locations, consisting of the first and second floors of each of the three sections (main, branch and annex) of Takamizawa House. "Direction" indicated the directional position of the element within its location. The categories were such structural components of the building as the ceiling, outer wall, and roof. "Member" was a further subdivision of categories into constituent elements, such as "galvanized iron" and "clapboard" for "walls." Finally, each item in a particular class of members was assigned its own number. These names were managed in a data table format viewable with a spreadsheet program. To every member we attached a label resembling a price tag with a bar code corresponding to the data list.

Scanning elements

In October, with the summer heat still lingering in Tokyo, we moved these dismantled, labeled elements to a building in the Takadanobaba district of Shinjuku. This was a three-story structure that stood empty as it awaited conversion from a print shop into offices, on loan to us by a cooperating business but only until the renovations got underway. The splatters of ink that covered the second-floor walls spoke of the fierce energy of the printing presses that had once run there, but now, deprived of their context, these traces of bygone days somehow resembled an index of emotions.

Here in these temporary quarters, we set about dividing the elements of the dismantled house into those that would be discarded and

て生まれ変わる直前のガランとした3階建ての建物は、リノベーションが始まるまでの期間限定で協力企業から借り受けられた。2階の壁に飛び散ったさまざまなインクの跡は、そこにかつて印刷機が猛々しく働いていたことを思わせると同時に、根拠を失った痕跡は、なにか感性的な示準をもつかのような佇まいを見せていた。

　解体現場からひとまずこの仮置場に移動された部材たちは、ここで廃棄するものとヴェネチアに移動するものに分けられる。いまとなっては役目すら失われた古い部材たちの一つひとつの名を確認しながら、状態を確認し、清掃・釘抜き・要不要の決定を行う。データリストと照合しながら情報がアップデートされていく。

　高田馬場の仮置場に移動した最大の理由は、仕分け作業のほかに、部材ごとのスキャニングを行うことにあった。3Dスキャニングの技術はさまざまにあって、《高見澤邸》の建った状態を記録した据え置き型のレーザースキャナがそうであるように、レーザーを対象物の表面に当てるものから、CTスキャンの画像を何枚も重ね合わせて内部構造まで立体形状としてつくりあげるものまである。今回のプロジェクトのように、古材や廃材利用において、材ごとのスキャンデータを採りデジタルデータベース化する試みは、まだ技術的に過渡期であることや実際の運用コストの問題から、あまり例がない。一方で、サステナビリティの観点から、資材の再利用にこのようなデジタル技術を用いたロジスティクス管理は、社会的にも期待されていることである。そこで、現段階の技術的状況で、今回のような住宅ひとつを解体新築するくらいのプロジェクト規模において、スキャニング技術がどの程度有効なものかを確かめる実証実験として、2種類のスキャニング方法を試した。

ハンディレーザースキャナ

　ひとつめはレーザー照射型のスキャニングで、ここでは据え置き型ではなく工業用のハンディタイプを用いた。使用した機材は協力企業から提供いただいた2019年に発売された最新のものである。この機材はリバースエンジニアリングとよばれる設計・生産のプロセスに多く用いられる。エンジニアリングが新しい物をつくりだすための技術であるのに対して、リバースエンジニアリングは図面が紛失しているなど、物としては存在しているが情報としては欠損している状態を直したり再度つくったりするための技術である。

　対象物に沿って手持ちのスキャナを動かしていき、リアルタイムで撮られた部分から3Dモデルがコンピュータ内に構築されていく。すでに3D上でデータ化された形態と、いまレーザーが当たっている部分の位置の重なりを、逐次コンピュータが認識しながらモデルを生成する。もし形態の連続性が認識できなくなると、かなりの確率でエラーが発生し、スキャニング不能となる。モデルの連続性は形態的特徴の重なり具合によって認識されるため、より多くの形があったほうが、よりスムーズにスキャニングが可能となる（※1）。すなわちフラットな平面は形の特徴がなくスキャニングができないのである。

治具

　この問題を解決するため、通常では魚の目のような小さいマーカーを対象物にランダムに貼る。コンピュータはそのマーカーを頼りにすることによって、位置関係を認識しモデルを連続的にスキャニングすることができる。しかしながら、この方法だと、マーカーごとスキャニングするため3Dモデルにマーカーの痕が残ったり、対象物実物にシールが貼り付いて取れなくなってしまうなど、じつに物理的な問題に直面してしまう。

　そこで本プロジェクトでは、柱や面材など比較的フラットで形態的特徴の少ない物を、マーカーの直接貼り付けなしでスキャニングするべく、特別な治具を設計し制作した。家具量販店のスチールユニットシェルフの支柱材とホームセンターで購入できる木材やクランプや透明フィルムなどを組み合わせ、対象物を覆うように木枠を組む。そし

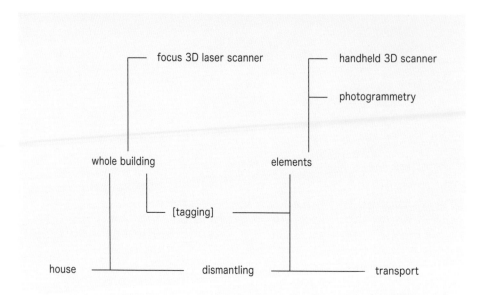

focus 3D laser scanner   handheld 3D scanner

photogrammetry

whole building   elements

[tagging]

house   dismantling   transport

1

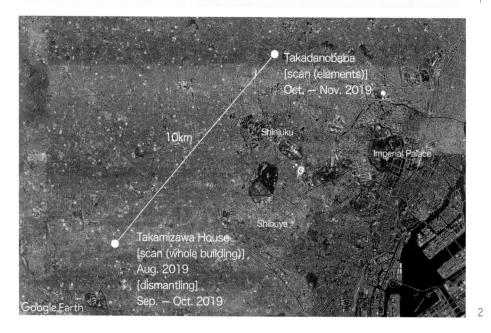

Takadanobaba
[scan (elements)]
Oct. — Nov. 2019

10km   Shinjuku   Imperial Palace

Shibuya

Takamizawa House
[scan (whole building)]
Aug. 2019
[dismantling]
Sep. — Oct. 2019

Google Earth

2

1   Scanning work flow and scan methods.
     スキャニングの作業フローとスキャンメソッド

2   Location of Takamizawa House and scanning sites.
     《高見澤邸》とスキャン現場の地理的位置関係

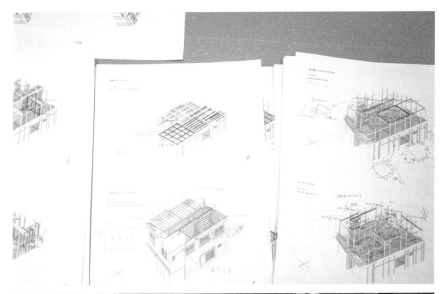

3

4

3   Elements are managed by constructing 3D CAD images from
     measurement data and applying ID tags.
     実測データをもとに 3DCAD を構築し ID 付けによる部材管理を行った

4   ID tags are attached to each clapboard and pillar.
     下見板や柱ひとつずつに ID タグが貼られる

3: ON DIGITAL DESIGN

Scanning jig

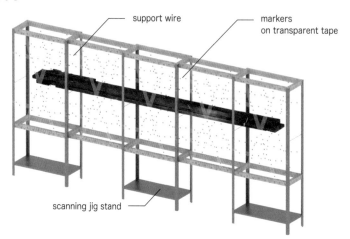

support wire

markers
on transparent tape

scanning jig stand

5

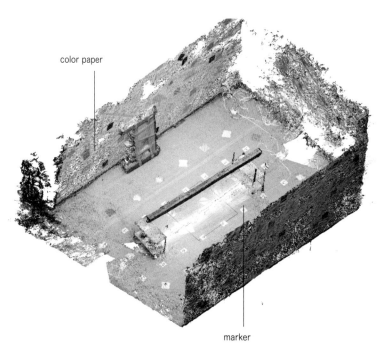

color paper

marker

6

5 Jig built to scan elements with a handheld 3D scanner.
Markers were affixed to transparent tape wrapped around
a steel and wood frame, and elements were mounted on
wires attached to steel supports.
ハンディ 3D スキャナーで部材をスキャニングするために制作した
治具。スチールと木材の枠に透明テープを貼りマーカーを施してい
る。部材はスチールの支柱に張ったワイヤーに乗せる

6 Scanning elements with photogrammetric technology. A
special room was prepared with calibration markers on the
floor and colored paper on the walls.
フォトグラメトリ技術を用いて部材をスキャニングする。壁にカラー
ペーパー、床にキャリブレーション用のマーカーを置いた専用の部
屋を準備して行った

7   Texture data generated by handheld scanner software.
     ハンディスキャナーのソフトウェアによって生成されたテクスチャ
     データ

3: ON DIGITAL DESIGN

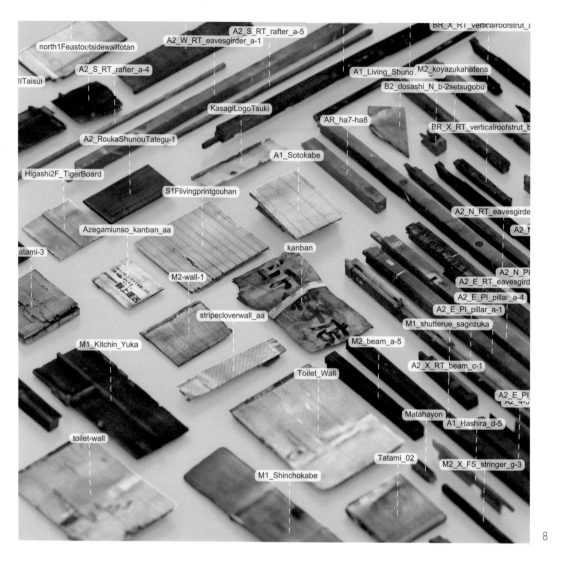

9

8 A portion of the element data scanned by handheld scanner.
   ハンディスキャナーでスキャニングした部材 3D データの一部

9 Scanning the entire building with a stationary 3D laser scanner.
   据え置き型のレーザー照射3Dスキャナーで建物全体をスキャニン
   グしている様子

3: ON DIGITAL DESIGN

10 Point cloud data of the entire building, showing the west façade.
建物全体の点群データ、西面ファサード

11 Point cloud data of the entire building, showing isometric
views of the main house first floor.
建物全体の点群データ、オモヤ１階部分のアイソメトリック

3: ON DIGITAL DESIGN

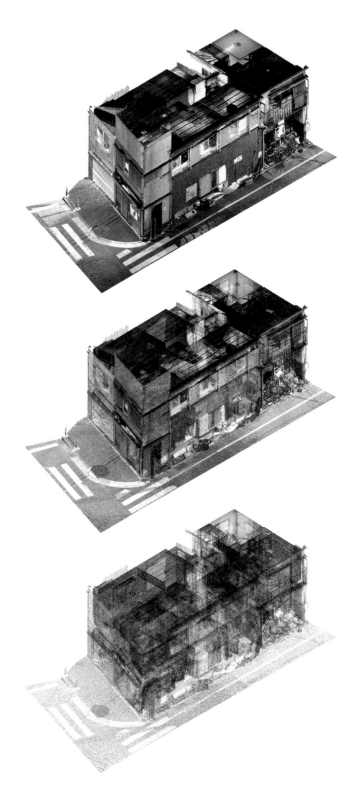

Point cloud data of the entire building, showing an isometric view and the south façade. From the top, point-cloud resolution pitches are 0.5, 1.5, and 2.5 mm.
建物全体の点群データのアイソメトリックおよび南面ファサード。上から点群の解像度 0.5mm、1.5mm、2.5mm ピッチと変化させている

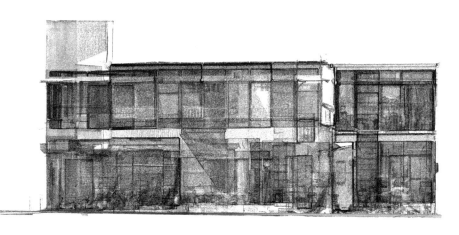

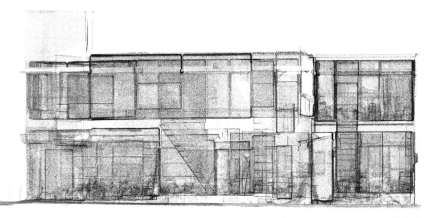

3: ON DIGITAL DESIGN

those that we would ship to Venice. Confirming the name of each of these old members, now deprived of their original raison-d'etre, we checked their condition, cleaned and de-nailed them, and decided whether they should stay or go, updating the information in our data list as we went along.

Besides the sorting process, however, another major reason for moving the house elements to this temporary location in Takadanobaba was so that we could scan them. There are several types of 3D scanning technology. They range from the stationary laser scanner we used to record Takamizawa House while it was still standing, which worked by striking the surface of objects with laser beams, to machines that produce a 3D image of an object's interior from multiple CT scans. Whether because the technology is still in the developmental stage or because the actual operating costs are steep, a project that attempts, as ours did, to create a digital database of scan data from every piece in a collection of old or scrap materials slated for reuse, is a rarity. From the standpoint of sustainability, however, society has need of logistics management utilizing digital technology of this sort for purposes of recycling building materials. In that light we tried out two different scanning methods as an experiment to determine how useful scanning technology at its current level might be for a small-scale project like this one involving the dismantling and rebuilding of a single house.

Handheld laser scanner

First, for laser scanning of individual elements we used a handy portable device made for industrial use instead of the stationary scanner we employed earlier for the entire house. The handheld scanner, a brand-new model that went on the market in 2019, was provided by the cooperating business. This type of scanner is often used in design and production work for reverse engineering purposes. If engineering is the process of making new things, reverse engineering is the process of reconstructing a product or information about it when the object itself exists but information about it is lacking—for example, when blueprints are lost.

As one moves the handheld scanner around an object, the computer compiles a 3D model in real time with the recording of each section. The computer recognizes and adds data on the position of each newly scanned section to the three-dimensional shape it has constructed from the incoming data so far, generating the model as it goes along. If the computer cannot recognize continuity between shapes, in most cases it will cause an error and the scan will fail. The model's continuity is determined by the degree of overlap in in the shapes' geometry, so the more morphological characteristics there are, the smoother the scanning will go.[*1] Thus a flat surface cannot be scanned because of its lack of such characteristics.

The jig

The usual solution to this problem is to stick little dot-like markers at random on the object to be scanned. The idea is for the computer to rely on these markers to ascertain positional relationships as it generates the model. However, this solution causes its own very

て、木枠の面に透明のフィルムを張り巡らせる。フィルム上にマーカーを付けることで、スキャニングのための3次元空間を作成する。あらかじめこの治具のスキャニングフレームと透明フィルムのマーカーの状態だけでスキャニングしておき、そして治具のなかに部材を入れてスキャンする。部材のデータからマーカーのデータのみを引くことで、マーカーの部分を消すことができる。すでに商業的に開発されている技術と、今回の目的に対してそれだけでは足りない部分を、DIY的に創意工夫してつくることで、通常では対応できない形状も、かなりの精度でスキャニングできることが証明された。

フォトグラメトリ

対象物を精緻に記録することができるレーザー照射形式の工業用ハンディスキャナは、近年ハードウェア性能も向上して普及も進んでいる。一方で、機材価格が高価なことや、モデルを生成するために機材本体以外にもコンピュータが必要なことなど、導入にあたってのハードルが高いことも事実である。このような問題点を克服している技術として、昨今のコンシューマーレベルで広く普及している「フォトグラメトリ」がある。フォトグラメトリとは、対象物を360度あらゆる角度から写真を撮り、その写真の視差角から、コンピュータが自動的に立体形状を類推して3Dモデルを作成するソフトウェア技術である。フォトグラメトリのスキャン精度は、ハードウェアのスペックに依拠するのではなくソフトウェア技術に規定されているといえる。すなわち、ある対象物の形を認識しうるに十分な視点の数の写真さえ撮っておけば、将来さらに(人工知能などによる)ソフトウェアの類推技術が発展することによって、より詳細なモデルが構築可能となると考えうる。

本プロジェクトでも、工業用ハンディスキャナを用いた実験をするとともに、フォトグラメトリ技術を用いたスキャニング実験を行った。フォトグラメトリが3Dモデルを構築するにあたって重要なのは、各々の画像の相対的な撮影位置をコンピュータが特定できることである。その位置特定の際、コンピュータは画像内のビットマップごとの色情報を手がかりとする。すなわち、単一色で輪郭に起伏などの特徴の現れにくい立体物は、フォトグラメトリには向いていない。逆に、石や木など色や形が変化に飛んでいる自然物などは最も得意としている。本プロジェクトが主たる対象としている柱梁などはあまり向いていない部類で、本実験においては視差角認識の助けになるよう壁一面に色紙を用いてさまざまな形状と色彩を施し画像記録を行った。しかしながら、まだ検証の余地はあると考えるものの、本プロジェクトに許された時間的制約のなかでは、柱梁など長物の撮影をした場合に、すべての画像の撮影位置をコンピュータに認識させるに至らなかった。また、仕口の形状や微細な表面の凹凸においても、その精度において試行した実験範囲のなかでは良い結果を得られなかった。

写真という100年以上前から続く記録技術を用い、そこにコンピュータによる類推のテクノロジーをハイブリッドさせる。写真をもとに3Dを構築するフォトグラメトリは、後処理にデジタルテクノロジーの力点が置かれた技術である。それはまるで複数の記憶のイメージをつなぎ合わせ、頭のなかでその形を再構築するような感覚に似ている。記憶された像をもとに、「後から」それが何であったかを取り戻す。記録されなかった部分を補完しながら、「あったであろう事実」を再構築する。かくして、記録されたものと後から類推されたものを継ぎ足して、ひとつ先に新たな創造をつくりあげる。

物と情報

関連ある物同士や物を解体したパーツを平面上に並べる「ノーリング」というレイアウトデザインの手法がある。物自体や物同士の成り立ちを2次元の平面の上に並べる。すると普段と異なった情報のレイヤーが立ちあがり、そのレイヤーから世界の成り立ちを別の角度で見つめ直すことができる。ところで、こうして2次元の平面に並べて置い

3: ON DIGITAL DESIGN

real problems, such as showing traces of the markers in the 3D model (the scan doesn't discriminate between the markers and the object), or difficulty peeling the markers from the actual object.

To avoid these drawbacks, we designed and built a special jig that would allow us to scan objects with relatively few morphological characteristics, such as pillars and other elements with flat surfaces, without affixing markers to them. We assembled the jig from braces for steel unit shelving purchased at a furniture outlet, and lumber, clamps, and transparent tape that could be obtained at any home improvement store. We constructed a wooden frame to surround the scanned object, and wrapped the frame in transparent tape. By affixing the markers to the tape, we were able to create a three-dimensional space for scanning purposes. First we scanned just the jig's frame and marker-covered tape, then inserted the target object and scanned again. By deleting the marker data from the object data, we could erase the marker traces from the model. Our experience proved that it is possible to scan even problematic shapes with a fairly high degree of precision simply by exercising a little do-it-yourself creativity to make tools that supplement the commercially available technology where it is inadequate to the task at hand.

Photogrammetry

Recent hardware improvements have made handheld laser scanners capable of highly detailed recordings of objects increasingly popular. However, there are barriers to their marketability, such as the high price of the equipment and the need for a computer to generate the model. One technology that currently enjoys popularity with consumers as a means of overcoming such hurdles is photogrammetry. This is a software technology that enables the automatic generation of a 3D model on a computer based on the angle of convergence among photographs taken of an object from many positions in a 360-degree arc. With photogrammetry, the degree of scanning precision depends on the software, not the hardware specifications. Therefore, as long as you take enough photos from enough angles to define the shape of an object, future advances in modeling software (using AI and whatnot) should make it possible to generate increasingly detailed models.

In this project we experimented not only with an industrial handy-scanner but also with scanning that uses photogrammetric technology. To build a photogrammetry-based 3D model, the computer must be able to identify the relative positioning of each photographic image, for which purpose it relies on color data from the bitmapped images. Consequently photogrammetry is not effective for monochromatic solid objects whose outlines are difficult to discern; conversely, it is excellent for natural objects like rocks and trees with highly varied colors and shapes. However, the pillars and beams that comprise many of the objects in this project fall into the "less effective" category. For purposes of our experiment we tried to facilitate recognition of angles of convergence by applying colored paper to walls to highlight variations in shape and color before taking the photos. Though we believed that further testing was in order, the time constraints our project faced

たとき、もともとあった位置関係の情報はどこにいくのだろうか。物の置き方や場所を変えたりすることは、その瞬間に、もともとあった位置情報がふわっとなくなり、新たな情報がそこに取って代わって入ってくるようなことである気さえしてくる。

　柱や梁、床、押さえ縁や下見板、それぞれの産業的来歴のなかで製造され、東京のあの場所にたどり着き、ほんの数十年、住宅の形をとどめていた物たち。これから遠くおよそ 1 万 km 離れた土地で別の意味と情報を与えられ、約半年の時を過ごし、また別の土地に移動する予定の物たち。数十年のアイデンティティをもとに名を与えられ、点の位置情報に還元されてデータの海に放流される物たち。

　予算や時間、重量、大きさ、さまざまな物理的要件と奮闘しながら行った一連の作業で情報化できたものは、4,000 あった部材の 1/10 にすぎない。しかし、技術的な向上にすべての期待をかけるのではなく、このような限界性にこそ想像性の本質を見る。

　フォトグラメトリは、記録された複数の視点から視点と視点のあいだを類推で補完し、ひとつの 3D モデルをつくりだす。一度解体された《高見澤邸》が部分ごとに別の場所で再構築されたとき、その場に居合わせる者は部分を頭のなかで結びつけながら、なんとなくもとの形を想像するだろう。データベースに収められた部材の 3D データを見た人は、それがもともとどこにあったのか思いを馳せるだろう。フォトグラメトリも人間が行っていることはさして変わらないが、人間と違い技術は、見えているけれど見えない世界、人間の目では捉えきれない世界を明確に映し出す。そしてそれら技術は現在において限りなく透明化し、私たちの現実感は、すでに常習化したデジタルの目を介してつくりあげられている。

　そもそも建築設計においてデジタル技術の活用はどのような意味があるのだろう。それは BIM に代表されるように、設計・生産の効率化など合理的な理想を完成形へと近づける。ないしそれは、アルゴリズムを駆使して人間の手では生み出せない形態をつくりだす。はたまたそれは、機械学習のように大量のデータから人間では導き出せなかった知の発見を行う。そしてそれは、設計と生産のナレッジをシームレスに共有することを可能にし、地域性から国際性などあらゆるスケールを横断する。その価値や意味は時代や状況に応じて変わるが、創造性を模索するにおいては、デジタル技術で何ができるかではなく、それが何であるか問うことを念頭に置きたい。

　《高見澤邸》は解体され、デジタル化された。写真が現実をそのまま光の集まりとして写し出すように、レーザー照射によるスキャニングは現実を「距離の集まり」として映し出す。物質から剝離した距離の集まりは、またもとの宿主に戻るのかもわからない。部材へと姿を変えたあの物質としての建築物は、いまは港に積まれたコンテナのなかで新たな意味の訪れを待っている。データ化された物たちは、物質世界に寄り添いながらも、また別の法則によって存在し始める。解体・移動・再構築のなかで起こりうる建築エレメントの誤用や転用をポジティブな営為として捉え直す本展。データ化された本プロジェクトにおいても、単なる古材管理のデジタル活用ではなく、情報の欠損さえも、誤用や転用の創造的契機として捉えたい。

　そして、ある日イタリアの街角で《高見澤邸》の柱が陽気な看板を支えている風景に出会う。あるいは VR ゲーム空間をさまよっていてあの夏の日に情報世界に送られた柱と出会う。そのような未来が到来することに期待したい。

註
※1――本実験では形のみで連続性を認識するタイプの機材を使用したが、機材ないし使用ソフトウェアによっては、レーザー照射とともに、写真画像認識を使った色の一致度によるモデル形態の統合をハイブリッドに行う技術もある（2019 年 11 月の時点で使用した機材も色の一致による認識ができるようになったが、本実験では都合により使用しなかった）。

データベース構築・3D スキャニング：砂山太一、奥泉理佐子、磯野信、松下千尋、吉田野土香、添田朱音
点群レーザースキャン（FARO）協力：クモノスコーポレーション株式会社
ハンディレーザースキャナ（EinScan Pro）協力：日本 3D プリンター株式会社
執筆協力：川久保美桜

3: ON DIGITAL DESIGN

prevented us from achieving computer recognition of the positions of all images taken of pillars, beams, and other long objects. We were also unable to obtain accurate results within the limits of our experiment when photographing complex shapes like joints and surfaces with minute irregularities.

A hybrid of computer modeling technology with photography, a recording technology first developed over a century ago . . . Photogrammetry's strong suit is that it harnesses the power of digital technology to process the 3D images it constructs from photographs. This bears a remarkable resemblance to the process by which we remember things: reconstructing the shape of a larger memory in our minds by linking images from multiple memories together. Based on these stored images, we recall what happened at a later time, filling in the gaps in our recollections to reconstruct the "probable facts." In this way we add our modeled inferences to what we have recorded to create something new.

Objects and information

There is a layout design method known as "knolling" in which you arrange a set of related tools or the parts of a dismantled object at right angles to each other on a flat surface. Organizing the relationships between objects, or between parts of an object, in two dimensions creates a new layer of information that enables us to view the organization of the world from a different perspective. But when we lay objects out on a flat surface in this manner, what happens to the information about their original positional relationship? When we alter the placement or location of objects, any previous positional information vanishes into thin air, as if the space it occupied a moment earlier had been usurped by new information.

Pillars, beams, floorboards, moldings, clapboards . . . These objects, each manufactured in its own industrial context, were brought to together in a particular place in Tokyo where they defined the form of one house for just a few dozen years. Now they will be assigned different meanings and information in a land some 10,000 kilometers distant, where they will spend half a year before moving on to other destinations. Under names reflecting the identities they maintained for those several dozen years, they have been reborn as point-clouds of information and tossed into a vast sea of data.

Grappling with such physical constraints as budget, time, weight, and volume, we were able to complete the digitization of only one-tenth of the 4,000-plus elements on hand. And yet, rather than place all our hopes on improvements in technology, we have come to see in these very constraints the essence of creative possibility.

Photogrammetry generates a 3D model by referencing a large number of recorded viewpoints and filling in the gaps between them. When the parts of the dismantled Takamizawa House are reconfigured at a different location, the people there will no doubt find themselves picturing the parts in their original configurations even as they contemplate how to join them together. When they view the 3D data for an element stored in the database, they will wonder where that element was originally located. Though there is little if any difference between what photogrammetry does and what the human mind does, technology offers a clear picture of a world that cannot be seen with the human eye, or one that we see but without truly seeing it. And now that today's technology has made everything infinitely transparent, our sense of reality is formed through digital eyes that have already become a force of habit.

What, ultimately, is the point of utilizing digital technology in architectural design? One purpose is to facilitate our pursuit of such rational ideals as efficiency in design and production, building information modeling (BIM) being a prime example. Another is to create forms, through the use of algorithms, that cannot be produced by the human hand. Yet another is to acquire knowledge from vast quantities of data that a human being alone cannot process, as with machine learning. Finally, digital technology enables us to seamlessly share design and production knowledge on any scale, from local to global. Its value and meaning will vary with the times and the circumstances. In seeking out new modes of creativity, however, the question we should ask is not what we can do with digital technology, but what digital technology itself is.

Takamizawa House has been dismantled and digitized. If photography captures reality as a bundle of light, laser scanning captures it as a bundle of distances. Removed from the physical substance it once adhered to, this bundle of distances may yet return to its host. Now transformed into its constituent elements, the house embodying that substance sits in containers on a dock, awaiting anointment with a new meaning. The digitized objects may keep one foot in the material world, but they have

begun a new life that follows different rules. This exhibition is an exercise in reassessing as a positive thing the diversions or misuses of architectural elements that are likely to occur in the process of dismantling, shipping, and reconfiguring them. Our digitization project, too, should not be viewed as simply for purposes of materials management, but as a source of the creative opportunities to be found in diversion or misuse—even the loss of information.

Someday, we may see pillars from Takamizawa House supporting a colorful signboard on an Italian street corner. Or we may be wandering through the space of some VR game and come upon the pillars we sent off to the world of data on that summer's day. I look forward to the arrival of that future.

Note
*1 The scanner we used in our experiment recognizes continuity only in terms of object shape. However, depending on the device and software, a technology is also available that integrates model shapes using a hybrid of laser scanning and color matching based on photographic image recognition. (As of November 2019 the model we used is also capable of color match-based recognition, but circumstances did not permit its use in our experiment.)

Database construction and 3D scanning: Taichi Sunayama, Risako Okuizumi, Makoto Isono, Chihiro Matsushita, Nodoka Yoshida, Akane Soeda
Focus laser scan (FARO) cooperation: KUMONOS Corporation
Handheld laser scan (EinScan Pro) cooperation: Japan 3D Printer Co., Ltd.
Assistance with manuscript: Mio Kawakubo

3: ON DIGITAL DESIGN

Primordial Noise in an Information Society
Takehiko Daikoku (Philosopher)

With: Kozo Kadowaki (Architect and construction studies)
+ Toshikatsu Kiuchi (Architect) + Sunayama (Architecture and art studies)

The separation of information and material in an information society

Kozo Kadowaki: One of the things we'd like to talk about with you today, Professor Daikoku, is the theoretical meaning of one of the major themes of this project, the movement of objects. In the course of transporting materials from Japan to Italy, we are bound to lose all sorts of things. However, we believe that we can find a positive meaning in the loss that accompanies this movement by treating loss as an opportunity for new creations. Through this approach, we also want to examine the meaning of living in a society that is constantly involved in movement or transport. Another theme is the meaning of digitizing objects. We have been making 3D scans of the elements of Takamizawa House to convert them into data. Here again, we believe that losses occurring in the process of making the move from real space to digital space can provide us with creative opportunities. Another concern is this: As the standardization of architecture proceeds apace on a global scale, one encounters buildings made in the same way all over the world. That's because building materials are standardized to facilitate mass transport. Yet at the same time, delivery systems like Amazon's are personalizing their logistics to match the needs of individual customers. Might personalized logistics suggest an alternative possibility for architecture as it becomes increasingly standardized?

Takehiko Daikoku: A while back I wrote an article, "A Social Philosophy of Distribution: The Significance of the Amazon Logistics Revolution for an Information Society" [in *Gendai Shi-*

so (Revue de la pensée d'aujourd'hui) Special Issue: Distribution Studies, March 2018 issue, published by Seidosha]. One reason I wrote it was a recognition that the ordinary perception of products as fundamentally consisting of objects no longer holds true today. If products have two aspects, as information and as material, then it is a characteristic of our information society that these two aspects must inevitably be separated. It is the Internet that made this possible, but in fact the problem itself has a long history in philosophy.

Platonic philosophy, for example, begins with the idealized notion of ideas, which are imitated in inferior copies through what is known as mimesis. Aristotlian philosophy, on the other hand, dismisses the existence of ideas, recognizing as real only objects composed of *eídos* (form) and *ýli* (matter). We can think of "form" in this sense as meaning "information."

Now, according to your concept for this exhibition, "movement" is a positive keyword. But in an information society, movement is eliminated wherever possible. As with Amazon's delivery system, information and material are separated, with information arriving first via the Internet, to be followed later by material. What Amazon has done is construct a vast and sophisticated distribution network to reduce that delay to as brief a time as possible.

Toshikatsu Kiuchi: I'm reminded of the "Bad Press" project by Diller and Scofidio [1993]. Men's dress shirts are normally ironed and folded so they will fit into a rectangular packing box, but without making the creases conspicuous. "Bad Press" was an installation that proposed pressing clothes in twisted, wrinkled patterns as a new style of expression. This notion of creating new expressions from losses and constraints that are an unavoidable consequence of the transport process relates to our project, too, I think.

Kadowaki: The project involves dealing with the large number of parts, or elements, lost in the process of dismantling Takamizawa House. We intentionally use the word "elements" because it also connotes the creation of some sort of whole. Furthermore, we anticipate that compensating for the loss of these elements will serve as a catalyst for creativity. I believe there is a critical aspect to finding a source of creation in movement that causes the separation of information and objects. I think that pretty much sums up our project.

Movement and potentiality

Daikoku: That makes perfect sense to me, and relates to a concept for which I use the term "virtuality." As it's used today, the word "virtual" is based on the Platonic distinction between the "real" thing and a copy, but originally it meant something like "potential." Potentiality and possibility are usually treated as synonymous, but they actually mean entirely different things. If we follow Kant, possibility is like a 500-yen coin you are only thinking about. You can use it only if that possibility becomes real: an actual 500-yen coin. Potentiality, on the other hand, refers to the properties of a material. It could become a 500-yen coin, or something else altogether—the possibilities are many and varied. So if we look to elements for a creative spark, we must view them as "potentialities" that could turn into any number of things.

Then, Aristotlian philosophy has it that form (i.e. information) and matter (i.e. materials) form a hierarchical structure. At the top is "pure form," which Aristotle defines as God, the supreme end. All materials aim toward becoming that supreme end of pure form. At the other end, the material at the very base of the hierarchy is "primary matter"—but the instant this is defined, it becomes form, so it is ultimately indefinable. It's really none other than *mu*—nothingness, the unformed void.

Until now, the paradigm for creation has been the supremacy of form. That is precisely why we assign importance to authorship, in the sense of "Who created that form?" In contrast, what you are attempting here is to see what will happen when the matter at the base of the hierarchy begins to make itself heard—when form is viewed from the standpoint of matter.

Kadowaki: You might say it's an experiment in treating design, traditionally considered a conceptual endeavor, as a conversation initiated by materials.

Daikoku: Form can be designed, but matter cannot, because it is one with nature.

The shift to a world of uncertainty

Kiuchi: Maybe it's because we've spent so much time doing 3D scans of the house elements, but our interest has tended to focus on the materiality of matter, and how that can be factored into the logic of assembling things. On the other hand, the more data we deal with, the more difficult we find to view it as matter and incorporate it into our concept of design.

Daikoku: As I mentioned before, primary matter doesn't exist. It can't appear as just form or just matter. In the past, form and matter were always bound together in "objects," but it became possible to separate them with the advent of the information society. That provided the opportunity for the birth of "virtuality." An information society is by definition one in which matter that is originally supposed to correspond to a certain form may correspond to other forms instead. We can also describe this phenomenon in terms of the shift from a world of certainty to one of uncertainty. In that sense, this project is extremely contemporary in its relevance to our information society.

Taichi Sunayama: In his *FedEx* series, the artist Walead Beshty packed glass cases in cardboard FedEx boxes, shipped them to international destinations, and exhibited the glass cases as they were, with the cracks they incurred in transit. You could interpret that as a depiction of a failure, caused by the transport process, in the integration of form and matter.

Daikoku: The work incorporates that deviation and finds a source of creativity there, doesn't it. Marx's theory of revolution talks about much the same thing. The Ancien Régime is the form, a space into which aristocrats, commoners, and slaves are all crammed. As far as the form is concerned they are mere matter, but when poverty gets too extreme, the matter—i.e., the slave class—revolts, altering the form as well. That's what revolution is, in a nutshell.

Kadowaki: A society that's entirely covered by a logistics network like Amazon's is ripe for a revolt by matter. The delivery of a different object from the expected one is like a small rebellion by objects. Nor can we overlook the possibility of a more large-scale uprising against chronic delivery delays and rising fees.

Kiuchi: What stance should architects adopt in such circumstances?

Kadowaki: What we can do for the time being, I think, is to lend our support to the struggles of matter. Up to now, design has consisted of mobilizing physical matter that conforms to an idealized form. We should change our way of thinking and provide matter in revolt with the optimum forms to patch it up.

"Primordial noise" as context

Kadowaki: Something else I would like to discuss is the issue of converting house elements to digital data. Our purpose in digitizing them was to manage objects that are inherently unmanageable. But doing 3D scans of every single element produced a quantity of data far beyond what we anticipated, so now the data itself is in revolt and quite unmanageable. We're currently confronted with a situation where both objects and information are out of control.

Sunayama: It feels as if the 3D scanning did

not generate information about matter so much as it generated a different kind of matter altogether—something that isn't just a copy of reality, but has its own distinct texture.

Kadowaki: Architects often draw what we call a framing plan that merely indicates the positional relationships of posts, beams and other elements. We might describe it as a medium that intentionally reduces information to an abstraction of architecture. The sensation you describe of information turning into matter via the 3D scan process may be due to the inclusion of lots of extraneous information beyond what we intended to gather.

Daikoku: In a system that assigns supremacy to form, it is desirable to eliminate noise to the extent possible. But if we assign supremacy to matter instead, we should preserve as much noise as possible. Ordinarily we think of noise as anything that interferes with whatever it is we wish to convey, but that premise needs to be challenged. Shouldn't we treat noise rather as the context that sustains what we wish to convey—like an ocean in which our little island of content floats? I refer to noise that serves as a condition for possibilities in this manner as "primordial noise." Perhaps we need to treat the 3D data as "primordial noise" in this sense.

Kadowaki: Digitization is the act of moving objects into the world of computers. When you tear objects away from their original context, other aspects of those objects come into view. If you think about it, that's the same thing as moving the house elements to Italy. We tend to think of the information society as a world of forms, but it may well be more of a world of matter than we thought.

129

情報社会における根源的ノイズ
大黒岳彦（哲学者）

聞き手：門脇耕三（建築家・構法研究）＋木内俊克（建築家）＋砂山太一（建築・芸術学研究）

情報社会における「情報」と「素材」の分離

門脇耕三： 今回は哲学をベースにメディア論や情報社会論、ロジスティクス論などを研究されている大黒岳彦さんにお話を伺いたいと思います。大黒さんとお話ししたい内容はいくつかあります。ひとつには、今回のプロジェクトではモノの移動が重要なテーマになっており、その理論的な意味づけをしたいということがあります。日本からイタリアに資材を運ぶと、じつにさまざまなものが失われます。解体と輸送の過程でモノを遺失してしまうばかりではなく、何もしなければ部材の組み立ての情報もほとんどが失われてしまう。そのときに、これらの欠損を新たな創造のための隙間とみなすことで、移動に伴うロストにポジティブな意味を与えられるのではないか。そうしたことを通じて、われわれが日々、移動や輸送に取り囲まれている社会に暮らしていることの意味も問いかけてみたいと思っています。

もうひとつお話ししたいのは、モノをデジタルデータ化することの意味づけです。これまで《高見澤邸》の部材を3Dスキャンしてデータ化してきたのですが、われわれにもまだその作業の意義がよくわかっていないところがあります。しかしここでも、現実空間から情報空間に移動することで生じる欠損にクリエイティブな契機を見出すことは可能でしょう。また、デジタル情報はコンピュータが見ている世界そのものですから、われわれが見ている情報世界の喪失を表現しているともいえる。そのあたりをいま一度言語化しておきたいという狙いがあります。

さらに付け加えるなら、いま建築の空間はグローバルなレベルで規格化・標準化が進んでいて、世界中どこに行っても同じようなつくり方の建物に出会う。それは建築に使われる資材が大量輸送に合うようにカスタマイズされてしまっているからなんですね。一方で、Amazonの配送システムなどを見ると、ロジスティクスが個々の顧客のニーズに合わせてパーソナライズしている側面もある。われわれとしては、個別化したロジスティクスが建築の規格化・標

準化に対する別の可能性の提示につながるのではないかという期待もあります。

大黒岳彦： 僕は以前、〈流通〉の社会哲学——アマゾン・ロジスティックス革命の情報社会における意義」という、現代の情報社会をロジスティクスの観点から分析した論文を書いたことがあります（『現代思想　特集＝物流スタディーズ』2018年3月号所収、青土社）。それを書いた理由はいくつかありますが、ひとつには、一般的に商品の原基形態はモノであると考えられていますが、もうそういう時代ではないだろうという現状認識があるからです。もう少し具体的にいうと、商品が「情報」と「素材」という2つの側面によって構成されているとするならば、それらが必然的に分離せざるをえないのが情報社会の特質なのではないかと思うのです。

それを可能にしたのはインターネットですが、この問題系自体は哲学史では古くからあるものです。例えばプラトン哲学の場合、最初に理想的な「イデア＝原形」があって、その劣化コピーが「ミメーシス＝模倣」と呼ばれる。プラトン哲学では、そのような本物／コピーの図式で世界が考えられている。基本的にファインアートの原理はミメーシスであるといえるでしょう。それに対して、アリストテレス哲学はイデアなんて理想的なものはない、あるのは地上にある個々のものだけだとする個体主義で、リアルな個物は「形相」と「質料」でできているという考え方をとります。形相はギリシャ語で「エイドス（εἶδος）」、質料は「ヒュレー（ὕλη）」といいます。あるいはラテン語で「フォルマ（forma）」と「マテリア（materia）」といってもいい。そして、この「エイドス」ないし「フォルマ」は、「情報」と読み替えることができる。そう考えるなら、「情報」という概念は、哲学においてはきわめて伝統的な考え方だということがわかります。

それから、今回のコンセプトでは「移動」がキーワードになっているとのことですが、情報社会においては、移動はなくせるのであればなくしたいものです。瞬間移動装置のようなものがあって顧客の要求する商品をすぐに届けるこ

とができれば、それに越したことはない。ところが情報社会においては、Amazonの配送システムを考えてもらえばわかるように、情報と素材は分離していて、インターネットを介して情報が先に届き、素材は遅れて手元にやってくる。Amazonがすごいところは、その遅れをできるだけ短くするために広大かつ繊細な流通網を構築した点にあります。ですから、移動にポジティブな価値を見出すというお話を聞いて、やや虚を突かれた思いがしたんですね。

門脇：　われわれも移動そのものをポジティブに捉えているわけではないんです。しかし、移動に取り囲まれている事実から出発したいということですね。

木内俊克：　お話を聞いていて、ニューヨークの建築家のディラー・スコフィディオが、かつてロジスティクスが孕む問題をテーマにした《Bad Press》(1993)というプロジェクトを行っていたことを思い出しました。Yシャツは普通四角い梱包箱に合わせて折り目がつけられています。それに沿って折り目がついていれば、きちっとしたものに見えるわけです。プロジェクトではそれを逆手にとって、ひねったりねじったりしてシワのパターンが新しいスタイルの表現になるということをインスタレーションとして提示しました。輸送によって不可避的に生じる欠損や制限や遅れなどの問題を、そのまま新たな表現に転換しようとする視点は、今回のプロジェクトにもつながるものだと考えています。われわれとしては、完成した状態のモノと移動のプロセスを切り分けずにシームレスに捉えることで、自分たちがどういう世界に生きているのかということをリアリティをもって示したいと思っているわけですね。

門脇：　今回は《高見澤邸》という古民家を解体することで出た大量の部材を扱っています。それらはあらかじめ欠損した部材です。僕はよく「エレメント」といういい方をするのですが、この言葉には全体の部分というニュアンスがあるので、明示されていない全体像を想像させるようなところがあります。さらにいえば、エレメントには何らかの全体性を生成していくようなイメージもある。「欠損」にしてもそうで、何かが欠けているがゆえに、そこを埋め合わせ

ようとする創造力──潜在しているものを顕在化させるような力──を喚起するところがあるのではないかと考えています。そのときに、大黒さんがおっしゃったような、情報とモノとの分離が起こる。Amazonなどはそこを一刻も早く埋め合わせようとするのですが、それでも情報が欠損したエレメントとしてあるからこそ顕在化の欲望を抱えるわけですね。そのこと自体は創作者としてポジティブに捉えていて、そうした分離を引き起こす移動には、なんらかの批評的側面があるのではないか。ひとまずはそのように整理できるかもしれません。

コンテクスト間の移動と潜在性

大黒：　なるほど、よくわかりました。それは僕のいい方でいえば「ヴァーチュアル」という概念に関連する問題です。ヴァーチュアルは普通「仮想」と訳されます。それはプラトン的な枠組みに基づいていて、まず本物があって、ヴァーチュアルなものはその劣化した再現であるという含意がある。僕は「ヴァーチュアル」という言葉はもうちょっと違うニュアンスで語られるべきだと思っているんですね。例えば、ジャン・ボードリヤールは1980年代の後半に、マスコミがつくり出す現実はVR（ヴァーチュアル・リアリティ）だといっている。つまり、現実と思われているものがそもそもヴァーチュアルなのだという見方を、ボードリヤールはその時点ですでに提示しているわけです。

もともとヴァーチュアリティとは「潜在性」を意味する言

3: ON DIGITAL DESIGN

葉です。一般的に「潜在性」と「可能性（ポシビリティ）」はイコールで結ばれがちですが、これらはまったく別のことを意味しています。これはジル・ドゥルーズや彼に影響を与えたアンリ・ベルクソンなどもいっています。カントに従えば、可能性とは考えられただけの500円玉のようなもので、実際に使うことはできない。それが現実化して500円玉という実体になることで、はじめて使えるようになるわけです。一方、潜在性とはそういうものではなく、素材の属性を意味しています。それは500円玉にもなりうるし、別のものにもなりうる、多様性を孕んだものなのです。よりわかりやすいモデルとして、植物の種子を考えてみればよいでしょう。種子は育つまではどんな植物になるかわかりません。どんな植物にもなりうる多様性を孕んでいる。それこそが「潜在性」というものなのです。ですから、素材やエレメントに創造性を求めるのであれば、それらを何になるかわからない「潜在性」として考える必要があるのではないでしょうか。

門脇： 面白いですね。このあいだ國分功一郎さんにお話を伺ったときにファインアートの話になりました（200頁参照）。20世紀のファインアートの典型的な方法論は、日常的なものを本来のコンテクストから切断するもので、わかりやすくいえば、美術館の白い空間のなかに置かれるとゴミでも作品に見える、といったものです。この場合はオブジェクトそのものよりも、コンテクストを脱却するという方法のほうが重要です。しかしわれわれはもはや、そうしたやり方にリアリティを感じられなくなっている。今回われわれがやっていることは、オブジェクトを違ったコンテクストに移動させると、オブジェクトが隠していた潜在性が発揮されて、別の発現の仕方をするということなのではないかと思うんですね。慣れ親しんだものが別のコンテクストに移動すると、最初は「不気味なもの」に見えるはずです。しかしそれに手を加えることによって、もう一度親しみのあるものへと回復していく。今回のプロジェクトではそういうことを試みているのではないかと國分さんはおっしゃっていました。そう捉えると、移動から潜在性の

議論まで、すべてつながってくるように思えてきます。

大黒： 方、情報はそれぞれのコンテクストのなかで再構築されるので移動しないんですよね。移動するのは素材です。だから遅れが生じるわけですね。

砂山太一： 移動はベクトルと位置情報の変化として捉えられます。位置情報には情報という言葉が含まれていますが、考えてみれば定義が難しいところですね。この世界では同じ位置に別のものがあることはないので、位置情報は固有のものと考えることができます。オブジェクト指向のプログラミング形式においては、「プロパティ」と「ビヘイビア」を分けて考えますが、位置情報は「ビヘイビア」で、それに付帯する共有可能な情報が「プロパティ」ということになる。一口に情報といっても、2つのレイヤーがあるわけです。解体した《高見澤邸》の各部材は位置情報が剥落しているので、世界における固有性がない状態、プロパティしかなくなっている状態といえます。それをイタリアに持って行き、再構築することで、新たなビヘイビア＝ふるまいが与えられる。そう考えると、移動というのは、新たなふるまいを与えることと捉えることもできます。

なぜこういうことを思ったのかというと、各部材をデータ化する際に固有の名前を振るのですが、その名前が位置情報に基づいているのです。「オモヤの2階の南面にあったn本めの柱」というように。それはイタリアに持って行ってもそのまま引き継がれるわけですが、関係性のネットワークが再構築される以上、それに由来する名前のほうも変わるべきではないかという気もするんですね。

門脇： それは位置情報というより、ほかの部材との相対的な関係性を表しているように思います。建築にはさまざまな部材の名称があります。同じ材質や形の木材であっても、「垂木」と「根太」は違うものですね。位置が保存されているというより、構築のための関係性が保存されていると考えるべきではないでしょうか。

大黒： SNSのコミュニケーション情報でも時間と場所がタグ付けされるじゃないですか。その場合の位置情報は、GPSという絶対的な座標軸に基づいているわけですね。

それはニュートン的な絶対的な時空間です。一方で、ライプニッツが考える時間や空間は相対的な関係性であり、トポロジカルな枠組みです。そういう意味では、建築の部材はライプニッツ的な閉じた関係性、つまりコンテクストのなかで意味をもつものだといえるでしょう。

木内： いまの砂山さんの部材の話と、先ほどの大黒さんの情報が先に届いて素材は遅れてくるという話は、微妙に違う気がするんですね。砂山さんは部材の固有名について考えていますが、素材というのは名札をもっておらず、匿名的なものですよね。

不確定的な世界への移行

大黒： そこは重要なポイントですね。少し整理していうと、アリストテレスの哲学では、「形相＝情報」と「質料＝素材」は階層構造をなしているんですね。その頂点にあるのが「純粋形相」で、アリストテレスはそれを究極目的としての神と規定している。あらゆる素材はその究極目的である純粋形相に向かっているというわけです。対して、最も底にある素材が「第一質料」と呼ばれるものです。これについてはどういうものか規定できない。規定した瞬間に形相になってしまうからです。だから「無」というほかないものなのです。

これを一般化していうと、形相から見るとき、素材は匿名的なものとしてしか捉えられない。ニクラス・ルーマンは、社会というのは人間から成るわけではなくてコミュニケーションから成るのだといっていますが、その含意はコミュニケーションによるネットワークこそが一次的なものであって、人間はその交点にあるノードにすぎないということです。だから人間は代替可能で、そこに AI が入ってきてもかまわないわけですよ。

門脇： そう考えると、われわれがやっていることと Amazon との違いが明確になりますね。Amazon が扱う商品は匿名的なものなので、どこに配達されても違和感なく受け取られるわけですが、われわれが扱っているのは名前

があるもので、イタリアに行くと不気味なものになる。

大黒： これまでの創作のパラダイムは形相優位だったわけですよ。だからこそ「誰が形相をつくったか」が、つまり作家性が重視された。それに対して、今回は基底にある質料が自己主張を始めるというか、質料から形相を見たときにどういうことが起きるかということを試みているのではないでしょうか。

門脇： いままでは理念的なものとして考えられてきた設計を、素材からの対話として捉える試みだと。

大黒： 形相は設計可能ですが、質料はどちらかというと自然と結びついたものなので、設計できないわけですよ。Google と Amazon という二大グローバル企業で考えると、Google が形相的であるのに対して、Amazon は質料重視の企業といえます。なので、Google と Amazon はセットで見ていく必要がある。さらにいえば、僕はロジスティクスというのは代謝のようなものだと思っているんですね。人体においては、構成している物質がある期間ですべて入れ替わるわけじゃないですか。そういう意味で、ロジスティクスは世界の代謝系だと考えるとわかりやすい。その際、形相は自己同一にとどまるわけですが、質料は代替可能です。というより、形相が自己同一にとどまるためには、質料が入れ替わる代謝系が必要なのです。

木内： お話を聞いていて、先日、構造設計の金田充弘さんに、部材をどうやって組み立てるか相談をしていた際の議論を思い出しました。しばらく部材の 3D スキャン作業をしていたせいか、形相と質料の言葉をお借りすれば、僕たちの関心は名前の付けようのない物質の質料性に傾倒しており、それを何とか組み立ての論理に組み込めないか考えてきている節がある。しかし考えれば考えるほど、データを質料として見る視点は捉えどころがなく、なかなか設計という概念には結びつかない難しさがあると感じています。

大黒： 先ほどもいったように、第一質料はないんですよ。形相も質料も実体化したらダメなんです。昔はモノというかたちで、形相と質料がつねに密着して存在していたので

すが、情報社会においては、それらが分離可能になってしまったわけです。そこにおいて「ヴァーチュアリティ」の生まれる余地が出てくる。つまり、本来はある形相と合致するはずの質料が、別の形相と合致する事態が起こりうるのが情報社会なのです。それは確定的な世界からより不確定的な世界への移行といういい方もでき、そういう意味では今回のプロジェクトはきわめて現代的であり情報社会的な試みだといえます。

門脇： Amazonは、いったん分離した形相と質料が顧客のもとで再び完璧に合致することを仮定したビジネスモデルなわけですね。

大黒： そうです。ZOZOが共同開発して話題になった「ZOZOSUIT」などはその典型で、それまで洋服はショップに行って試着して買うことが普通だったわけですね。ところがZOZOの場合は、最初に専用アプリによって体型などのデータを採って、その後で合う服を買う。要するに、形相が先行してあって、それに完璧に合致する質料を後から埋めるというモデルなんですね。

砂山： ワリード・ベシュティという美術作家の作品に、ガラスケースをFedEx便の段ボール箱に詰めて国際輸送し、輸送過程でひび割れたガラスケースを作品としてそのまま展示する《FedEx》というシリーズがありますが、あれなどは逆に、移動によって起こる形相と質料の統合の失敗を表現していると解釈することもできますね。

門脇： AmazonにしてもZOZOにしても形相と質料を完璧に統合することに血道を上げていたわけですが、もしかしたら両者を統合しない方向に次の可能性があるのかもしれませんね。

大黒： 昔は製品が手元に届くまで、どんなものが届くかわからなかったわけですよ。ところが、Amazonでは写真や詳細な製品情報によって最初からわかりきっている。だからこそ、最初のイメージとズレが生じたときには不満が爆発するわけですね。

門脇： 一方で、現在はイメージのズレに気づかせないようなデザインもいろいろと出てきています。最近の若い人た

ちはほとんどショップに行かず、eコマースで服を買うようになっていますが、結果として数が出せない新進のブランドのデザインほど、フリーサイズやユニセックスを前提にすることが多くなっている。ここしばらくダボッとした服が再び流行っているのはこうしたことが関係していると思いますが、体型と服の型紙が切り離されたデザインがどんどん出てきているんですね。

大黒： ズレが生じることを織り込んで、それをクリエイティビティにつなげていっているわけですね。マルクスが革命理論でしているのがまさにこういう話で、アンシャン・レジーム（旧体制）というのは形相＝形式なんですね。その空間に貴族や平民や奴隷などが押し込められている。彼らは形式にとっての質料＝素材にすぎず、一人ひとりは代替可能なのですが、貧窮してくると素材である奴隷層が反乱を起こすわけです。それで形式のほうが変わっていく。これが革命なんですね。

門脇： Amazonのようなロジスティクス網が覆い尽くした社会は、質料が反乱を起こす契機に満ちています。日常的な例でいうと、思っていたモノと違うモノが届くということはモノの小さな反乱だといえるし、慢性的な遅配や配送の高騰など、もっと大規模な反乱の予感も絶えません。

木内： そうした状況に対して、われわれ建築家はどういうスタンスを取るべきなのか、もう少し明確にしておきたいところです。

門脇： さしあたり建築家としてできることは、質料の蠢きに悪ノリしてみることだと思うんですね。イデア的な形相に合うよう自在に質料を呼び出すというのがこれまでの設計でしたが、発想を転換して、質料が暴れているからそこに最適な形相をパッチ的にあてがう。そういうスタンスですよね。

大黒： やはりイデアを追い求めるよりは、どこまでも個体に即してつくることがこれからの設計なのではないでしょうか。

134

コンテクストとしての「根源的ノイズ」

門脇： もうひとつ考えておきたいのは、部材のデジタルデータ化にまつわる問題です。もともとは制御できないモノを管理する目的でデータ化を試みたわけですが、部材を一つひとつ 3D スキャンしたところ、情報量が想像以上に大きくて、今度はデータのほうが暴れて制御できない。われわれはいま、モノも情報もどちらも制御できない事態に陥っているわけです。

砂山： モノと情報をただ単に対応させるだけであれば、別に 3D スキャンではなく写真でもいいんです。ただ、3D スキャンであれば精確な形と寸法が採れるわけですね。ところがいざスキャンしてみたら、物質に対する情報というよりも、別の物質が現われてしまったという感じでしょうか。写真においても写真特有のリアリズムがあると思いますが、3D スキャンにおいても、ただの現実の写し身ではなく固有の質感が現れている。

門脇： 例えばわれわれ建築家は、柱や梁などの部材の位置関係だけを表現した伏図という図面を書くことがありますが、これはあえて情報を少なくして建築を抽象化するメディアだともいえる。砂山さんが 3D スキャンによって情報が物質化する感覚を抱くのは、取得したい情報以外のたくさんの過剰な情報が入ってしまっているからではないでしょうか。

大黒： 博物館などでは、貴重な文物を 3D スキャンして展示することがありますね。あの展示は来館者に複製としての 3D データを見てもらう目的がありますが、展示物としての 3D データは基本的に完全無欠でノッペリしています。これは、初源の文物にはノイズがないことを前提としているからですね。しかし、このプロジェクトにはそういう目的があるわけではなく、扱っている部材は初源からノイズだらけですし、管理のための情報化だといってもノイズが管理の邪魔をしてくる。ですから、ここは見方を 180 度転換して、この強烈なノイズ性をどのように利用できるかという観点に立つべきではないでしょうか。

形相優位の体制では、ノイズはできるかぎり排除されることが望ましい。しかし、質料優位で考えるなら、逆にノイズはできるかぎり保存されるべきです。ノイズこそが不確定性と深く結びつき、想像を超えた何かを生み出す要因になるわけですから、そこにクリエイティブな契機を見出さなければ。ビッグデータというのはそういうもので、膨大な情報を集めるとノイズにしか見えないのだけれど、データマイニングして解析してみると、そこから考えもしなかったような新たなパターンが見えてくるのです。今回のデータにしても、一つひとつ単体で見ていくと単なるノイズなのだけれど、それらを集めることでパターンが見えてくるということもありうる。そういう活用の仕方もあると思いますね。

門脇：「ミラーワールド」構想などでは、情報空間のなかに現実世界とパラレルな世界を構築することで、世界の検索性が高められるだろうといわれています。しかし今回の試みを通じて、その企図はおそらく想像以上に困難で、情報空間はノイズだらけになるではないかと思うようになりました。逆にいうと、われわれが見ている安穏としたこの現実世界は本来ノイズだらけで、普段はそのことに気づかないのだけれど、情報化によってはじめてそのことに気づかされるのではないか。だとすれば、情報化によって世界の検索性が上がるという単純な話ではないように思えてきますね。

大黒： 一般的にノイズというのは、伝えたいことがまずあって、それを攪乱するものと思われていますが、そもそもその前提を疑ってみる必要があります。ノイズというのはむしろ、伝えたいことを成り立たせるコンテクストであり、ノイズの海のなかにコンテンツという小島が浮かんでいると捉えたほうがいいのではないか。そのような情報の可能性の条件としてのノイズを、僕は「根源的ノイズ」と呼んでいます。そう考えるとこの 3D データは「根源的ノイズ」として捉えるべきなのではないでしょうか。

門脇： 建築における基本的なコンテクスチュアリズムでは、世界を「図」と「地」に見立てて、どういう設定をすれ

ば何が「図」として浮かび上がってくるかという操作をします。いまのお話を聞くと、3Dデータにコンテクスチュアリズム的な操作を施すと、まったく違った「図」が浮かび上がってくるはずで、それこそが「潜在性」と呼ぶべきものだということですね。

大黒： そのとおりです。ですから、最初に目的を設定してはダメなんです。目的もわからないまま、とにかく何でもかんでも集めるというのがビッグデータの発想です。ノイズだらけの状態からなんらかのゲシュタルトが浮かび上がってくる。それこそがクリエイションではないでしょうか。

門脇： 実際の展示では、ある部材のデータから別の潜在性を浮かび上がらせるという見せ方を試みてもいいかもしれませんね。情報化というのはオブジェクトをコンピュータの世界に移すことであり、もとのコンテクストから引き剥がすことでオブジェクトの別の側面が立ち上がるわけですから、考えてみれば、イタリアへの輸送と同じようなことをやっているといえる。情報化社会というのは一般的には形相的と考えられていますが、あらためて意外と質料的な世界なのかもしれませんね。

大黒： そうだと思いますよ。今回の展示で「エレメント」と呼んでいるものは、僕の言葉では「メディア」といい換えられます。メディアというと普通は「媒体」と訳されますが、美学の分野では第一に絵具や石膏といったメディウムを指します。つまりメディアの本義は素材性であり、その意味において、「情報社会はメディア社会である」というべきなのです。

4:
REASSEMBLAGE
OF
ELEMENTS

エレメントの
再構成

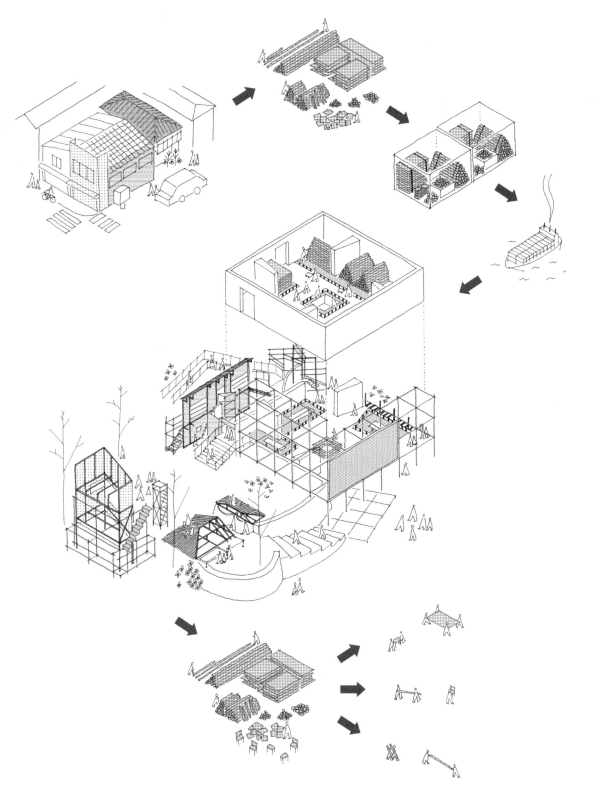

Exhibition Layout
Kozo Kadowaki
(Architect and construction studies)

Built in 1956, the Japan Pavilion of the Venice Biennale was designed by Takamasa Yoshizaka, an architect who studied with Le Corbusier and taught at Waseda University. The pavilion sits in a corner of Venice's largest park, the Giardini di Castello. In typical Yoshizaka fashion, the building is erected atop pilotis so as to harmonize with the rolling terrain of the park.

Unique among the national pavilions at the Biennale, the Japan Pavilion has its own garden, intended, it is said, for exhibiting sculptures. Though it contains some large trees, the garden is not ostentatiously designed and blends naturally with the open space of the surrounding park.

In contemplating how to hold our exhibition at this pavilion, the first thing we considered was the construction process. Most of the exhibition materials will come from the dismantled Takamizawa House. Brought by ship, these bits and pieces of the house need to be stored in a safe, secure, dry place where they can be easily managed. The natural candidate is the interior of the pavilion. And so the pavilion itself has become our "warehouse."

The construction work will require adequate space for processing and test-assembling these materials. The piloti space under the pavilion provides shelter from rain and wind, making it ideal for this purpose. So the piloti space is our "workshop."

That leaves only the garden to serve as an exhibit space, so that is where we decided to reassemble Takamizawa House. Visitors will be encouraged to tour the exhibit space, warehouse, and workshop in that order. I have described each of these spaces in detail below.

(1) Exhibit space (garden)

Here we will exhibit Takamizawa House as it appeared when it served as a residence. The house itself will be reassembled into components of the display space for the exhibits. The façade that faced the main street will be appropriated as a screen, the roof of the annex as benches facing the screen, and the corrugated iron sheeting from the south wall as display paneling. Videos showing the original configuration of these elements will be projected on the screen. In this way visitors can simultaneously view the past and present of the house. Some sections of the pipe scaffolding used during the assembly process will be left in place to provide structural reinforcement. However, a key aspect of these exhibits is that there will be no moment of "completion."

Extending as it does beyond the spatial boundaries defined by the Japan Pavilion building, our exhibit space will lack any clear-cut boundary of its own, becoming a place where all kinds of objects gather together in wobbly, haphazard fashion. This configuration is itself an implicit critique of the rigid framework of the Venice Biennale, which is predicated on competition among nation-states, each holding its own exhibition.

(2) Warehouse (pavilion interior)

Any elements of Takamizawa House not used in the exhibit space will be displayed inside the pavilion. Our plan is to arrange them according to the era in which they were installed and the type of industry that produced them. This should give viewers a clear idea of how the industries that created Takamizawa House transitioned from handicrafts to heavy industry.

　　To protect the floor, we plan to cover it with the type of "blue sheet" tarpaulin commonly used for such purposes in Japan. We will leave the blue sheets in place even after the show opens, but our aim is for a design that uncouples the sheets from their usual symbolic association with work sites and temporary structures.

(3) Workshop (piloti space)

The piloti space under the pavilion will be used as our workshop for processing and test-assembling the elements of Takamizawa House. Our plan is to build all the workbenches and other furniture used by the artisans from elements of the house.

We will also erect scaffolding on the walls of the pavilion and hang blue sheets for signage there, with the space between the walls and sheets serving as a workspace for the architects.

Of the huge quantity of elements generated by the dismantling of Takamizawa House, a substantial portion consists of wooden members, particularly those used as structural and backing materials. After the exhibition opens we plan to hold workshops where people can use this surplus wood to make furniture, which will be displayed as part of the exhibition. After the show is over, interested parties will be welcome to take these items. Thus our exhibition will continue to grow even after opening. What we will be designing over the course of the show is the trajectory of the surplus elements emerging from Takamizawa House as they set out on yet another journey, this time from Venice to points unknown.

展覧会の会場構成
門脇耕三（建築家・構法研究）

ヴェネチア・ビエンナーレ日本館は、ル・コルビュジエのもとで学び、
早稲田大学で教鞭を執った建築家である吉阪隆正により
設計され、1956年に竣工した。日本館は、カステッロ地区にある
ヴェネチア最大の公園、通称ジャルディーニの一角にあり、
吉阪の設計らしく、公園の起伏をそのまま活かすために
ピロティで床を持ち上げた設計となっている。
日本館は、彫刻を展示するために設けられたという庭園をもつが、
これも他国のパビリオンにはない大きな特徴である。
庭園には大きな樹木が生い茂っているが、庭園として
整えられすぎることもなく、周囲のオープンスペースとごく
自然に連続している。
ここで展覧会を開催するにあたって、まず考えたのは、
その施工のプロセスである。展示の主材料となるのは解体された
《高見澤邸》であるが、日本から届いたバラバラの《高見澤邸》は、
雨がかからず、施錠ができて資材の管理も容易な日本館内に
運び込むことが自然に思われた。
そこで館内は「資材庫」と見立てることにした。
施工のためには、資材を加工したり、仮組みするためのスペースが
必要となる。ピロティは雨もかからず、風も抜け、
こうした作業には都合が良さそうだ。
そこでピロティを「工房」と見立てることにした。
そうなると、残されたスペースは庭園しかない。
そこで《高見澤邸》は庭園で組み上げることとし、ここを
「展示スペース」と見立てることにした。
観客は、展示スペース、資材庫、工房の順に展覧会を
めぐることになる。
それぞれの詳細は、以下の通りである。

(1) 展示スペース（庭園）

ここで展示されるのは、《高見澤邸》が住宅として使われていた頃の
姿である。また、展示物を展示するために用いられるのは、
組み立てなおされた《高見澤邸》自身である。
《高見澤邸》の大通り側のファサードはスクリーンへ、シンタクの
屋根はスクリーンを眺めるベンチへ、南側のトタンの壁面は展示壁
面へと転用されて、かつての姿を映した映像などが展示される。
一軒の住宅の過去と現在を同時に眺めるような展示である。
組み立てのために用いた単管足場は、一部が残置されて構造的な補
強として用いられているが、ここでは「完成」という一瞬をつくらな
いことが強く意識されている。
なお、われわれの展示は、日本館という建物がつくる空間的枠組みを
離れて、その外部に展開したわけだが、結果として、展示スペースは
明示的な境界を失い、あらゆるものがふらふらと
迷い込んでくるような場所となった。
この会場構成には、各国間が独自の展示を行って国別に競い合う、
ヴェネチア・ビエンナーレのネーション・ステート的な枠組みへの
批評も込められている。

(2) 資材庫（日本館内）

展示スペースで使われなかった《高見澤邸》の部材や部品は、
日本館内に展示される。これらは取り付けられた時代と、その生産を
担った産業の性格に従って並べられる予定で、
《高見澤邸》をつくった産業が、手工業的なものから重化学工業的な
ものへと変質していったことが読み取れるような計画としている。
床の養生のため、日本では養生用シートとして一般的な
ブルーシートを使う予定である。
ブルーシートは開幕後もそのまま残されるが、
残されたブルーシートが「現場」や「仮設」といった記号性から
切り離されて見えてくるようなデザインを目指している。

(3) 工房 (ピロティ)

《高見澤邸》の部材の加工や仮組みを行うため、ピロティは
工房として用いられる。職人が用いる作業台などもすべて
《高見澤邸》の部材を用いてつくる予定である。
日本館の壁面には足場を立て、ブルーシートを貼ってサイネージと
しているが、壁面とブルーシートの隙間は建築家のための
作業スペースにあてられる。
《高見澤邸》の解体で生じた部材や部品の数はおびただしく、
特に構造材や下地として用いられていた木材は膨大である。
開幕後は、この木材を使って家具などを製作するワークショップを
開催する予定だが、製作した家具は会場内に置いて展示物とし、
さらに閉幕後は、希望する人に使ってもらうことを考えている。
この展覧会は、開幕後も成長を続けるのであり、開幕後にわれわれが
デザインするのは、《高見澤邸》から生まれた余剰のエレメントが、
ここからさらに別の場所へと旅立っていく、その軌跡である。

　　　　　4: REASSEMBLAGE OF ELEMENTS

146

Jo Nagasaka
長坂常

Born in 1971. President of Schemata Architects. He works on projects in diverse genres both in Japan and abroad. His interest is in gleaning new perspectives and values from everyday objects and existing environments, and sharing them with people through his designs. He is co-author of *When B Side Becomes A Side* (revised edition, Kajima Institute Press, 2009), *Jo Nagasaka: On My Mind* (LIXIL Publishing, 2016), and *Joe Nagasaka / Schemata Architects* (Frame Publishers, 2017).
http://schemata.jp

Representative projects
Artek ColoRing (2019)
DESCENTE TOKYO (2019)
HAY TOKYO (2018)
House in Nobeoka (2017)
Blue Bottle Coffee Kyoto Cafe (2017)
VITRA STAND in Milan (2015)
DESCENTE BLANC Daikanyama (2015)
Aesop Aoyama (2012)
HANARE (2011)
LLOVE (2010)
House in Okusawa (2009)
Sayama Flat (2008)

1971 年生まれ。スキーマ建築計画代表。国内外でジャンルを問わず活動の場を広げる。日常にあるもの、既存の環境のなかから新しい視点や価値観を見出し、デザインを通じてそれを人々と共有したいと考えている。共著書＝『B 面がA 面にかわるとき［増補版］』(鹿島出版会、2016)、『常に思っていること』(LIXIL 出版、2016)、『JO NAGASAKA/SCHEMATA ARCHITECTS』(Frame Publishers、2017) など。
http://schemata.jp

主な作品など
《Artek ColoRing》(2019)
《DESCENTE TOKYO》(2019)
《HAY TOKYO》(2018)
《Blue Bottle Coffee Kyoto Cafe》(2018)
《House in Nobeoka》(2017)
《VITRA STAND in Milan》(2015)
《DESCENTE BLANC Daikanyama》(2015)
《HANARE》(2011)
《LLOVE》(2010)
《Aesop Aoyama》(2010)
《House in Okusawa》(2009)
《Sayama Flat》(2008)

1 *HAY TOKYO* (2018)
ⓒMasataka Nishi
《HAY TOKYO》(2018)
ⓒMasataka Nishi

2 *Blue Bottle Coffee Kyoto Cafe* (2018)
ⓒTakumi Ota
《Blue Bottle Coffee Kyoto Cafe》(2018)
ⓒ太田拓実

3 *Sayama Flat* (2008)
ⓒTakumi Ota
《Sayama Flat》(2008)
ⓒ太田拓実

4 *Artek ColoRing* (2019)
ⓒArtek
《Artek ColoRing》(2019)
ⓒArtek

5 *House in Nobeoka* (2017)
ⓒTakumi Ota
《延岡の家》(2017)
ⓒ太田拓実

6 *HANARE* (2011)
ⓒTakumi Ota
《HANARE》(2011)
ⓒ太田拓実

4: REASSEMBLAGE OF ELEMENTS

1

2

3

4

5

6

Learning Things We Didn't Know,
Thinking Things We Never Thought

Twenty years have passed since I began designing furniture immediately upon graduation from university. During those two decades I expanded my scale of production to interiors, and then to buildings. Today, in addition to furniture, interiors, and buildings, I also work on the scale of cities, designing everything from houses to commercial facilities and schools.

In 2007, members of my staff said they wanted to work in an office that was open to the surrounding neighborhood, not closed off from the outside world. Together with the Aoyama|Meguro art gallery and the professional painter Shuhei Nakamura, I rented a space facing the street in Nakameguro, Tokyo, which formerly belonged to a shipping company, and opened the shared office Happa there in 2007. At Happa we designed and built things, went about our daily lives, and invited people to visit. We built not only desktop models but actual 1:1-scale objects, held exhibits so we could gauge the reactions of people firsthand, and sometimes threw parties where our staff and visitors could intermingle. Being in this environment opened my eyes to the creation of spaces that have "reality."

The global financial crisis known in Japan as the Lehman Shock occurred the year after we opened Happa. Around that time the president of a real estate firm said to me, "You and your staff are sneaky. Why is your own office so much nicer than the places you design for everyone else? Can you make my apartment houses as nice as this?" Acceding to his request, we undertook the renovation of a 30-unit apartment building. The project, *Sayama Flat* (2008), for which we created spaces simply by "subtraction," proved to be a turning point in our approach to making things. For the first time I was pleased by the sight of residents of one of my works using it and adding to it as they liked. Previously, whenever I visited a residence of my design after the owner had moved in, I felt a twinge of disappointment at the sight of laundry hanging out to dry or furniture scattered around a room. With this project, though, no such feelings arose. If anything, I wanted to engage in more such undertakings.

Continually moving space, invisible development

My previous attitude of making everything from scratch has evolved to one of thinking that the world around us already has some good things in it that can be improved with just a little work. Moreover, the things we make will, in time, be altered by other people. When I realized this obvious truth, it changed my approach to architecture. I designed *Hanare* (2011), a new residence that is meant to be modified while lived in. For the *MAKE HOUSE: New Prototypes of Wooden House* exhibition (2015), I thought of a house to be lived in while being built. As part of a proposal for a new campus for the Kyoto City University of Arts (2017), I designed "semi-architecture"—structures that are neither buildings created exclusively by a professional nor pieces of furniture to be moved around at will by the user, but which can be moved by the proprietor. Through these designs I hoped to enrich the activities of people both inside and outside a building. I began to think about spaces that continue to move, where completion is not the peak but the start of a process. This idea came to fruition in *Hay Tokyo* (2018). In 2020 we will complete part of the Arario in Jeju project, an example of what we call "invisible development" that will transform activities on a neighborhood scale by simultaneously renovating several adjacent older buildings. Then, in 2021, we plan to see the continually-created space we developed for the Kyoto City University of Arts proposal realized in a building for Musashino Art University.

The work of renewing knowledge

Along with architectural endeavors of this sort, we also continue, via the furniture making we began at Happa, with the work of "knowledge renewal"—learning things we didn't know, thinking about things we never thought about before. *Flat Table* (2008) is the result of realizing that if you pour colored epoxy resin on a tabletop, the uneven surface produces different shades of color, yielding attractive patterns. Subsequently we created *Udukuri* (2012) for London's Established & Sons, using the traditional *udukuri* finishing technique of scrubbing the wood surface to bring out the grain, yielding vivid color gradations. Then we combined the *Tsugaru-nuri* lacquering technique with *udukuri* for our ColoRing furniture line (2013), which led to a special ColoRing edition (2019) of Alvar Aalto's Stool 60 that was presented at the 2019 Milano Salone international furniture fair; it is now mass-produced in collaboration with Artek.

Not long after I introduced *Sayama Flat* as well as *House in Okusawa* (2009) in the book *When B Side Becomes A Side* (Yamato Press, 2009), orders for residential renovations suddenly dried up, but work on commercial spaces just as abruptly increased. Aesop Aoyama (2010), in which we utilized old materials reclaimed from a demolished house for the shop interior, was representative of that period. The next few years produced a variety of projects both at home and abroad, ranging from the brands Takeo Kikuchi (2012) and Today's Special (2012) to apparel shops for Descente Blanc (2015) and cafés for Blue Bottle Coffee (2015). My next commission for a residential renovation, after a five-year hiatus, was *House in Hatogaya* (2015). This order came from a very ordinary family, evidence of the extent to which "naked architecture" has achieved acceptance in Japan. Around the same time Kozo Kadowaki, the curator of this exhibition, consulted with me on the renovation of *House in Tsutsujigaoka* (2015), and *House in Nobeoka* (2017) followed after that.

知らなかったことを知り、思いもしなかったことを思う

大学を卒業してすぐに家具のデザインを始め、その後インテリアから建築へと制作のスケールを上げながら20年ほどが経過した。現在では、家具、インテリア、建築のほかにまちづくりも手がけ、設計ジャンルも住宅から商業施設、学校などへと広がっている。

2007年に、外界から閉ざされたオフィスではなく、街に開かれたオフィスで働きたいという希望がスタッフから上がり、アートギャラリー「青山｜目黒」と塗装職人のなかむらしゅうへいとともに、中目黒の路面に立つ元運送会社のスペースを借りてシェア・オフィス「HAPPA」(2007)を始動した。われわれは「HAPPA」でデザインし、ものをつくり、生活し、外から人を招き入れた。デスクトップだけではなく、実際に手を動かして1/1のものづくりをしたり、展示をして目の前で人々の反応を確認したり、時にパーティを開いて集まった人たちとスタッフの皆でコミュニケーションをとる。そんな環境のなかで、改めてリアリティのある空間づくりに目覚めていった。

「HAPPA」を始めた翌年、リーマン・ショックが起きた。その頃、「HAPPA」を訪れた不動産会社社長から「先生たちはずるいですよね。自分のところはこんなに素敵なのに、何でよそではよそいきの設計をするんですか？ うちの集合住宅もこんな素敵な場所にしてくれませんか？」と依頼を受けて、30室ある集合住宅の改修が始まった。これがわれわれが「引く」だけで空間構成を行った《Sayama Flat》(2008)で、ものづくりの転換点となったプロジェクトだ。このプロジェクトではじめて、自分の作品に住人が自由に手を加えたり、自由に使っている光景を素敵だと感じた。それまでは、施主が入居した後の住宅に行くと、干されている洗濯物や置かれている家具を見ては身勝手にもガッカリしたりしていたのだが、このプロジェクトでは一切そんな感情が湧かず、むしろこんな感じのプロジェクトをやっていきたいと思ったのだった。

動き続ける空間、見えない開発

すべてのものを白紙からつくるというこれまでの考えが、われわれの周りにはすでにまんざらでもない世界があり、そこに少し手を差し出すだけでより良いものになるという思いに変わった。そして、われわれが手がけたものもゆくゆくは他人によって変えられていく。そんな当たり前なことに気づいた時、建築へのアプローチが変わったのだ。住みながら変化していく新築の住宅《HANARE》(2011)を設計し、「MAKE HOUSE 木造住宅の新しい原型展」(2015)でつくりながら住む家「つくる家」を考え、京都市立芸術大学移転設計プロポーザル

（2017）ではプロだけがつくる「建築」でも、人が自由に動かせる「家具」でもない、運営者が動かせる「半建築」を設計し、室内外で人のアクティビティを豊かにすることを考えた。竣工はピークではなくスタートであり、動き続ける空間を考え始めた。こうしたことが《HAY TOKYO》（2018）で実を結び、2020年にはわれわれが「見えない開発」と呼ぶ、隣り合う複数の古いビルを同時に改修して街の規模でアクティビティを変える「Arario in Jeju プロジェクト」の一部が完成する。そして2021年には、京都市立芸術大学プロポーザルの際に考えていた育てる製作空間が、武蔵野美術大学の校舎で実現する予定だ。

知の更新作業

　このような建築活動と同時に、HAPPAで始めた家具づくりを通じた「知の更新」作業（知らなかったことを知り、思いもしなかったことを思う作業）は現在も続いている。テーブルの天板に色のついたエポキシ樹脂を流し込むことで表面のわずかな凸凹の深さの差が色の濃淡を生み、模様をつくることに気づいた《FLAT TABLE》（2008）をつくり、その後、木の表面をこすり木目を浮き上がらせる仕上げ技法「うづくり」による色のグラデーションが鮮やかな《UDUKURI》（2012）をロンドンの Established & Sons から発表した。また津軽塗とうづくりを掛け合わせた《ColoRing》（2013）は、2019年のミラノサローネ国際家具見本市で発表したアルヴァ・アアルトの「Stool 60」を使った《ColoRing》（2019）へと展開し、Artek 社とのコラボレーションによって量産化が実現した。

　書籍『B面がA面にかわるとき』（大和プレス、2009）では満を持して《Sayama Flat》と《奥沢の家》（2009）の両住宅を発表するのだが、その後、ぱったり住宅リノベーションの依頼がなくなる一方、急激に商業空間の仕事が増えた。その頃の代表作に、古い住宅の解体ででた古材を利用した店舗の内装《Aesop Aoyama》（2010）がある。その後、《TAKEO KIKUCHI》（2012）や《TODAY'S SPECIAL》（2012）、アパレル《DESCENTE BLANC》（2015−）からカフェ《Blue Bottle Coffee》（2015−）など多種多様なプロジェクトを国内外で展開している。再び住宅リノベーションの依頼を受けたのは約5年後の《鳩ケ谷の家》（2015）だった。ごく普通の家族からの依頼で、日本におけるネイキッドアーキテクチャーへの理解への高まりを表している。同時期に本展キュレーター門脇耕三からも住宅リノベーションの相談を受けて《つつじヶ丘の家》（2015）ができ、その後《延岡の家》（2017）を手がけた。

4: REASSEMBLAGE OF ELEMENTS

Ryoko Iwase
岩瀬諒子

Born in 1984. President of Studio Iwase and Assistant Professor, Graduate School of Engineering, Kyoto University, where she also graduated from the Faculty of Engineering and completed her master's program. After working for EM2N Architects in Switzerland and at Kengo Kuma and Associates, she established her own office after winning the 2013 Kizu River Waterfront Competition held by Osaka Prefecture; her prizewinning waterfront renovation, *Tocotocodandan*, was completed in 2017. Her practice covers multiple areas from architectural spaces to public-works infrastructure and public space design. She has received the grand prize of The Japanese Institute of Landscape Architecture Award, the Good Design Gold Award, the Tokyo University of the Arts Emerald Award, and the Best Debutant Award.
http://ryokoiwase.com

Representative projects
W city Street project (2018-)
Children's home project (2019-)
Tocotocodandan (2017)
Doboku no Heya (2014)
Kamakura of Light (2014)
KUSANAMI (2013)

1984 年生まれ。岩瀬諒子設計事務所主宰。京都大学建築学科助教。京都大学工学部卒業。同大学工学研究科修了。EM2N Architects（スイス）、隈研吾建築都市設計事務所を経て、2013 年大阪府主催、河川沿いの広場設計業務実施コンペにおける最優秀賞受賞を機に、岩瀬諒子設計事務所を設立。当該作品を堤防のリノベーション《トコトコダンダン》として 2017 年に発表。建築空間から土木インフラやパブリックスペースのデザインまで、領域横断的に設計活動を行う。主な受賞に日本造園学会賞、グッドデザイン金賞、藝大美術エメラルド賞、ベストデビュタント賞など。
http://ryokoiwase.com

主な作品など
《W市街路計画》(2018－)
《子どもの家プロジェクト》(2019－)
《トコトコダンダン》(2017)
《ドボクノヘヤ》(2014)
《光のカマクラ》(2014)
《KUSANAMI》(2013)

1 *Tocotocodandan* (2017)
Top: Overhead view photographed by drone. The area contains a mix of residences and factories. / Photo by Shinkenchiku-sha
Bottom: The landscaping is designed to provide both a flood-prevention embankment and a riverfront space for people to enjoy. / © Masato Ikuta
《トコトコダンダン》(2017)
上：上空よりドローンで撮影。住宅と工場とがまじりあうエリアに立地する／撮影＝新建築社写真部
下：防災施設としての堤防と人の居場所としての水辺を両立するランドスケープ／© 生田将人

2 *Tocotocodandan* (2017)
Porous concrete planters. / © Shingo Kanagawa
《トコトコダンダン》(2017)
ポーラスコンクリートの花壇／© 金川晋吾

3 *W City Street Project* (planned for 2022)
The street and the private lots on either side blend into a seamless whole. / © studio IWASE
W市街路計画（2022予定）
隣接する民有地と道路が連続的な風景となる／© 岩瀬諒子設計事務所

4 *KUSANAMI* (2013)
Top: Model of the work aligned with the direction of the wind. / © studio IWASE
Bottom: A landscape created by shimmering glass, light and shadows. / © studio IWASE
《KUSANAMI》(2013)
上：風向きに沿うよう配置された計画案／© 岩瀬諒子設計事務所
下：揺れるガラスと光と影で風景をつくる／© 岩瀬諒子設計事務所

1

2

3

4

4: REASSEMBLAGE OF ELEMENTS

The Materiality of Interfaces

Architecture/civil engineering/landscaping

Treating architecture, civil engineering, and landscaping in a continuum as a means of seamlessly relating people, infrastructure, and the natural environment, I engage in spatial practices that seek to incorporate feedback from the new perspectives found in fields that differ in their systems, scales, and philosophies.

Through architectural-scale projects in which I design interfaces between public spaces, streets, embankments and other forms of infrastructure, I search for ways in which people can relate to their surrounding environment them in a manner appropriate for such future contingencies as disasters and downsizing.

Material/scale

The objects dealt with by these different fields vary in use, scale, and dimension (solid or flat), but such universal concepts as "material" and "scale" serve as clues toward treating them in seamless fashion. For example, the *igusa* rush grass used in traditional Japanese architecture can function as flooring in the form of tatami mats, or as a wall finish for plastering. By the same token, concrete can be turned into floors or walls, or molded into curbstones which are treated as works of "civil engineering" rather than "architecture." Materials, as we all know, are universal entities that seamlessly apply to diverse elements and fields. At the same time, they are fascinating presences with a broad range of distinct identities, each varying in its physical properties, origins, impact on human sensibilities, aging, and meaning.

A tidal wall that enriches lives

Tocotocodandan (Osaka, 2017) is a riverfront embankment for which I added tiers and sloping terrain to an existing vertical tidal wall as part of the construction of a 240-meter promenade and a 4,300-m² public space. I inserted new topography that incorporates traces of the wall's half-century history of improvements, which were discovered midway through the design stage. The design offers people the opportunity to use the embankment as furniture, to observe changes in tide levels, and to participate in maintaining the city's infrastructure by tending to the plantings there.

The dampness-free surface of porous concrete is ideal for people who want to lie down, while the tiny crevices in it provide a habitat for moss and other plant life, contributing to the growth of a small ecosystem. Also, because we built the retaining walls by layering paving materials like a *mille-feuille* pastry, a pattern resembling geologic strata emerged on the surface. From a slight distance the multi-tiered form of the embankment takes on a textured appearance, creating a landscape embracing such diverse elements as people, plants, railings and planters.

Dynamism underground

A project for W city—a 240-meter-long, 11-meter-wide street extension scheduled for completion in 2022—drew my attention to the property boundaries between the street and the private land along it, as well as to the presence of infrastructure trunk lines beneath the surface. Despite this being an improvement project for a "symbol road" for the city, most of the streetside properties were parking lots, and the roadway itself was not sufficiently wide. My proposal was to re-edit this landscape. First, I proposed securing adequate pedestrian space by modifying the roadway width and alignment. In addition, I proposed making the sidewalk match the asphalt pavement of the parking lots (the roadway was block-paved), thereby blurring the visual boundary between the private land and the sidewalk, and giving the parking lots—private properties in terms of administration—the appearance of public spaces maintained as one with the road space.

Most streets have infrastructure trunk lines buried under them in alignment with the road surface. Whenever a streetside building is erected, the roadway gets dug up due to the construction work required to connect the building to the trunk lines. Over time the street—particularly if it is paved with asphalt—comes to resemble a chaotic patchwork of old and new surfaces. For this project I envisioned dividing up the asphalt surface from the outset so that, with the passage of time and the discoloration of the pavement, the history of the town's repairs creates a collage-like pattern on the surface.

Depicting light and wind

Kusanami (Tokyo, Osaka and Düsseldorf, 2013), a glass construction that shimmers in the wind, is my expression of the presence of light and wind through the medium of glass. I used 0.5 mm thin sheets of chemically strengthened glass, the kind that covers smartphone screens, in the largest possible dimensions (1800 mm maximum height). The single sheets were not freestanding. Altering their shapes without applying heat, I joined two or three sheets together to form structures that could stand on their own. Light entering the room is scattered by the twisted glass surfaces, filling the space with curtains of light that sway gently in the breeze.

Among my other projects are furniture-scale works that utilize the same strand rope used for suspension bridges in civil-engineering projects; hedge landscaping integrated into architecture; and the reorganization, for disaster prevention purposes, of public facilities covering an entire city block.

Just as the shapes of buildings and other structures can be perceived as textures when viewed from a distance, I strive to seamlessly arrange forms and textures, including those of such organic elements as mountains, trees and foliage, via the lens of scale. Through such arrangements and choices of materials, I try to weave new relationships together and imbue them with multiple layers of meaning, always bending my ear to the voice of the "place."

Through this practice, my hope is to take the imaginative stimuli offered by the natural environment, urban infrastructure, history and time—macro-scale elements normally difficult to perceive directly—and distill them into a fresh source of joy and stimulation we can experience at eye-level, in our daily lives.

マテリアリティ・ オブ・インターフェイス

建築／土木／ランドスケープ

「人間」「インフラ」「自然環境」をシームレスに思考していくための手段として「建築」「土木」「ランドスケープ」という分野を連続的に捉えながら、制度やスケール、思想の異なる分野で発見した新しい視座をフィードバックしていくような空間的実践に取り組んでいる。

建築スケールのプロジェクトから、広場や堤防、道路というインフラ、それらのインターフェースのデザインを設計対象とし、来るべき災害の時代、ダウンサイジングの時代にふさわしい、人間ととりまく環境との関わり方を模索している。

マテリアル／スケール

各分野で扱う対象は、用途、規模、立体／平面なども異なるが、「マテリアル」や「スケール」というユニバーサルな概念を使って、連続的に思考する手がかりとしている。

例えば日本の伝統技術において、イグサが畳という「床材」にも、左官として「壁仕上げ」にもなるように、コンクリートも床や壁に変化し、それが「縁石」の形状に成型されれば「建築」ではなく「土木」というラベルがつく。当然ながらマテリアルは、分野やエレメントを横断するきわめてユニバーサルでシームレスな存在である一方、物質としての材料特性や出自、人の嗜好、エイジングや意味など、きわめて具体的な意味や広がりを伴ってしまうという魅力的な存在でもある。

日常に寄り添う防潮堤

《トコトコダンダン》(大阪、2017) は垂直型の既存護岸に、ひな壇状とスロープ状の地形を描き加え、240mの遊歩道と4,300㎡の広場空間の機能を付与した防潮堤である。設計途中に発見された「半世紀にわたる護岸の改修の歴史」に仲間入りをするように新しい地形を挿入し、人々に堤防を家具のように使いこなす機会、潮位変動を観測する機会、植栽の手入れを通じて都市インフラのメンテナンスに参加する機会を提供している。

ポーラス状のコンクリートの湿り気のない表面は、人にとっては寝転ぶのに最適である一方、小さな間隙はコケや植物の棲み処ともなり、小さな生態系を形成するのに寄与している。この表面は、舗装材をミルフィーユ状に積層させて打設したため、近景の表面には地層のような様相が現れ、遠景では、小さな段々に分割された堤防のフォルムが

4: REASSEMBLAGE OF ELEMENTS

テクスチャのように知覚され、人、植物、手すり、プランターなどとともに風景を形成している。

地面の下のダイナミズム

　W市街路計画（竣工：2022年予定、延長240m、幅員11m）では街路と沿道の民有地との「敷地境界」や、地面の下に張り巡らされている「インフラ幹線」の存在に着目した。シンボル街路の整備計画であったが、道路幅員も狭く、沿道の民有地の大部分は駐車場であった。そこで車道幅や線形の変更による歩行者空間の充実に加え、両端の歩道部分を沿道駐車場のアスファルト舗装に揃える（車道部分はブロック舗装とする）ことで視覚上の境界を曖昧にし、管理上は民地である駐車場が道路空間と一体で整備された広場にも見えてくるような、風景の再編集を提案した。

　また、道路の下にはインフラ幹線が埋設されており、沿道建物の建て替えのたびに幹線への接続のために道路が掘り返されるため、特にアスファルト舗装の道路には新旧さまざまな表面が無秩序に現れることになる。本計画ではあえて舗装表面を事前に分割することで、時間経過と素材の退色によって、街の修繕の履歴が地表面にコラージュされていく風景を構想している。

光と風の描写

　風に揺れるガラス建築《KUSANAMI》（東京、大阪、デュッセルドルフ、2013）では、ガラスという素材を通じて光と風の存在を表現した。スマートフォンのディスプレイなどに使用される化学強化薄板ガラス（t＝0.5mm 最大高さ1,800mm）を最大寸法で用い、一枚では自立しないガラス板を、熱を加えずに変形させながら2-3枚連結して造形し構造的に自立させることで実現している。

　空間に入射した光は、ねじれたガラスの表面によって拡散され、風にふわふわと揺れる光の襞の空間を創出させた。

　このほか、土木のつり橋に使われるストランドロープを家具スケールで用いた作品や、生垣の風景を建築と一体的に表現したプロジェクト、一街区全体の公共施設を防災の観点から再編するプロジェクトなどがある。スケールを介することで「フォルム－テクスチャ」を行き来し、また山肌－樹形－葉振りなどの有機物と人工物を連続的に捉える手法や、マテリアルを介することで新しい関係性を紡いだり、重層的な意味を宿す手法などを、プロジェクトごとに模索している。

　こうした実践を通じて、自然環境や都市基盤のシステム、歴史など、意識されにくい「巨視的視点や時間への想像力」を、アイレベルでの新鮮な喜びや日常の実感として還元したいと考えている。

Toshikatsu Kiuchi
木内俊克

Born in 1978. President of Toshikatsu Kiuchi Architect Office.
He engages in a multidisciplinary practice ranging from art and
furniture production to welfare facility and public space design.
He also conducts research at the University of Tokyo on the
datafication of people's interests and involvement in urban life.
http://www.toshikatsukiuchi.com

Representative projects
Fukuchiyama-Gakuen Social Welfare Corp. New Miwa Suikouen
(2019-)
Whenever Wherever Festival 2018 (2018)
Hybridization and Learning (2018)
Kirikiri Community Center (2018)
Territory of the Obscure (2017)
Object Disco (2016)
Tanada (2016)
Under Blue Sky (2015)
Once In A Blue Moon (2014)
double bed (2014)
Otsuchi Town Central District Spatial Planning (2012)

木内俊克 (きうち・としかつ)
1978 年生まれ。木内建築計画事務所代表。美術、家具制作から、福祉
施設やパブリックスペースのデザインに至る領域横断的な活動を行う
傍ら、東京大学にて、都市における人々の関心のデータ的把握と都市介
入について研究を行う。
http://www.toshikatsukiuchi.com

主な作品など
《福知山学園みわ翠光園》(2019-)
《Whenever Wherever Festival 2018》(2018)
《Hybridization and Learning》(2018)
《大槌町中央公民館吉里吉里分館》(2018)
《注意散漫な世界の領域》(2017)
《オブジェクトディスコ》(2016)
《たなだ》(2016)
《Under Blue Sky》(2015)
《Once In A Blue Moon》(2014)
《double bed》(2014)
大槌町町方地区中心市街地空間イメージ検討 (2012)

1　Fukuchiyama-Gakuen Social Welfare Corp.
　New Miwa Suikouen (2019-)
　©Toshikatsu Kiuchi Architect
　《福知山学園新みわ翠光園》(2019-)
　©木内建築計画事務所

2　*Hybridization and Learning* (2018)
　©Toshikatsu Kiuchi Architect
　《Hybridization and Learning》(2018)
　©木内建築計画事務所

3　*Territory of the Obscure* (2017)
　©Toshikatsu Kiuchi
　《注意散漫な世界の領域》(2017)
　©木内俊克

4　*Object Disco* (2016)
　©Toshikatsu Kiuchi+Taichi Sunayama+Yamadabashi
　《オブジェクトディスコ》(2016)
　©木内俊克+砂山太一+山田橋

5　*Object Disco* (2016)
　©Toshikatsu Kiuchi+Taichi Sunayama+Yamadabashi
　《オブジェクトディスコ》(2016)
　©木内俊克+砂山太一+山田橋

6　*Whenever Wherever Festival 2018* (2018)
　© Toshikatsu Kiuchi
　《Whenever Wherever Festival 2018》(2018)
　© 木内俊克

　4: REASSEMBLAGE OF ELEMENTS

1

2

3

4

5

6

Measurement / Tautology / Body

We desire new images and seek their source in our environment.

Light entering our eyes, sounds entering our ears, smells we breathe, pressure and heat on our skin . . . Vibrant images arise in the instant we absorb this jumble of sensations. Even when we try to name these images using words and objects we have on hand, they are lost in the next instant. We can never keep up with them—and that is precisely why they keep us stirred up. The body achieves its true function when it is in communion with these bundles of images.

Creation through measurement

To measure something is to name it; in a fundamental sense this is the same as creating it. Measurement makes it clear that something is there, and defines how it manifests itself in our experience.

Territory of the Obscure (2017) was an installation project in which we attempted to measure the "ground" we dimly perceive on the periphery of our consciousness, at the very edge of our field of vision, vis-a-vis the "figure" on which we focus. If we cannot see the peripheral ground as a figure when we focus our attention, it simply slips into the next periphery. This obscured reality that we can never grasp is like a parallel world that always encloses our experience. Only measurement makes it possible to approach that territory asymptotically.

From 16:20 to 17:14 on September 13, 2016, we carried out a photoscan of 1,275 intermittent photographs of an exhibition room, producing a point cloud containing color and coordinate information that indicated view angles and times over a 54-minute period. An accumulation of "looks," the photoscan provided a reverse illumination of places where the gaze did not reach. These gaps, which manifested as errors appearing in the surfaces of the digital space created as a copy of the exhibition room, were measurements of traces of absence. The digitized room surfaces containing these gaps were restored to the exhibition room as full-size

copies printed on paper. These markers of absence were turned into figures that were nothing more than sloughed skins of ground. But the physical body, in perceiving these sloughed skins, hinted at their potential for measurement. The exhibition room was sculpted into a space that, however slightly, gave form to the possibilities of the parallel world.

Hybridization and Learning (2018) was also a research project on the theme of measuring the environment. Semantic similarity was measured for captions of a group of spatial images, which were vectorized by text analysis utilizing machine learning. This made visible the fact that, for example, the sentence "Plants, white pipes, and a beige wall are visible in the back through a wire mesh behind the brick" is semantically slightly closer to "Yellow and round, pink and square, clear acrylic sheets and pebbles are embedded in the grooves of concrete flagstones, casting shadows" than it is to "A yellow wall and a LED light bulb glow under the white eaves of a building with beige-colored tile walls." Here, too, measurement subtly expands our senses.

Copying tautologies

Object Disco (2016) was a project for a small urban plaza where people could rest or meet. We found elements in the surrounding area for which we created tautologies by copying the characteristics of each element, then assembled those copies and laid them out in the plaza. In its fundamental sense, the creation process was completed when we extracted the elements of an object by figuring out which attributes to copy and how to measure them.

In the extraction process, everything from infrastructure to furniture was treated as equivalent. For example, galvanized-finish steel frames that support planters parallel the slant of the plastic cover around the utility pole guy-wire next to them. Corrugated-sheet dividers for gravel are in the same colors as the roofs and walls of nearby houses. A bench copies the brick pattern of the wallpaper in a neighborhood shop. Meanwhile, another bench is given a rough finish to show that it is made of

4: REASSEMBLAGE OF ELEMENTS

real brick. These copies are intentionally distinguished from their objects in different ways, incorporating multiple stimuli that encourage the gaze to seek out these commonalities and differences.

Renewing the body

The *Object Disco* mini-plaza was devised as a place offering new discoveries with every visit that connect the visitor to the city at large. It provides "hooks" that attract and stimulate our simplest, most intuitive senses. In this manner it promotes bottom-up urban change by renewing our bodies as they pass through the city, turning them into engaged bodies actively exploring the place we are in.

Based on the same concept, *Whenever Wherever Festival 2018 (WWFes18)* was a performance-art event that simulated an urban plaza in a theater space for four days, completely integrating the stage and seating as one entity. Six separate performance spaces were set up as adjacent cells, with each cell holding a different program simultaneously and repeatedly. The attraction of the gaze to multiple, discontinuous objects, and the creation of undirected time in spaces where nothing was going on, expanded the possibilities for spontaneous activity.

The reconstruction of New Miwa Suikouen, a facility of Fukuchiyama Gakuen, is what one might call a city-scale project currently in progress. It entails the gathering of multiple facilities—from residential to day-care—for intellectually disabled people in one campus. It is also under consideration for use as a local disaster center, thus functioning as part of the city's infrastructure. At the beginning of this essay I wrote that our bodies achieve their true function when in communion with our environment. Moreover, we make up an assemblage of bodies of overwhelming diversity. Taking these facts as a point of origin, we are building an institutional environment centered around a network of minute commonalities and differences.

測定／同語反復／身体

私たちは新しいイメージを欲望し、環境にその源泉を求める。

　目に入る光、耳に入る音、吸い込む香り、肌に触れる応力、温度。そのすべてが一緒くたに私たちに入ってくる瞬間に立ち上がる、イメージの瑞々しさ。ありあわせの言葉や事物で名指そうにも、それは瞬間に失われ、追いつけないイメージに、だからこそ私たちは駆り立てられる。身体はイメージの束との交感において、はじめてその機能を保つ。

測定という造形

　測ることは名指すことであり、根源的な意味においてつくることと同義だ。それがそこにあることを明らかにし、いかに経験の俎上に浮かび上がってくるかを規定する。
　《注意散漫な世界の領域》(2017) は、像を結ぶ「図」に対し、視野の広がりが途絶えるぎりぎりの端、認識の周縁であいまいに意識される「地」の測定を試みた、インスタレーションのプロジェクトだ。周縁の「地」は、「図」として捉えられない以上、注意を向ければまた次の周縁に横滑りする。辿り着けないこの「注意散漫な世界」は、さながら平行世界として、つねに私たちの経験を取り囲んでいる。測定だけが、その領域への漸近に可能性をつなぐ。
　2016 年 9 月 13 日 16 時 20 分－17 時 14 分のあいだ、断続的な 1,275 枚の写真による展示室のフォトスキャンを行い、54 分間の視線と時間を写し込んだ色彩・座標情報をもつ点群を得た。眼差しの集積であるフォトスキャンは、視線が抜け落ちていた不在のありかを逆照射する。展示室のコピーであるデジタル空間の室表面に生まれるエラーとしての穴は、不在の痕跡の測定値だ。デジタル化され、穴を孕んだ室表面は、紙に印刷した室の原寸コピーとして展示室に差し戻される。不在のマーカーは「図」化し、「地」の抜け殻でしかない。だが「地」の抜け殻を知覚した身体は、その測定可能性に触れる。展示室は、わずかに平行世界の可能性を帯びた空間として造形される。
　《Hybridization and Learning》(2018) も、環境の測定を主題としたリサーチプロジェクトだ。空間イメージ群のキャプションを、機械学習を利用したテキスト解析によりベクトル化し、意味的な類似度を測定する。例えば「レンガの奥にあるメッシュを通して見える奥に、植物と白い配管とベージュの壁がある」は、「ベージュ色のタイルの外壁の建物の白い庇下に黄色い壁と LED 電球が光っている」より、「黄で丸く、ピンクで四角い、透明なアクリル板と砂利がコンクリートの敷石の溝

にはまって影を落としている」に、意味的にわずかに近似していることが可視化される。ここでも測定は、知覚をささやかに拡張する。

同語反復、なぞること

《Object Disco》(2016) は、休憩や待合を機能とする都市の小広場のプロジェクトだ。周辺領域の広がりから要素を発見しては、要素の属性をなぞり書きした同語反復により、広場にそのコピーを持ち込み、レイアウトする。根源的な意味での造形は、何を捉え、どんな属性でどう測定し、コピーするかの要素抽出の時点で完了している。

　抽出には、インフラから家具までが等価に扱われる。例えば植栽を支持する溶融亜鉛めっき仕上げのスティールフレームは、隣接する電信柱補強のプラスティックカバーの傾きと平行する。砂利を保つ波板の仕切りは、周辺住宅の屋根や外壁の色彩を拾う。ベンチは、近隣店舗のレンガ「柄」の壁紙をなぞる。実際のレンガであることを隠蔽するよう、精緻なレンガと目地をさらにサンダーで平滑化し、レンガ「柄」がコピーされる。一方、もうひとつのベンチでは、レンガは本物であることがそのまま露呈された粗い仕上げだ。コピーは対象ごとに意図的に差別化され、その共通性や差異を視線が追い始める契機が、幾重にも織り込まれている。

身体の更新

《Object Disco》の小広場は、都市に連続し、訪れるたびに発見されるべきものとして意図されている。単純で直感的な知覚を誘い、触れることを促すフックを提示する。そして、都市を通り過ぎるだけの身体を、場を探索する能動的な身体へ更新し、ボトムアップな都市変化を促す。

《Whenever Wherever Festival 2018》(2018、以下WWFes18)は、同じ問題意識のもと、劇場空間で都市広場を4日間にわたりシミュレーションした、舞台と客席が渾然一体となったパフォーマンスアートの舞台美術だ。独立したパフォーマンス空間を6つ隣接し、一つひとつのセルで同時進行的にさまざまなプログラムを繰り返す形式だ。断続的な多対象への視点の飛び火、何もない空間での無目的な時間の創出が、創発的な行為可能性を拡張する。

《福知山学園新みわ翠光園》の建て替えは、居住型から通所型まで、複数の知的障がい者福祉施設が集まった、現在進行中の都市規模といってよいプロジェクトだ。地域の災害拠点として具体的に都市機能

の一部を担うことも検討されている。冒頭で、私たちの身体は環境との交感においてはじめて機能を保つと述べたが、さらに私たちは圧倒的な多様性をかかえる身体の群であるということを再度起点とし、微細な共通性と差異化のネットワークを軸とした施設環境を計画している。

Taichi Sunayama
砂山太一

Born in 1980. President of Sunayama Studio and Associate Professor, Department of General Science of Art, Kyoto City University of Arts. He engages in production, design, planning and criticism rooted in a discourse on the informational and material aspects of artistic expression. After studying sculpture in Japan he lived in France from 2004 to 2011, where he studied the use of digital technology in architectural design and worked in and with architectural and structural design offices. In addition to running a design studio in Tokyo, he pursues theoretical research on contemporary art and design at Kyoto City University of Arts.
https://tsnym.nu/

Representative projects
KAMINOISHI (2019, with Hideyuki Nakayama)
Einstein Doll, Raccoon Left Humerus (2017)
fnss.show (2016)
Object Disco (2016, with Toshikatsu Kiuchi, Rick Yamakawa, Izumi Soeda, Yoshifumi Hashimoto)
Kyoto Mokuzai Kaikan façade design (2016)
Materializing exhibitions (2013–15)
Continuous Rectangular Timbers (2015)
LowLife (2014)
DoubleBed (2014, with Toshikatsu Kiuchi, Kosuke Nagata)
she (2013, with Tomohisa Goko, Kosuke Nagata)
Unsorted Scene (2009, with Jean-Phillippe Sanfourche, Yoichi Ozawa)

1980 年生まれ。sunayama studio 代表。京都市立芸術大学美術学部総合芸術学専攻教授。芸術表現領域における情報性・物質性を切り口に、制作・設計・企画・批評を手がける。日本で彫刻を学んだ後、2004 年渡仏。フランスでデジタル技術を用いた建築設計手法を学び、設計事務所や構造事務所において勤務・協働する。2011 年帰国。現在、東京にデザインスタジオを構えつつ、京都市立芸術大学において現代芸術、デザインの理論研究を行う。
https://tsnym.nu/

主な作品など
《かみのいし》(2019、中山英之との共同)
《アインシュタインのぬいぐるみとアライグマの左上腕骨》(2017)
《フィットネス.》(2016)
《オブジェクトディスコ》(2016、木内俊克、山川陸、添田いづみ、橋本吉史との共同)
京都木材会館ファサードデザイン (2016)
「マテリアライジング展――情報と物質とそのあいだ」(2013–15)
《角材の軸を連続させる》(2015)
《LowLife》(2014)
《DoubleBed》(2014、木内俊克、永田康祐との共同)
《She》(2013、御幸朋寿、永田康祐との共同)
《Unsorted Scene》(2009、Jean-Phillippe Sanfourche、小澤洋一との共同)

1 *MIRROR* (2019, AGC Studio) / ©Taichi Sunayama (Sunayama Studio)
《MIRROR》(2019, AGC Studio) ／© 砂山太一 (sunayama studio)

2 *Einstein Doll, Raccoon Left Humerus* (2017-)
Algorithm development: Taichi Sunayama (Sunayama Studio)
©Taichi Sunayama (Sunayama Studio)
《アインシュタインのぬいぐるみとアライグマの左上腕骨》(2017−)
アルゴリズム開発：砂山太一 (sunayama studio)
© 砂山太一 (sunayama studio)

3 *paper stone* (2017-)
Design: Hideyuki Nakayama (Hideyuki Nakayama Architecture)
Digital design and operation: Taichi Sunayama (Sunayama Studio)
©Taichi Sunayama (Sunayama Studio)
《かみのいし》(2017−)
デザイン：中山英之 (中山英之建築設計事務所)、デザイン、ワークフロー設計およびデジタルオペレーション：砂山太一 (sunayama studio)
© 砂山太一 (sunayama studio)

4 *Continuous Rectangular Timbers* (2015)
Design, production: Taichi Sunayama (Sunayama Studio)
©Taichi Sunayama (Sunayama Studio)
《角材の軸を連続させる》(2015)
設計・制作：砂山太一 (sunayama studio)
© 砂山太一 (sunayama studio)

5 *Or Moonwalk* (2015, Materializing Exhibition III)
©Taichi Sunayama (Sunayama Studio)
《あるいはムーンウォーク》(2015、「マテリアライジング展 III」より)
© 砂山太一 (sunayama studio)

6 gh/e (Taichi Sunauama + Kosuke Nagata + Tomohisa Goko)
she (2013, Materializing Exhibition I)
© Takeru Koroda
gh/e（砂山太一＋永田康祐＋御幸朋寿）
《she》(2013、「マテリアライジング展 I」より)
© 来田猛

4: REASSEMBLAGE OF ELEMENTS

Chasm of Reality

Architecture can be thought of in terms of two worlds. One is the world of buildings in which people dwell. These entities have space and are subject to time, both of them finite phenomena. The other world is that of numbers—the dimensions and geometries of design. Whether performed with a computer or pen and paper, design belongs to this numerical world, which is predicated on infinite space and time. For example, a broken, warped tile floor appears in a drawing as an arrangement of straight lines, with none of the complexities of the real thing. Meanwhile, information technology has brought the objects of the numerical world into the physical world in which we live. When we head toward a destination while checking location data on a smartphone map app, we feel virtually no distinction between the digital and analog components of our actions.

Quantified reality

At Sunayama Studio we contemplate the production logic of architecture and art. Since our early days of operation in the late 2000s, we have utilized computer programming and digital fabrication in design and production. For the Paris boutique interior project *Hermès Rive Gauche* (2010), for example, we were commissioned by the Parisian structural design office Bollinger + Grohmann S.A.R.L. to handle the basic design of geometry-generation programming for double-layered structures that resemble basket stitchery. To build three-dimensional curved wooden members, we developed a program for calculating optimal shapes based on physical requirements such as flexural strength. We conducted a simulation of real conditions, extracted physical data, adjusted it via computer, then retested it under real-world conditions in a back-and-forth process that might be termed the present-tense version of fabrication by computer.

In the chasm between quantity and perception

As our thoughts drag our bodies along amid the accelerating fusion of the worlds of information and matter, what sense of reality do we maintain? What new expressions do these sensations produce? In 2019 we designed the installation *Mirror* with this question in mind. Using an augmented-mirror display with a mirrored surface, we created an experimental work in which video images, reflected images, and actual objects blend with one another. Is what you see the real thing, or a video, or a reflection? Our aim was to design a work that renders ambiguous our sense of the reality of existence itself.

Einstein Doll, Raccoon Left Humerus (2017–) is a more speculative design research project in which we developed an algorithm that hybridizes data for two 3D mesh models. This enables us to mathematically generate shapes that we cannot imagine, even if we can put them in words—for example, "a shape midway between an apple and a shoe." However, the perceiver is a human being, and there will often be a gap between what people imagine when they hear the words "midway between an apple and a shoe" and the shape derived from numerical calculations. Our aim here was to objectively analyze human creativity in terms of the chasm between the world of numbers and the world of perception.

Meaning as function

The Einstein Doll and the Raccoon Left Humerus may be equivalent in the eyes of a machine, but human eyes impart meanings derived from memory and experience that give birth to a gap in values. So what exactly happens during the process of looking at something and recognizing it? *Paper Stone* (2017–) is a joint project with fellow architect Hideyuki Nakayama involving furniture made of paper. We scanned simple pebbles and generated polyhedral data to output three-dimensional objects on paper. The stones themselves had no special meaning, yet through the process of being captured and designed through the eyes of a 3D scan machine, they acquired an individual uniqueness of sorts. Treating this uniqueness as a "function," we built furniture that possessed "meaning as function."

How much identity resides in the "mereness" of a "mere pebble"? There is a difference between 1 cm and 1.1 cm, but few people can make that distinction. *Continuous Rectangular Timbers* (2015) was a prototype project for a structural system using 45-mm square lengths of rough-hewn cedar. In reality these rough pieces varied in size from around 42 to 48 mm square, but the system we proposed was able to tolerate a certain degree of variation in these dimensions. Thus what we proposed was a way of handling objects that allows us to utilize irregular objects as they are.

On the one hand we have the actual, complex world of objects, all of them different from one another; on the other hand we have the world of information with which human beings provisionally capture the real world so as to make rough sense of it by imposing the order of numbers, geometry, symbols. The world of things is finite, while the world of information is not. When we deal with the finite world, we must contend with the limits of that finitude—that is to say, we cannot know everything about the world, nor can information technology describe everything about the world. That is why defects, discrepancies, and deficiencies occur. But instead of treating this finitude as something negative, we can find an ongoing source of creativity in the bugs and errors that occur between the two worlds. Sunayama Studio is currently searching in that web of finitude for a real-time methodology for constructing the world.

現実裂け目

建築に2つの世界を考える。1つは人が住まう建物の立つ物の世界。そこには、空間があり、時間があり、どれもが実質的に有限なものである。もう1つは、建物ができる前の、設計における寸法や幾何学などの数の世界。コンピュータによる設計も、ペンと紙による設計もこの数学世界に属し、時間も空間も無限にある前提で考えられる。例えば、ガタガタで歪みのあるタイル貼りの床は、図面上では実際の複雑さは表現せず、抽象的な直線で表される。一方で、情報技術によって数の世界のものたちは、私たちの暮らす物質世界にもやって来ている。スマートフォンの地図アプリ上で位置データを確認しながら目的地に向かう一連の行動に、デジタルとアナログの差を感じることはほとんどない。

定量化された現実と

sunayama studio は、建築や美術の制作論理を思索するスタジオだ。2000年代後半の活動初期より、コンピュータプログラミングやデジタルファブリケーションを活用した設計・制作を行ってきた。例えば、パリのブティック内装のプロジェクト《Hermès Rive Gauche》(2010)では、パリの構造設計事務所 BOLLINGER + GROHMANN S.A.R.L. からの依頼を受けて、2層の籠編みのような構造地のジオメトリ生成プログラミングの基本設計を担当した。木材による3次元的な曲線部材をつくり出すために、曲げ強度など物質的な条件から最適な形状を計算するプログラムを作成した。現実をシミュレーションし、物質的な情報を抽出してコンピュータ上で制御し、再び現実の物質世界に返すという往還は、コンピュータを用いたファブリケーションの現在形といえる。

数量と認知の裂け目にある

加速する情報世界と物質世界の融和のなかで、身体を引きずりながら思考する私たちはどのような現実感をもつか。その感覚によって発見される新たな表現とはいかなるものか。2019年に制作したインスタレーション作品《MIRROR》は、そのような問いのもと制作された。表面が鏡になっている拡張ミラー型ディスプレイを用いて、映像と鏡像、そして実際に置かれたオブジェクトの3者が溶け合うような実験的な作品である。目に見えるものが、実物なのか、映像なのか、鏡像なのか。存在自体の現実感を曖昧にする設計を目指した。

《アインシュタインのぬいぐるみとアライグマの左上腕骨》(2017−)は、より思弁的なデザインリサーチである。ここでは、2つの3Dメッ

4: REASSEMBLAGE OF ELEMENTS

シュモデルデータを混成するアルゴリズムを開発している。これによって、例えば「りんご」と「靴」の中間の形という、言葉としてはいえても、イメージとして想像できなかった形を数学的に導き出すことができる。ただ、認知するのは人間である。人が「りんごと靴の中間」と聞いたときの想像と、算出された数値的な形にはしばしば乖離がある。ここでは数学世界と認知世界のあいだの裂け目から、人間の創造性を客観的に見つめ直すことを目的としている。

意味の機能を

　「アインシュタインのぬいぐるみ」も「アライグマの左上腕骨」も、機械の目には等価に見えるが、人間の目では記憶や経験からくる意味が付与され、価値のギャップが生まれてしまう。では、人が何かを見て認識する過程では一体何が起こっているのか。《かみのいし》(建築家中山英之氏との協働プロジェクト、2017-) は紙の家具のプロジェクトである。ただの石ころをスキャンし、多面体にして作成したデータを紙に出力して立体にした。石自体に特別な意味はない。しかし、3D スキャンの機械の目で捉えられ、デザインされるプロセスを通じて、ある固有性を帯びるようになる。それ自体を「機能」としてとらえ、「意味の機能」をもつ家具をつくった。
　ただの石ころの「ただの」の部分に、どれだけ多くの固有性があることか。1cm と 1.1cm は違うが、1cm と 1.1cm は多くの人にとって識別するのは難しい。《角材の軸を連続させる》(2015) は、45mm 角の杉荒材を用いた構造システムのプロトタイププロジェクトである。45mm 角の杉荒材は、実際には 42mm 前後から 48mm 前後と寸法に幅がある。ここで提案したシステムは、材ごとにある程度のばらつきを許容しながら成立させることができる。雑多なものを雑多なまま運用できるようにするための操作対象の捉え方を提案している。
　具体的で複雑でどれも違っている物の世界と、数字や幾何学や記号など秩序立っていて、人間が世界を大まかに認知するために仮止めしている情報の世界。有限な物質の世界と無限の情報の世界。有限の世界を扱っている限り、そこでは有限性の限界が生じる。つまり私たちは、世界のすべてを知ることはできず、また情報技術も世界のすべてを記述することは不可能だ。そこにはつねに不具合や不整合・欠損が発生しているが、しかしこの限界をマイナスに捉えるのではなく、2 つの世界のあいだに生じるバグやズレに創造性の継起を発見する。sunayama studio はその限界性の網のなかで、いま、現在進行中の世界構築のための手立てを探す。

166

Daisuke Motogi
元木大輔

Born in 1981. President of DDAA/DDAA LAB, member of CEKAI and Mistletoe Community, and lecturer at Musashino Art University. In 2010 he founded DDAA design studio to pursue projects in architecture, city planning, landscaping, interior and product design, concept making, and hybrids thereof based on an architectural perspective. In 2019 he established DDAA LAB with Mistletoe to conduct research and experimental design.
http://www.dskmtg.com

Representative projects
Bang & Olufsen flagship store GINZA (2019)
BANG & OLUFSEN ESTNATION ROPPONGI HILLS (2019)
MISTLETOE OF TOKYO (2019)
The National Museum of Modern Art, Kyoto/Dress Code: Are You Playing Fashion? (2019)
Sushi Yoshii (2019)
avex artist academy aoyama studio (2018)
Mori Art Museum/Japan in Architecture: Genealogies of Its Transformation (2018)
NIKE ATELIAIR (2018)
Dappled House (2018)
Nikelab × Undercover "GYAKUSOU" Global Retail Direction (2017-)
That Pipe in time, So Gold (2016)
Bench Bomb (2016)

1981年生まれ。DDAA/DDAA LAB 代表。CEKAI 所属。Mistletoe Community。武蔵野美術大学非常勤講師。2010 年、建築、都市、ランドスケープ、インテリア、プロダクト、コンセプトメイク、あるいはそれらの多分野にまたがるプロジェクトを建築的な思考を軸に活動するデザインスタジオ DDAA 設立。2019 年、Mistletoe とともに実験的なデザインとリサーチのための組織 DDAA LAB を設立。
http://www.dskmtg.com

主な作品など
《Bang & Olufsen flagship store GINZA》(2019)
《BANG & OLUFSEN ESTNATION ROPPONGI HILLS》(2019)
《MISTLETOE OF TOKYO》(2019)
《The National Museum of Modern Art, Kyoto/Dress Code: Are You Playing Fashion?》(2019)
《Sushi Yoshii》(2019)
《avex artist academy aoyama studio》(2018)
《Mori Art Museum/Japan in Architecture: Genealogies of Its Transformation》(2018)
《NIKE ATELIAIR》(2018)
《Dappled House》(2018)
《Nikelab × Undercover "GYAKUSOU" Global Retail Direction》(2017-)
《That Pipe in time, So Gold》(2016)
《Bench Bomb》(2016)

1 *MISTLETOE OF TOKYO* (2019)
ⓒKenta Hasegawa
《Mistletoe of Tokyo》(2019)
ⓒ長谷川健太

2 *A Gallery* (2019-)
ⓒKenta Hasegawa
《A Gallery》(2019-)
ⓒ長谷川健太

3 *Stacking Stool Studies* (2019-)
ⓒDDAA
《Stacking Stool Studies》(2019-)
ⓒDDAA

4 *Stacking Stool Studies* (2019-)
ⓒDDAA
《Stacking Stool Studies》(2019-)
ⓒDDAA

5 *Stacking Stool Studies* (2019-)
ⓒKenta Hasegawa
《Stacking Stool Studies》(2019-)
ⓒ長谷川健太

6 *Bench Bomb* (2016)
ⓒDDAA
《Bench Bomb》(2016)
ⓒDDAA

4: REASSEMBLAGE OF ELEMENTS

1

2

3

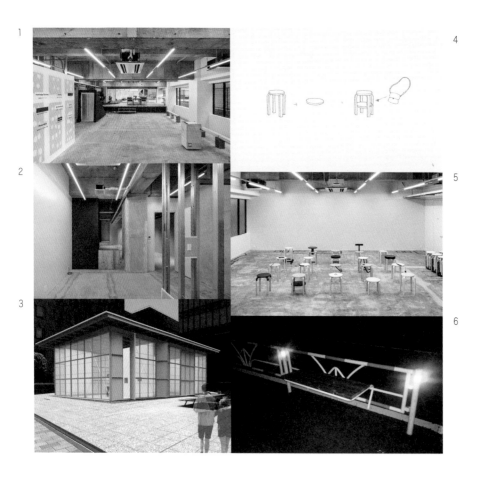

4

5

6

Architecture
for New Perspectives

Although design is the work of making something, I sometimes feel a bit guilty about making something new. The world is already overflowing with things—good, bad, big, small, new, old, classy, cheap. In an age of diverse values, the difference between a neighborhood bar and a Michelin-star restaurant is not one of objective superiority or inferiority, but only of concept. Our interest lies in the design of architectural perspectives that enable people to enjoy all of these diverse concepts and values equally. By slightly reinterpreting existing objects and ways of thinking, we should be able to create entirely new landscapes without rejecting the all too familiar things we see before us. As it entails closely observing objects and redesigning their relationships, this approach also serves as a methodology for finding new ways of looking at architecture, cities, and society.

Details, connections, repairs

The plan for *A Gallery* (2019–), a venue specializing in contemporary art, called for a temporary structure that would be removed after a few years. Since it seemed a terrible waste to simply scrap the building once its allotted time was up, we envisioned a structure that could be moved elsewhere after its term of duty on this site had ended. The conditions we established for this purpose were that the building could be dismantled, and that the components would be small enough to hand-carry. Ordinary steel columns would be far too heavy for people to carry, so we arranged 60 x 45 mm C-channel steel members at a 900-mm pitch in the manner of lightweight steel or wood columns. These are the same size as the light-gauge steel columns used for the interior, so the structure itself can also function as interior backing. To make the building easy to dismantle, all details, i.e., places where components connect to one another, are exposed. Details are like the conjunctions and punctuation marks of written text. Consider that the meaning of these three phrases—"columns, steel, glass, sheets"; "columns

with steel and glass sheets"; "columns of steel, glass in sheets"—changes with just the presence or absence of conjunctions and prepositions. Similarly, we wanted to devise a method whereby, through careful design, one can transform an entire structure with a minimal manipulation of connections and details.

For example, consider *kintsugi*, in which the repair process and the repairs themselves dominate the entire design. *Kintsugi* is a traditional method of fixing cracks in pottery with lacquer to which gold or other metal powder has been added for ornamental effect. The original vessel doesn't matter; it's not meant to be the expression of an artist's ego or a profound concept. The accumulation of defects and noise is acceptable—and since the vessel is fated to undergo repeated repairs every time it cracks, notions of perfection or completion do not apply. In architecture, too, we may expose details, equipment, and structural elements to anticipate the likelihood of future repairs or improvements. Instead of treating a building as "finished" with the initial conclusion of the construction process, let us consider design over a slightly longer timeline. If we do, we should be able to base our design on a state of perpetual incompletion that will itself determine the design.

Perpetually unfinished

Mistletoe of Tokyo (2019), an incubation facility in Tokyo, is an office that will never be finished. This is a space for a community of people investing in or otherwise supporting socially significant startups. Because their interests extend in all directions and undergo continual change, we thought an appropriate space would be one predicated on "continual evolution." Typical buildings have a moment at which they are clearly finished. Even after being occupied, however, this space continues to change as it undergoes perpetual verification, with concomitant rethinking of the design. To continue designing this unfinished space we established DDAA LAB, an organization for conducting

4: REASSEMBLAGE OF ELEMENTS

experimental research and prototyping, where we are now pursuing several projects that contemplate residential environments of the future. For example, we are working with a startup that develops compact water circulation systems to design a shower and kitchen that can be used in places lacking a water infrastructure. What we envision is a mobile architecture that does not depend on existing infrastructure.

The smallest unit and the whole

Bench Bomb (2017) is a project involving the arbitrary graffiti-like installation of benches around a city, using roadside guardrails as mounts. We designed and open-sourced 23 types of bench to fit the individual guardrail designs of Tokyo's 23 central wards. With *Stacking School Studies* (2019–), we are designing and open-sourcing joint parts in over 100 patterns that can be easily attached to Alvar Aalto's Stool 60. We are also developing products that utilize local industries for the smallest units that make up a city—interlocking blocks for sidewalks, roadside tree planters, central dividers, guardrails, traffic signals, braille blocks, and so on. For example, we are designing stainless steel guardrails and traffic signals for Tsubame-Sanjo, twin cities in Niigata Prefecture known for stainless steel products, to create a townscape unique to that area. By incorporating the local environment in this manner, we can devise components and repair methods that themselves transform the whole with a minimum of effort. We believe that this *kintsugi*-style methodology can be effectively applied at scales ranging from the smallest products to entire cities.

新しい眼差しのための建築

デザインは何かをつくる仕事なのだが、新しい何かをつくることに少し罪悪感を感じることがある。世界はとっくにもので溢れているからだ。良いもの、悪いもの、大きいもの、小さいもの、新しいもの、古いもの、高級なもの、安いもの。価値観が多様な現代においては赤提灯の居酒屋とミシュラン星付きレストランのあいだに優劣はなく、そこにはコンセプトの違いがあるだけだ。そして僕たちの関心は、多様なコンセプトと価値観をすべて平等に楽しむための建築的な視点をデザインすることだ。すでにある「もの」や「考え方」を少し読み替えることで、目の前のありふれたものを否定することなく、まったく新しい風景をつくりだすことはできないだろうか。ものをよく観察し、関係をデザインしなおすことで建築、都市、社会への新しい眼差しを発見するための方法論でもある。

ディテール、接合、修復

《A Gallery》(2019–) はコンテンポラリーアートのためのギャラリーだ。期間限定の仮設建築物という条件で、数年で撤去される計画だった。期間終了後、撤去し、廃棄するのはとてももったいないので、役目を終えた後も移動可能な建築を考えた。そのために僕たちが設定した条件は「分解可能にする」ことと「建材を人の手で運べるサイズにする」ということだ。通常の鉄骨造の柱は、とても人の手で運べる重さではないので、軽量鉄骨造や木造のように 60mm × 45mm のスチールの C チャンネルを構造材として 900mm ピッチで並べる。これは内装で使う LGS のサイズと同じなので、構造をそのまま内装下地として使っても機能する。この建物は分解をしやすくするために、すべてのものとものがぶつかる箇所、つまりディテールがむき出しになっている。ディテールは文章の接続詞や句読点のようなものだ。「柱、スチール、ガラス、板」「柱にスチールとガラスの板」「柱はスチール、ガラスは板」では文章自体の意味が変わってくるような、接合部やディテールをできるだけミニマムな操作でていねいにデザインすることで、全体に大きな影響を与えることができる方法を考えてみたい。

例えば金継ぎのように、接合部や補修方法そのものが全体の意匠を支配している状態はどうか。金継ぎは、割れや欠け、ヒビなどの陶磁器の破損部分を漆によって接着し、金などの金属粉で装飾して仕上げる伝統的な修復技法だ。器は何でもよい。一人称やだれかの強いコンセプトでつくるのではなく、欠損やノイズを受け入れる。そして、割れれば直すことが繰り返されるので、完成や竣工という概念もない。建築において、ディテールや設備、構造がむき出しになるということは、

今後の改修や修繕の可能性を想定している、ということでもある。竣工時点で完成するのではなく、もう少し長いタイムラインでデザインを考えたい。そしてその「完成しないこと」そのものが意匠を決定しているような状態をデザインの根拠にすることはできないだろうか。

完成しないこと

　東京にあるインキュベーション施設《Mistletoe of Tokyo》(2019)はけっして完成しないオフィスだ。ここは社会的意義の高いスタートアップに投資や支援をするコミュニティのための空間だ。彼らの関心は全方位に広がり、変化し続けていくので、「進化し続けること」が前提の空間がふさわしいように思えた。典型的な建物には、明確な完成の瞬間がある。この場所は、使い始めた後でも検証しさらにデザインを考え続けることで空間が変化続ける。僕たちはこの完成がない空間をデザインし続けるための実験的なリサーチとプロトタイピングの組織「DDAA LAB」を組織し、さらにいくつかの未来の住環境を考えるプロジェクトが進行している。例えば小さな水循環システムを開発するスタートアップとともに水インフラがない場所でも使用することができるシャワーやキッチンを考え、自動運転で動き回るインフラに依存しない建築のあり方を想像する。

最小単位と全体

　《Bench Bomb》(2017) は、道路上のガードレールを支持体としたベンチをグラフィティのように街に勝手に設置するプロジェクトだ。東京都心にある 23 の自治体それぞれのガードレールのための 23 種類のベンチをデザインし、オープンソースで公開する。《Stacking Stool Studies》(2019-) は、アアルトの「Stool 60」に簡単に取り付けることができる 100 パターン以上のジョイントパーツをデザインし、オープンソースで公開していく。そのほか、歩道用のインターロッキングブロック、街路樹帯や中央分離帯、ガードレールや信号、点字ブロックなどの都市を構成する最小単位のプロダクトを地場産業を使って開発する。例えばステンレスで有名な燕三条であればステンレス製のガードレールや信号機などをデザインすることで、その地域だけの風景をつくることができるのではないか。現状を受け入れることと、最小限の手数による、部分や補修方法そのものが全体の性格を決定しているような状態。ミニマムなプロダクトから都市のスケールまで、金継ぎ的な手法は有効なのではないかと考えている。

Rikako Nagashima
長嶋りかこ

Born in 1980. Graphic designer and president of village®. Her graphic design work extends to such diverse areas as book design, identity design, signage, and spatial design. She sees design as a way to contribute to the environment, culture, and social welfare, as well as to cultivate interest in the relationship between production and waste that affects our lives and the natural environment.
http://rikako-nagashima.com

Representative projects
David Lynch: From the Fringes of the Mind (2019)
Dojima River Biennale (2019)
Scrap_CMYK at Kinnasand (2019)
DESCENTE BLANC exhibition using waste fabric (2018)
Night Cruising documentary film about a blind filmmaker (2017)
Concept of Happiness: Anish Kapoor's Outline of Collapse exhibition (2017)
Tohoku Youth Orchestra (2016-)
ASSEMBLE: Community Fantasy and Future exhibition (2016-17)
City and Nature at Sapporo International Art Festival (2014)

1980 年生まれ。village® 代表、グラフィックデザイナー。ブックデザイン、アイデンティティデザイン、サイン計画、空間構成など、グラフィックデザインを基軸としながら活動。デザインを用いて、環境／文化／福祉に寄与すること、また自然環境や私たちをとりまく生産と廃棄の関係への関心を深めることを目指す。
http://rikako-nagashima.com

主な作品など
デヴィッド・リンチ「精神的辺境の帝国」展 (2019)
堂島ビエンナーレ (2019)
kinnasand「Scrap_CMYK」(2019)
廃生地による DESCENTE BLANC Exhibition (2018)
全盲者の映画制作を追うドキュメンタリー映画「ナイトクルージング」(2017)
アニッシュ・カプーア「アニッシュ・カプーアの崩壊概論」展 (2017)
東北ユースオーケストラ (2016-)
アセンブル「共同体の幻想と未来」展 (2016-17)
札幌国際芸術祭「都市と自然」(2014)

1 *Scrap_CMYK* (2019) / Kinnasand
Test-print ink stains printed in patterns on fabric made of recycled plastic bottles. / ©Kinnasand
kinnasand「Scrap_CMYK」(2019)
プラスチックボトルを再利用した生地にヤレ紙のインク汚れをパターン化してプリント ／©Kinnasand

2 *David Lynch: From the Fringes of the Mind* (2019) / Gyre Gallery
An experiment in eliminating waste by incorporating printer-generated ink stains into designs. / ©village®
デヴィッド・リンチ「精神的辺境の帝国」展 (2019)
印刷機によるインク汚れを廃棄せずむしろ率先してエラーを減らすデザインに取り込む事で廃棄物を出さない試み ／©village®

3 *yo* Takakura New Industries (2019)
Package designs for a 100% plant-derived hair care series, devised to minimize waste and maximize recycling of resources. / ©Chinami Uematsu
《余》たかくら新産業 (2019)
100% 植物由来のヘアケアシリーズのパッケージデザインはゴミの小量化と資源の再利用を徹底 ／©植松千波

4 Folding Screen, SUMIDA CONTEMPORARY (2018)
Hand-made paper recycled from scraps of test-print waste divided by color. / ©Sumida Contemporary
屏風 SUMIDA COMTEMPORARY (2018)
ヤレガミを色別にちぎり漉いて再生紙を制作／©Sumida Contemporary

5 DESCENTE BLANC exhibition (2018) / DESCENTE BLANC
An exhibition space created from recycled fabric. / ©Kenta Hasegawa
廃生地による DESCENTE BLANC Exhibition (2018)
廃生地を再利用して作った展示空間 ／©長谷川健太

1

4

2

David Lynch　David Lynch

From
the Fringes
of the Mind

of the Mind

3

5

　4: REASSEMBLAGE OF ELEMENTS

A Raison-d'etre for
Colors and Forms

During my ten years as an art director for an advertising agency, I began to feel uneasy about the way our society, and we as individuals, are driven by the premise that we must constantly strive for material and economic growth and consume natural resources without regard for the effect on the environment. Only after going independent and opening my own office did my suppression of those misgivings, while continuing work that promoted mindless consumption, provoke a reaction in me that included feelings of guilt. To what end is this growth, for whose sake is this quality, for what purpose are these designs? As I confronted my misgivings and pondered the point of design, I began to ask myself why I give colors and forms to things, why I fabricate exits where there really are none, and ultimately, how I should live as a human being. Since going independent I turn down advertising work and try to accept only projects related to the environment, culture, and social welfare.

Bruce Mau, a graphic designer known for his collaborations with Rem Koolhaas, advanced the notion of "massive design" as a force for public good according to the hierarchical relationship design > nature > culture > business. When I first encountered that line of thought, I was a bit disturbed by its implication that design is at the top of the heap and should control all aspects of life. Such a dynamic attitude may be necessary in countries or regions like the Netherlands that must survive by creating land for themselves through reclamation. But for the first 18 years of my life, my family cut firewood on the mountain behind our house and heated water with it for an hour to take a bath; we spent six months of the year tending rice fields, grew our own fruits and vegetables in season, and collected eggs every morning from the chickens in our yard. Having grown up like that, I picture the bounty and energy of nature that lies behind the services that deliver food to your door with the press of a button, and I feel that the designs created by human beings also owe their existence to that bounty.

My objectives in design are very modest. Just as people can use their buying behavior to take a stand in support of environmental movements, cultural activities, and efforts to improve social welfare, I try to apply the same awareness to my design work, which usually comes through commissions. When choosing whether to accept a job I think about what it stands for and what sort of contribution it makes. I also try to come up with designs that generate as little waste as possible, proposing (sometimes overtly, sometimes tacitly) the use of recycled, recyclable, or environmentally friendly materials. Recently my colleagues and I have been trying to recycle the waste paper that the printing process generates in the form of test-print sheets for ink adjustment. Recycling the industrial waste from one's own work is not just interesting in terms of working with this waste "noise"; more importantly, it raises our awareness by forcing us to confront the very real problem of waste produced by our designs. For the David Lynch exhibition *From the Fringes of the Mind* (Gyre Gallery, 2019), I created printed works that eliminated the very existence of test-print waste, intentionally producing ink-stained sheets on a printer and treating the ink patterns as "differentiated graphics." For Sumida Contemporary (2018) I divided test-print waste paper by colors, tore it into large scraps, and blended it into a pulp with which I hand-made terrazzo-like paper sheets, then used these to make folding screens. For *Scrap_CMYK* at Kinnasand in Denmark (2019) I experimented with the use of test-print ink stains as a graphic element by scanning the stains to create patterns, then printing the resulting graphic designs on fabric made of recycled plastic bottle waste to produce textiles on the theme of "design-generated waste." At present I continue to pursue small-scale experimental projects of this sort.

What is growth for? Who is this quality for? What purpose does design serve? Is there a raison-d'etre for the colors and forms we come up with? As environmental crises grow increasingly severe, I can't help feeling that time is running out. What should a person who works in design do? I will continue to seek answers to that question.

A few words about this catalog for the Japan Pavilion at the 17th International Architecture Exhibition of the Venice Biennale: It has been made as environmentally sound as possible within the limitations on format, binding, and printing process imposed by budgetary constraints and publishing and distribution conditions. The cover, jacket, wrapper, and pages are all made with Forest Stewardship Council (FSC) certified paper, which is manufactured from trees that were grown under sustainable forest management practices and legally logged. The ink is VOC-free, i.e., it contains no petroleum solvents so as to avoid the use of volatile organic compounds, which are known to be a health hazard when released into the environment. We used the LED UV printing process to conserve energy and polyurethane reactive (PUR) binding to optimize recy-clability. Following the example of Takamizawa House, which will be transformed into a variety of formats in Venice, then further recycled, we plan to cut up the plastic sheeting used at the Japan Pavilion, convert it into bags by thermocompression bonding, and use them as cases for a special edition of this book after the exhibition is finished.

色と形の存在意義

環境配慮もなしに天然資源を消費し続け、物質的／経済的成長を目指すべきという前提のもとに社会や人々が動かされていることに対して違和感を感じながらも、広告代理店でアートディレクターを10年続けていた。しかし違和感に蓋をして闇雲に消費を助長する仕事をしていたことは、その後独立して自分の事務所を構えてからの嫌悪感を伴った反動源となっていった。何のための成長か、誰のための質か、何のためのデザインなのか。違和感を直視して、何のためにデザインがあるのかを考えることは、自分は何のために何に対して色や形を与え、出口のないものに出口をつくる姿勢をとるのかを考えることでもあり、つまるところ人としてどう生きるのかを考えることとなった。独立後は広告の仕事の依頼は断り、できる限り環境／文化／福祉の仕事ができるよう取捨選択していくようになる。

レム・コールハースとの協働でも知られるグラフィックデザイナーのブルース・マウがかつて謳った「マッシブ・デザイン」は、「デザイン＞自然＞文化＞ビジネス」という構図とともにデザインによる公益を目指そうというものだったが、当時この考え方を知った私は、ヒエラルキーの最上位にあるデザインが生命のあらゆる領域をコントロールしようとする態度に通じるようにも思え、少し恐ろしくも感じた。オランダのように干拓によって国土を造らねば人々が生きられなかったような国や地域を背景とした場合ではこのダイナミックな考え方は前提になるのかもしれない。しかし生まれてから18年間、風呂は裏山から切ってきた薪を使って1時間かけて沸かし、米は半年かけて育て、野菜や果物は季節ごとに畑で育て、卵は毎朝庭先の鶏から恵んでもらうような、そんな日常を過ごした私は、ボタンひとつで食べ物やサービスが目の前に届くことの向こうにある自然の恩恵とエネルギーを想像しては、人為によるデザインもまたそうした恩恵とともにあると考えてきた。

私がデザインで試みることは、とても地味で地道なものだ。個人が暮らしのなかで、購買行動によって環境運動や文化活動や福祉向上のための活動の支援を表明することができるように、主に受注から始まるデザインの仕事には同じ意識で、その仕事は何に加担することになるのか、何の意義があるかを考えたうえで、取捨選択をする。そして廃棄物ができるだけ出ないようなデザインを提案し、時にあからさまに時にしれっと、再生マテリアルの利用やマテリアルの再利用の提案、環境対応素材の提案をしてアウトプットするよう心がけている。最近は印刷のプロセスで排出さ

4: REASSEMBLAGE OF ELEMENTS

Naritake Fukumoto
福元成武

れるヤレ紙（インク調整のために使用する損紙）は、自分たちで引き取って再利用を試みており、自分の仕事で発生する産業廃棄物を自分で再生することは、廃棄物というノイズを扱う面白さもあるけれど、それ以上にリアリティをもって自分のデザインがもたらす廃棄の問題を直視することになり、その事実に自覚的でいることにも繋がっている。デヴィッド・リンチ「精神的辺境の帝国」展 (2019) では、ヤレ紙のインク汚れをそのまま "個体差のあるグラフィック" とみなし積極的にインク汚れを印刷機で起こすことでヤレ紙という存在自体をなくした印刷物を制作した。「SUMIDA CONTEMPORARY」(2018) では、ヤレ紙を色ごとに仕分け大きめにちぎって攪拌し手漉きしてつくったテラゾーのような紙で屏風を制作。またヤレ紙のインク汚れをグラフィックの要素として活かす試みとして、kinnasand「SCRAP_CMYK」(2019) では、インク汚れをスキャンしてパターン化したグラフィックデザインを、使用済みプラスチックボトルゴミを再利用した生地にプリントすることで、"デザインが産む廃棄" をテーマにしたテキスタイルを制作した。このように地道ではあるが、さまざまに試みつつ、現在も次のプロジェクトを進行中である。

　何のための成長か、誰のための質か、何のためのデザインなのか。自分が考える色とカタチに、存在の意義はあるのか。自然環境は今後ますます厳しくなる。時間はないと切に感じる。デザインをする自分がすべきことは何か、自分自身に問い続けている。

　今回の第17回ヴェネチア・ビエンナーレ国際建築展日本館カタログに関して。出版流通環境と予算環境により判型や造本や印刷手法に制限があったが、そのなかでできることをした。表紙、カバー、帯、本文用紙は、違法伐採ではないと承認され持続可能な森林管理が行われている木材をもとに生産された FSC 森林認証紙を使用し、インクは揮発性有機化合物（環境中へ放出されると公害などの健康被害を引き起こすといわれている）の発生を防ぐために、石油系有機溶剤0%のノン VOC インキを使用した。またエネルギーを抑え印刷するために LED-UV 印刷にて印刷をし、リサイクル適正の高い PUR 製本にしている。リサイクルに関しては、ヴェネチアに持ち込まれた《高見澤邸》がさまざまに形を変えさらに再利用されていくように、日本館で使用されるビニールシートは切断し熱圧着して袋を作成し、会期後に特別版として本のケースに再利用されていくことを計画している。

Born in 1978. President of the design and construction company TANK. He works with architects on many projects, always with the aim of creating quality structures by considering how to build them with changing technologies and economic needs in mind, without being confined to conventional construction methods.
https://tank-tokyo.jp/

1978年生まれ。株式会社TANK代表。建築施工。建築家のプロジェクトに多く携わる。変化し続ける技術と経済性をもって既存の工法に対し "いま" どうつくるべきかを考え、良質のものを提供したいと考えている。
https://tank-tokyo.jp

1　Transforming construction methods
　Photo: Jumpei Kato
　Text: Yuka Uchida, courtesy of Casa BRUTUS
　工法の転換
　写真：加藤純平、テキスト：内田有佳、企画：『Casa BRUTUS』

2　Replacing construction methods
　©Kenta Hasegawa
　工法の置換
　©長谷川健太

3　Experimenting with new construction methods
　Planning: David Glaettli＋TANK
　©Takumi Ota
　新しい工法の試み
　プランニング：ダヴィッド・グレットリ＋TANK、
　©太田拓実

4　*A Cat Tower* (2015)
　©Kenta Hasegawa
　《A Cat Tower》(2015)
　©長谷川健太

5　*A Dog Run* (2016)
　©Kenta Hasegawa
　《A Dog Run》(2016)
　©長谷川健太

4: REASSEMBLAGE OF ELEMENTS

How Should We
Make Things Now?

While engaged in the day-to-day management of construction projects, it occurs to me that the world is full of superb products ready-made for use in building construction, as well as superb construction systems for making use of those products. Moreover, these systems are subdivided into tasks, each with its own professional specialists. This arrangement makes it possible to create very well-built structures rationally and efficiently.

However, the projects I undertake often incorporate designs into the construction process itself. In such cases we are sometimes compelled to come up with unique solutions that preclude the use of ready-made components or the work of the usual specialists.

Most construction companies treat requirements like these outside the purview of the usual professionals as an onerous nuisance, and wind up substituting conventional construction methods. The result is a situation in which construction methods per se cannot be included in the design process.

At TANK we are interested in the design of unconventional construction methods. We find meaning in our activities and potential in our designs through the development of optimum means for realizing the objectives of those designs without clinging to conventional processes. We strive to create new construction methods, sometimes by engaging in construction ourselves through the building of mockups.

Transforming construction methods

We proposed a contemporary DIY project of customizing open-source furniture designs by Enzo Mari, as featured in the June 2017 issue of the magazine *Casa BRUTUS* (published by Magazine House). The concept Mari advanced in the 1970s, of building products using straight-cut materials assembled with nails, was revolutionary and praiseworthy. But it struck us that the accompanying noise, sawdust, and tool maintenance present high hurdles for apartment dwellers in cities today, not to mention the fact that a certain degree of skill is required to cut materials straight and join them properly with nails or screws. As a solution we offered free Internet access to wood processing and 3D printing data that can be used with commonly available DIY services to assemble a table from precut plywood and 3D-printed plastic joints ordered online. Since there is no need to cut the materials or use screws to attach them, anyone can build this table with ease. We sought out methods and dimensions that would make assembly as simple as possible, conducting repeated tests to make the plywood thin (hence light) and the joints easy to assemble. The ever-expanding choices of colors and materials that can be output by 3D printers, as well as the many varieties of plywood available, allow users to customize their work in keeping with Mari's original concept. As 3D printers come into increasingly general use, they will serve as a primary DIY tool, which should in turn drive prices down.

Replacing construction methods

Employed as a construction material since around 6,500 BCE, mortar continues to enjoy widespread use today. However, cracks often appear in mortar-finished surfaces. Clients tend to view cracks as undesirable, but are they really? Can't we transform cracks, so typically treated as a construction error, into a design element? We got the idea of repairing floor cracks in a Kyoto renovation project in the manner of *kintsugi* — the traditional method of repairing pottery with lacquer mixed with gold or silver.

Instead of lacquer we used epoxy, which we colored gold for decorative purposes. The amount of cracking is unpredictable since it depends on site conditions and worker skills, and the patterns made by the cracks will also vary from site to site. We also use mortar-type materials that do not crack, but the fineness of the grains creates a different texture and hence a lighter sound with some base materials, affecting one's sense of the weight of the space. Therefore we use such materials differently from mortar.

Experimenting with new construction methods

To enhance perceptions of the scale of the space and spark the imagination of visitors to a furniture exhibition room, we placed the furniture on footplates on which we drew a 100-mm pitch grid with Posca brand water-soluble felt-tip pens. We made it a priority to generate lines that were not precisely measured, but appeared soft and hand-drawn. However, there was little time available to complete the project, so we built a device that could draw 26 lines at a time. Since Posca pens require that you keep pumping the ink to draw a smooth, unbroken line, and to prevent the ink from cutting off or overflowing due to the unevenness of the plywood surface, we attached a suspension device to the back end of each pen so as to accommodate such irregularities. This allowed us to achieve the line texture and work speed we desired.

In experiments like these, we are actively searching for approaches to the development of new designs by recombining current production and construction methods in a variety of ways—diverting conventional methods to other uses, modifying them within existing frameworks, or devising entirely new methods.

いまどうつくられるべきか

日々施工管理を行っていて思うことは、世の中には建物をつくるための優れた既製品が溢れていて、それを利用して施工を行うための優秀な施工体制が整えられているということである。またその施工体制は職種ごとに細分化され、それを専門とする業者が存在することによって合理的、効率的に完成度の高いモノをつくることができる仕組みが形成されている。

一方でわれわれが受けもつ案件では、つくり方自体にデザインが組み込まれることが多く、その場合既製品では適切に対処できなかったり、業者では対応できないような特殊な納まりを考える必要がある。

多くの施工会社は、このようなどの業者にも頼むことができない案件を厄介で面倒なものだと捉えがちであり、既存の一般的な工法に置き換えて施工を行うことが多く、工法自体をデザインとして扱うことができない状態にある。

われわれTANKはその一般的ではない工法をデザインすることに関心を持ち、既存の工法に捕われることなく、デザイン意図を最適な方法で具現化することに活動の意義とデザインの可能性を感じており、時には自らモックアップを製作し、実際に自主施工することによって、新しい工法を生み出す取り組みを進めている。

工法の転換

『Casa BRUTUS』(マガジンハウス、2017年6月)におけるエンツォ・マーリがデザインした家具図のオープンソースをカスタマイズするという企画で、現代のDIYを提案した。1970年代に発表された"直線のカット"と"釘で固定"をすればプロダクトをつくることができるという彼のコンセプトは画期的で尊ぶが、よく考えてみると、現代都市に住む人の多くにとっては、マンションでの音出し、木材をカットするときの粉塵、道具の保管だけでもハードルが高く、材料を直線にカットしてビスまたは釘で固定すること自体も、相当程度に慣れていない限り難しいのではないかと感じた。そこで、ベニヤのカットと3Dプリンターで出力される樹脂のジョイントをインターネットでオーダーし、届いた材料を組み立ててテーブルをつくるという、一般化されたサービスを使ってできるDIYの方法を使い、木材加工用と3Dプリンター用のデータをネットで公開し、誰でも入手できるようにした。材料をカットしなくていいし、組み立てにビス留めも必要なくなるため、誰でも簡単につくることができる。ベニヤをなるべく薄く(軽く)して、組み立てやすいジョイントの形を何度もつくって検証し、誰でも組み立てられる方法と寸法を探した。3Dプリンターで出力できる色も素材も増え続け、ベニヤも種類があるから、利用者はカスタムもできるし、エンツォ・マーリのオリジナルのコンセプトに適している。今後さらに普及す

る3Dプリンターは DIY の主要なツールとなり、低価格化を推し進めると
いうメリットを生むだろう。

工法の置換

　紀元前6500年頃から建材として使われていたというモルタルは、現在
でも一般的に使われている材料である。モルタルを仕上げで使う際には
表面にクラックが生じる可能性が高い。クライアントはクラックをネガ
ティブな要素として認識するが、はたして本当にそうだろうか。施工のエラー
とみなされることが多いクラックをデザインとして転換することはできな
いのか。京都のリノベーションプロジェクトで床のクラックを「金継ぎ」の
ように補修することを考えた。
　金継ぎに使う漆ではなく、クラックの補修で使われるエポキシを使って
金色で飾った。現場の状況や職人の加減によりクラックの量は推測でき
ず、現場ごとに異なる模様もデザインの特徴となる。クラックの入らない
モルタル系の材料も使用するが、粒子が小さく質感が異なるうえに下地
によっては軽い音がして、現場で感じる空間の重さが違うため、モルタル
とは区別して使っている。

新しい工法の試み

　家具の展示スペースを、空間の規模が認識しやすく、人々の想像力が
より働く場所にするために、什器の下にポスカ（水性インクのサインペン）
で100mmピッチのグリッドを描いた土台を製作した。その際に大切にし
たのは、精密な線を引くのではなく、手の痕跡が残ったような柔らかい線
を引くこと。納品までの時間的余裕もない。そこでわれわれは、一度に26
本の線が引ける装置を製作した。ポスカなのでインクを出し続けなけれ
ば安定した線が引けないのと、合板表面の凹凸で線が途切れたりインク
が出すぎないよう、凹凸に追従できるサスペンションを各ペンの後端部
に設けた。これにより、目標としていた線の質感と作業スピードを得るこ
とができた。
　以上のように、現在の生産方法・施工方法を組み替えることによって
新しいデザインをつくりだす方法として、一般的に使用されている工法を
転用したり、同じ仕組みの工法を改変したり、またはまったく新しい工法
を考えてみたりと、さまざまな方向からのアプローチを積極的に模索して
いる。

Kozo Kadowaki
門脇耕三

Born in 1977. Associate Professor, Meiji University. Partner in
the architectural firm Associates. Specializing in architectural
construction methods and design, he applies his research on
the material construction of buildings to activities ranging from
architectural design to criticism. His theory and practice aim
toward the development of an architecture rooted in a richness
of detail that has been lost in the modern era. He has co-
authored and co-edited such books as *Philosophy of "Sharing"/
Or, The Relationship between Love, Systems, and Space* (LIXIL
Publishing, 2015).
https://www.kkad.org

Representative projects
Annex of Metal Lab (2019)
Kadowaki House (2018)
Former Hayami Clinic (2017)
House in Tsutsujigaoka (2015, with Jo Nagasaka/Schemata
Architects)

1977年生まれ。明治大学准教授。アソシエイツパートナー。建築構法、
建築設計。建物の物的なつくられ方についての研究をベースにしなが
ら、建築設計や建築批評などの活動も展開。近代に入ってから失われ
た、細部の豊かさを根拠とする建築のあり方を見出すべく、理論と実
践を積み重ねている。編著書＝『「シェア」の思想／または愛と制度
と空間の関係』（LIXIL 出版、2015）など。
https://www.kkad.org

主な作品など
《メタルラボのアネックス》(2019)
《門脇邸》(2018)
《元速水医院》(2017)
《つつじヶ丘の家》(2015、長坂常／スキーマ建築計画と協働)

© Takeshi Shinto

1　*Annex of Metal Lab* (2019)
Design: Kozo Kadowaki + Kazuki Imai + Takashi Yamamoto/Building
System Design Laboratory at Meiji University
Top: Conversion of a residence-with-storefront into an office,
featuring diverse elements and construction methods.
Bottom: Looking up the stairs from the 1st floor.
© Building System Design Laboratory at Meiji University
《メタルラボのアネックス》(2019)
設計：門脇耕三＋今井一貴＋山元隆史／明治大学構法計画研究室
上 (top)：店舗付き住宅からオフィスへの改修。多様な構法によるエレメント
の多様な現れ
下 (bottom)：1 階から階段を見上げる
© 明治大学構法計画研究室

2　*Kadowaki House* (2018)
Design: Kozo Kadowaki/associates + Building System Design
Laboratory at Meiji University
Top: The designer's house.
Middle: View of the living area from the 2nd-floor kitchen via the
dining area.
Bottom: Exterior view toward the adjacent house, an accumulation
of miscellaneous elements.
© Takeshi Yamagishi
《門脇邸》(2018)
設計：門脇耕三／アソシエイツ＋明治大学構法計画研究室
上 (top)：設計者の自宅
中 (middle)：2 階キッチンからダイニングを通してリビングを見る
下 (bottom)：隣棟側の外観。雑多なエレメントの集積
© 山岸剛

3　*Former Hayami Clinic* (2017)
Design: Kozo Kadowaki + Ryutaro Kawade + Yojiro Nonaka +
Ryosei Inayama/Building System Design Laboratory at Meiji
University
Conversion to a residence with cuts through the concrete slab and a
louvered floor. Other cuts expose sections of the interior.
© Building System Design Laboratory at Meiji University
《元速水医院》(2017)
設計：門脇耕三＋川出隆太郎＋野中陽次郎＋稲山凌生／明治大学構法計画
研究室
コンクリートを切断してルーバー床を架けた住宅の改修。既存の内装も切断
されたため、断面が露出している
© 明治大学構法計画研究室

1

2

3

Elements, Non-totality, and Relational Freedom

I base a variety of activities, including architectural design and criticism, on my research into building construction methods. If there is an underlying keyword in my work it is "elements," by which I refer to the physical parts that make up buildings. However, my concept of elements is grounded in a critique of the conservative architectural view that a building must by definition constitute a complete, unified whole, or totality.

Why must buildings—particularly what we call architectural works—possess "totality"? Granted, a building governed from top to bottom by a consistent logic or geometry gives it a coherent organization, making it easy to grasp as a form of architectural expression. But a building's primary purpose is not to express something, so expression alone does not justify clinging to totality for its own sake. Furthermore, a rigorous adherence to totality creates a fully-formed interior world that tends to close the building off from its environment.

One might also be able to justify totality in the interests of productivity. In point of fact, mass production facilitated by standardization was the objective of the simple, straightforward geometries introduced by modern architecture. Today, however, Japan has left the era of mass production behind, and architects find themselves forced to contemplate what architecture should be like in an era of small-scale production. In the realm of construction methods we see chimera-like composites of fundamentally different industries, as when an aluminum sash is inserted in a wooden frame. It seems to me that the impulse to subordinate such phenomena to notions of totality only serves to limit the possibilities offered by architecture as a junction of diverse industries.

In light of such considerations, the point of totality in architecture appears increasingly dubious. Below I will summarize the conclusions I have drawn from my own research. [*1-5]

Such elements as floors, walls, and ceilings are parts of a building; at the same time they themselves are assemblages of multiple components. There are practical reasons and historical precedents for treating such elements as self-contained units. In other words, an element is a semi-autonomous entity with its own existential logic. One might also say it possesses an incomplete totality. Therefore, if we let the unique existential logic of individual elements develop unfettered, it will enhance a building's character as a space in which disparate logics converge and intermingle. Conversely, if we wish to impose a consistent totality on a building, we must exercise some sort of control over these elements.

This framework could just as easily apply to any whole-vs.-parts relationship. If we see a city as the whole and buildings as its parts, then we might argue that that the personalities of individual buildings must be suppressed to maintain a proper totality for the city. The question "Does a building require totality?" is nothing more than a question of whether the space occupied by a building is to be made to conform to the domain assumed to constitute a "whole."

But what we really need to be wary of is that this framework defines "parts" as objects of control, while "the whole" functions as an abstract pattern determining the manner of control. In other words, totality is a false focal point devised as a component of a simplistic methodology that attempts to design an interior environment by controlling its elements, which it identifies by defining boundaries demarcating this interior. In that case, why can't we design buildings by eliminating this peculiar entity "totality" with its potential for delusions of transcendence, eschew defining arbitrary boundaries, and let complex elements thrive in their complexity? In my own works I put this approach into practice by designing them according to the following method.

An effective method of eliminating "totality" from a building is to treat its elements as specific and individual. A clue to this is context. A mature city is rich with context, so I design elements in such places such that their own existential logic is continuous with

4: REASSEMBLAGE OF ELEMENTS

that of their surroundings, giving them a presence that transcends boundaries. One might describe this as designing them as elements of a local context rather than of a building. It is also effective to let the elements conform straightforwardly to the structural principles inherent in the elements themselves. These strategies allow the elements scattered throughout a building to grow and thrive according to their own individual logics.

When the density of elements gets to a certain level, it's time to begin designing the parts that link them. The work of designing relationships between elements that just happen to adjoin one another is essentially ad hoc, with unanticipated issues constantly cropping up, but my view is that these parts should relate as critiques of one another. The result is a significant attrition of the tendency to construct a "whole" by establishing an architectural order, whether geometric or structural or dynamic.

Deciphering the parts of a building designed in this manner does not lead to a grasp of the whole. Understanding of one part may enhance understanding of some other part, but not necessarily the rest of the building. No standardization of parts, no shortcuts from the parts to the whole are permitted, so an overall image does not readily materialize. In short, a birds-eye view of the entirety is unattainable.

What manifests itself there is nothing more than a physical sequence of adjacent elements or spaces. But precisely because this sequence of elements and spaces has no preordained relations, it has the potential to expand indefinitely. It is the freedom offered by that expansiveness that gives the details of a building—i.e., of the world that appears before our eyes—the opportunity to reclaim the richness of the past.

Notes
*1 Planner and editor, "Special Feature 2: Elements for Building—Architects Talk about Construction Methods," *SD [Space Design] Review 2012*, Kajima Institute Publishing, 2012, pp. 65–108
*2 Article, "Elements as Anti-space," *10+1 website*, LIXIL Publishing, February 2015, http://10plus1.jp/monthly/2015/02/issue-01.php
*3 Article, "Escape from Architectural Prison: Thoughts on Sayama Flat," in Jo Nagasaka, *When B-Side Becomes A-Side* (revised edition), Kajima Institute Publishing, 2016, pp. 151–155
*4 Article, "The Paradox of Disconnection and Connection," *10+1 website*, LIXIL Publishing, December 2016, http://10plus1.jp/monthly/2016/12/issue-01-3.php
*5 Article, "Overcoming the Tension between the Whole and the Parts," *Shinkenchiku Jutakutokushu* (New Architecture / Housing Special) No. 38, Shinkenchiku-sha, August 2018, p. 53

エレメント／非－全体性／
関係性の自由なひろがり

建物の構法についての研究をベースにしながら、批評や建築設計など、活動はさまざまな方向に展開している。通底するキーワードとして、建物の物的な部分を意味する「エレメント」を挙げることができるが、その根底には、建物はそれ自体で完結する全体性を備えるべきであるとする、保守的な建築観への疑念がある。

建物、とりわけ建築作品と呼ばれるものには、なぜ全体性が必要とされるのか？もちろん、首尾一貫した論理や幾何学によって建物のあり方を隅々まで統制すれば、成り立ちが明快になり、建築表現としてわかりやすくなるし、その結果として、建物にはここでいう全体性が付与される。しかし建物は、第一義的には何かを表現するために存在するのではないのだから、表現は全体性に拘泥する理由にはならない。また厳格な全体性は、それによってできあがった世界を内部で完結させ、建物にある種の閉鎖性をもたらしてしまう。

あるいは、生産性の観点から全体性の存在意義を説明できるかもしれない。実際、近代建築に導入された直截簡明な幾何学は、規格化と標準化を通じて大量生産を実現するためのものであったが、現代の日本では大量生産の時代は過ぎ去って、むしろ少量生産時代の建築のあり方を本気で考える必要に駆られている。また構法は、例えば木造の躯体にアルミサッシが取り付くといった具合に、由来の異なる産業のキメラ的複合体の様相を呈しているが、これを全体性によって統制しようという考え方は、多様な産業のジャンクションとしての建築の可能性をかえって狭めてしまうようにも感じられる。

このように考えていくと、建物の全体性の意義は疑わしくなってくる。検討を続けるうちに明らかになってきたのは、以下のようなことであった（※1－5）。

そもそも床・壁・天井などといったエレメントは、建物の部分であると同時に、複数の部材が組み合わさったまとまりでもあり、ひとつのまとまりと見なされる合理的理由や歴史的経緯をもつ。つまりエレメントは、独自の存在論理をもった半自律的な存在である。不完全な全体性をもつといってもよい。したがってエレメントそれぞれに固有の存在論理を素直に展開するならば、建物は異質な論理が輻輳する場としての性格を強める。反対に、建物に首尾一貫した全体性をもたせようとするのであれば、エレメントには何らかの統制が敷かれねばならない。

ただし、この構図はあらゆる全体と部分の関係に敷衍できる。例えば都市を全体、建物を部分とみなせば、都市の良好な全体性を保つために、建物の個性は極力削ぎ落とすべきとの議論も成立する。「建物に全体性は必要か？」という問いは、「全体」というかたちで仮定された領域を、建物が占める空間的な範囲と一致させるかどうかという問題にすぎない。

しかし、むしろここで注意すべきなのは、この構図における「部分」が制御の対象と同義であり、また「全体性」は制御のあり方を方向づける抽象的なパターンとして働いていることである。つまり全体性とは、境界を規定することで内部とその要素を同一視し、要素の制御を通じて内部環境をデザインしようとする、素朴な方法論の部品として現れる虚の焦点である。だとするならば、そこに超越性さえ幻視しかねない全体性という特異な存在を取り去って、複雑な要素を複雑なままに、排他性を発揮する自明な境界をなるべくつくらないように、建物をデザインすることはできないか。自身の建築作品はその実践であり、具体的には、次のような方法で設計を行っている。

建物から全体性を取り去る有効な方法は、エレメントを具体個別に考えていくことであり、その手がかりのひとつがコンテクストである。成熟した都市はコンテクストに満ちており、そうした場所におけるエレメントは、その存在の論理が周辺と連続し、越境的な位置づけを獲得できるように設計する。建物ではなく、局所的なコンテクストのエレメントとして設計するといってもよい。また、エレメントが内在するモノとしての構築の原理に、エレメントを素直に従わせることも有効である。これらの操作によって、建物全体に散らばったエレメントは、それぞれが別の論理に導かれて豊かに育っていく。

エレメントの密度が高まってきたら、それらをつなぐ部分の設計を始める。たまたま隣り合ったエレメントの関係を構築する作業は本質的にアドホックで、思いがけない取り合いが次々と生まれるのだが、そこで部分と部分は、互いの存在をクリティークするものになるよう意識する。その結果として、幾何学的だったり構成的だったり力学的だったりする建築の秩序、つまり全体を組織化しようとする動きは、その勢いを大きく削がれることになる。

そのようにしてできあがった建物では、部分を読み解いても、全体を把握することには繋がらない。ある場所について理解することが、別の場所の理解を促すことがあったとしても、それがすべての場所にあてはまるとは限らない。部分から全体への短絡や、部分の一般化は禁じられていて、全体性は容易には立ち上がらない。すなわち、そこでは全体を俯瞰する視点が失われている。

だからそこに実現するのは、エレメントや場所がいくらか即物的に隣り合う、その連なりにすぎない。しかしエレメントや場所の連なりは、あらかじめ決められた関係性をもたないことによってはじめて、どこまでもひろがっていく可能性へと開かれるのだ。その広がりが担

4: REASSEMBLAGE OF ELEMENTS

Kayoko Ota
太田佳代子

保する自由によってこそ、建物の細部、つまりわれわれの目の前に現れる世界は、かつての豊かさを取り戻すことができると考えている。

註
※1——拙企画・構成（『SD2012 構築へ向かうエレメント——構法と建築家の言葉』鹿島出版会、2012、65−108頁）
※2——拙論「反−空間としてのエレメント」（「10＋1 website」LIXIL出版、2015年2月号、http://10plus1.jp/monthly/2015/02/issue-01.php）
※3——拙論「建築的牢獄からの脱走——《SAYAMA FLAT》について」（長坂常『B面がA面にかわるとき［増補版］』鹿島出版会、2016、151−155頁）
※4——拙論「切断と接続のパラドクス」（「10＋1 website」LIXIL出版、2016年12月号、http://10plus1.jp/monthly/2016/12/issue-01-3.php）
※5——拙論「全体と部分の緊迫した関係を超えて」（『新建築住宅特集』No. 38、新建築社、2018年8月、53頁）

Curator of CCA c/o Tokyo and lecturer at the Graduate School of Design, Harvard University. As an architectural curator, she endeavors to advance architectural thought through communication in a variety of formats about architecture and cities. She recently co-authored *SHIBUYA! The Graduate Students of Harvard Think about Shibuya in Ten Years* (CCC Media House, 2019). Among the books she has edited is *Project Japan: Metabolism Talks...* (Taschen, 2011).
https://www.cca.qc.ca/en/cca-c-o/58179/tokyo

Representative exhibitions
In the Real World, The Venice Architectural Biennale (2014)
Shenzhen and Hong Kong Biennale of Urbanism and Architecture (2009)
Waist Down: The Creation of Miuccia Prada (2005–09)
Content: A Retrospective of OMA/AMO, Berlin and Rotterdam (2003–05)

Edited books
Rem Koolhaas and Hans-Ulrich Obrist, *Project Japan: Metabolism Talks...*, Taschen (2011)
Inside Outside: Petra Blaisse, The Monacelli Press (2009)
AMO / Rem Koolhaas, *Post-Occupancy*, Domus d'Autore, Editoriale Domus (2005)

CCA c/o Tokyo キュレーター、ハーバード大学デザイン大学院講師。建築キュレーター。建築・都市をめぐるさまざまな形式のコミュニケーションをつくりだし、建築的思考の開拓を目指す。共著＝『SHIBUYA! ハーバード大学院生が10年後の渋谷を考える』(CCCメディアハウス、2019)、主な編書＝『プロジェクト・ジャパン』（平凡社、2012）、共訳書＝『S,M,L,XL＋——現代都市をめぐるエッセイ』（ちくま学芸文庫、2015）など。
https://www.cca.qc.ca/en/cca-c-o/58179/tokyo

主な展覧会など
Content: A Retrospective of OMA/AMO, Berlin and Rotterdam (2003-05)
Waist Down: The Creation of Miuccia Prada (2005-09)
Shenzhen and Hong Kong Biennale of Urbanism and Architecture (2009)
In the Real World, The Venice Architectural Biennale (2014)

主な書籍編集など
AMO/Rem Koolhaas, *Post-Occupancy*, Domus d'Autore, Editoriale Domus (2005)
Inside Outside: Petra Blaisse, The Monacelli Press (2009)
Rem Koolhaas, Hans-Ulrich Obrist, *Project Japan: Metabolism Talks...*, Taschen (2011)

A Site for Regenerating the Role of the Architect

Time and space beyond one venue

The exhibition *Co-ownership of Action: Trajectories of Elements* is extremely ambitious in its conception. The curator has "seized" the unique opportunity offered by the Venice Biennale to enact an elaborate scenario that will "drag" the exhibition into it in the process of its execution.

In other words, the exhibition will not simply end with its conclusion at the Biennale. The aforementioned scenario is for a process of circulation between objects and production that extends in space and time beyond the exhibition itself. The plan is to present a vibrant reenactment of that process within the limited space of the exhibition venue.

The following is a simplified description of the scenario. It begins with the dismantling of a very ordinary *machiya* town house built in a residential area of Tokyo in the 1950s, when industrialization had begun to accelerate in the postwar era. Kozo Kadowaki and his team salvage all of its components and subject them to a sophisticated analysis. As anticipated, they make some surprising and exciting discoveries. That alone might be enough to build an exhibition around, but the scenario goes on from there.

The components of the house are sorted, loaded on a ship, and transported to the Japan Pavilion at the Venice Biennale. Architects and carpenters from Japan arrive in Venice and select components from those stored inside the Japan Pavilion, which has been turned into a warehouse. They begin to convert the components into workpieces, which they set up in the outdoor area of the pavilion. Working in the piloti space under the pavilion, the architects and carpenters come and go during the six months of the exhibition, sometimes joined by local practitioners, as a variety of workpieces accumulates in the outdoor area. As the exhibition progresses, the interior of the pavilion empties out while the exterior fills up with these workpieces, fomenting a festive atmosphere . . .

If this bold scenario unfolds as planned, the exhibition will be a grand achievement indeed. That will require the fulfillment of two conditions, however. The first is the vibrant transmission of the initial half of this recycling scenario—the history in Japan of the architectural components of the dismantled townhouse. The second is the successful creation of a means of vividly conveying to visitors the sequence over time from objects to production, from production to society, and from society to objects or production.

Reassigning spatial functions

It is rare, and even thrilling, for the Japan Pavilion to host an exhibition in a format according to which visitors follow a circuit (ideally, more than once) that enables them to vicariously experience a sequence of this sort. Downgrading the interior space on the second floor of the Japan Pavilion—normally the exhibition venue—to a mere warehouse, and instead assigning to the ground-floor piloti space—normally put to superficial use at best—the critical function of artisans' workshop, is a highlight in itself. Meanwhile, the outdoor area plays the starring role.

This agreeably piquant role reassignment sharply articulates the functions of three spaces. The second-floor interior is a space for "objects," i.e., the Tokyo townhouse components that are the primary subject of the first half of the scenario. The piloti level is a space for "production." It also admits elements of diversity and randomness that may even clash with the concept of creation. The outdoor area, including the garden, could be described as a "users' space or society" sustained by this cycle of objects and production.

As visitors to the Japan Pavilion circulate from the outdoor area to the interior space to the pilotis and back to the outdoor area, they are also experiencing the chain linking society to objects to production and back to society. If each space is conceived as representing a distinct part of this cycle, then the more pronounced the articulation, the better.

In that regard, one concern is the plan to use the

4: REASSEMBLAGE OF ELEMENTS

outdoor area to exhibit information on the "objects" shipped in from Tokyo. The definition of the warehouse as serving exclusively as a storage space for these objects is clearly articulated. But how can the intermingling of objects and society in the outdoor area be made comprehensible as an "intermingling"? This aspect, too, is surely crucial to conveying the intent of the exhibition. When I wrote earlier that visitors should follow the circuit "ideally more than once," it was because the message of the exhibition is likely to penetrate the hearts of visitors only after repeated circuits along this chain of spaces.

Redefining the exhibition format

What is the ultimate statement conveyed by an exhibition like this one, in which so many things are going on at once? Let me try to surmise it from the standpoint of one visitor.

The structural components of the dismantled *machiya* can be expected to include numerous damaged, defective, or missing parts due to many years of addition, modification, and aging. It is these "losses" that intrigue Kadowaki and his colleagues. The damaged or lost components were created by the unique destiny of this particular house, plus the actions of time and nature. Now, along with all the other components, they are reverting to the state of neutral "objects" with no relation to standards or plans.

That Kadowaki et al. are able to view these liberated components with a pragmatic eye is doubtless because they have the sensitivity and motivation to grasp the infinite potential that emerges in the instant such components are freed from the code of a particular system. Having anticipated that transformation, they have prepared a scenario that "plunges" these architectural components—which have now become "objects"—into a different societal context. This involves setting up a pseudo-production space at a Biennale venue into which they actively introduce randomness and anonymity. The result should be a spectacle, catalyzed by these liberated elements, of regeneration of the role of the architect.

The goal of the curator appears to be to inject new hope into today's architectural environment. This may become evident during even one circuit of the stimulating ambience in the outdoor and piloti areas of the pavilion. But the deeper the understanding one gains of this concept of circulation, the more richly it will sublimate into something that touches the heart.

Key to this project is the vision of a new image of the architect as someone who, liberated from the role of all-seeing, dictatorial creator, chooses to collaborate with others in the creative process. It is a vision that resonates with the general theme of this year's Biennale: "How will we live together?" What this exhibition purports to showcase is not the recycling of a house, but the regeneration of the architect's function. Its indisputable value lies, I believe, in its presentation of this regenerative experience not on the merely symbolic level, but through actual practice with actual objects.

建築家像が再生される現場

会場を超える時空

「ふるまいの連鎖：エレメントの軌跡」展は、展覧会としての構想がきわめて野心的である。

キュレーターはビエンナーレという独特の機会に乗じてある周到なシナリオを設定し、展覧会を巻き込みながら実践する。

つまり、この展覧会は会場だけでは完結しない。周到なシナリオとは、展覧会を超える時空の出来事からなる、いわばモノと生産の循環のプロセスであり、それを展覧会場の限られた空間で生き生きと再現し、実践してみせようというのだ。

シナリオは次のように単純化できる。

工業化が加速し始めた1950年代に東京の住宅街に建てられたごく平凡な町屋が一軒解体される。門脇耕三とチームはその部材をまるごと引き取り、高度な分析調査を行う。彼らの期待どおり、そこには驚きの発見があり、彼らを興奮させる。この段階ですでに展覧会ができてしまいそうだが、シナリオはさらに進む。

部材は選別のうえ船積みされ、ヴェネチア・ビエンナーレの日本館に運び込まれる。日本から建築家や大工職人がヴェネチアに到着し、資材庫と化した日本館の屋内から部材を選び出しては工作物に変え始め、屋外エリアに設置していく。ピロティで作業する建築家や大工職人は6カ月の会期を通して入れ替わり、時には現地の人々も参加して、多種多様な工作物が屋外エリアに設置されていく。会期が進むにつれ、日本館の屋内はガランとしていく一方、屋外は工作物で賑わい、祝祭的な雰囲気さえ漂う……。

この壮大なシナリオがうまく実現されれば、展覧会の構想としてまず快挙となるだろう。そのためには2つのことが必要になると考えられる。ひとつは、循環のシナリオの前半部分、つまり解体された町屋の建築部材が日本で経てきた出来事を、生き生きと伝えることである。もうひとつは、モノから生産、生産から社会、社会からモノや生産へという時間をともなう連鎖を、観客に実感してもらう仕掛けをつくり、成功させることだ。

空間構成の読み替え

観客が順路を（できれば何度か）巡回することで、連鎖を追体験する仕組みになっている、という展覧会形式もやはり日本館としては異例であり、痛快でさえある。

展覧会場である日本館2階の屋内空間は資材庫に格下げされる一

方、いつも中途半端な使用感が否めないピロティは職人たちが使う工房という重要な役割を与えられ、ひとつの見せ場となる。主役を張るのは屋外空間だ。

小気味よいほどの読み替えにより、3つの空間の役割は明快にアーティキュレートされる。2階の屋内空間は、シナリオ前半の主題となる東京の町屋の構成部材、つまり「モノ」の空間である。ピロティは「生産」の空間。そこには多様性や偶然性といった、創造の概念とぶつかりかねない要素も入り込む。庭園を含む屋外エリアは、「モノと生産の循環」が支えている「利用者たちの空間、社会」といえばよいだろうか。

観客は日本館の屋外エリア→屋内空間→ピロティ→屋外エリアを巡ることで、「社会→モノ→生産→社会」という連鎖をも体験する。各空間が「循環」の異なる部分を表象してもいるというコンセプトであれば、アーティキュレーションは明快なほどよいだろう。

そこで気になるのが、東京から運び込まれた「モノ」の情報が、屋外エリアで展示されることだ。資料庫はあくまで、モノの集積場として成立させたいという意向も理解できる。ならば、屋外エリアでの「モノ」と「社会」の混在を、いかに「混在」として理解してもらえるかが、展覧会の本意を伝えるうえでのもうひとつのポイントになるだろう。先に「できれば何度か巡回すること」と書いたのは、空間の連鎖を1度よりも2度、繰り返したどることで、展覧会のメッセージは観客の心に刺さると思うためだ。

展覧会という形式の読み替え

さまざまなことが同時に起こるこの展覧会だが、そこから伝わってくる最大のステートメントは何だろう？ 観客のひとりとして想像してみる。

解体された町屋の構成部材は、長い年月をかけて行われた継ぎ足しや変更、経年といった要因からなんらかの欠損をきたしているものが多かったという。この欠損に、門脇たちは引きつけられた。欠損した部材はその家固有の成り行きや時間と自然がつくったもので、ほかのすべての部材同様、標準化とも計画とも無縁の、ニュートラルなモノに回帰している。

彼らが解放された部材を即物的に見ることができたのは、ある体系のコードから解放された瞬間に現れる無限の可能性をそこに感じとる感性と動機があったからに違いない。

そのことを想定してもいた彼らは、モノ化した建築部材を別の社

4: REASSEMBLAGE OF ELEMENTS

会的文脈のなかに投げ込むというシナリオを用意する。ランダム性、無名性を積極的に巻き込んでいく擬似的な生産の場を、ビエンナーレの会場に設定したのだ。それは、解放されたモノに触発された、建築家という主体が「再生」されていく光景となるはずだ。

　この展覧会のキュレーターの本意とは、建築をめぐる現代の新しい希望を描き出すことではないだろうか。それは楽しげな屋外やピロティを一巡しても受け取れるのかもしれないが、循環の構想を理解することで心を掴むものに昇華するのだと思う。

　作者という権威的で一貫性をもつ主体像から解放され、創造の過程で他者と共存することを選びとる新しい建築家像。それは「How will we live together?」という今回の総合テーマに共振するビジョンでもある。だから家屋のリサイクルなどでは毛頭なく、建築家像の再生をこの展覧会は示すだろう。しかもそれが表象ではなく、現実の実践とモノによって示されることが、この展覧会のゆるぎない魅力となるはずだ。

A Communism of Action
Koichiro Kokubun (Philosopher)

With: Kadowaki (Architect and construction studies)

A communism of action

Koichiro Kokubun: First of all, I'm intrigued by the exhibition's focus on the concept and technology of "completion" of a construction project. It reminds me of a dam in Tokushima, the Daiju Weir on the Yoshino River. In 2000, after the central government decided to build a movable-gate dam on the river, voters in a local referendum responded with a resounding "no." The Yoshino had always been susceptible to inflows of seawater in time of drought, causing salt damage to crops. The Daiju Weir was built about 250 years ago to redirect the river's course to prevent this, and has survived for many generations with occasional modifications. However, the Construction Ministry at the time declared that the permeable structure of the rock weir allowed flooding in times of heavy rain, so it decided to build a movable-gate dam in its place, ignoring local citizens' arguments that serious flooding would not occur. When a weir of the same structure was tested in an experiment, there was apparently no problem with flooding—when the river's waters rise, the flow through the weir's rock filter simply increases. The filter structure also cleans the water passing through, whereas a movable-gate dam would stop the flow and cause sludge to build up.

Martin Heidegger cited the ancient Greek concepts of *physis* [nature] and *techne* [craft-like knowledge], defining the latter as the human yoking of the power of the former. In the way it harnesses the power inherent in water and land, the Daiju Weir is a superb example of *techne*. A movable-gate dam would be far more low-tech. What's more, the weir, which

has undergone continual modification over the generations, is the perfect example of a project to which the notion of "completion" doesn't apply.

Ever since writing *The World of Chu-Dou-Tai [the Middle Voice]: An Archaeology of Will and Responsibility* [Igaku-Shoin, 2017], I have been thinking about something I call "communism of action." The modern era is one in which actions were assigned the attribute of private ownership in the sense of treating a certain action as belonging to a certain person. Supporting this notion was the concept of the will. In his book *The Use of Bodies* [2014; Japanese translation by Tadao Uemura, Misuzu Shobo, 2016], Giorgio Agamben writes that "the will is, in Western culture, the apparatus that allows one to attribute the ownership of actions and techniques to a subject." In my book I vigorously criticized the fictional concept of "will." Surprisingly, a word for "will" did not exist in ancient Greece, nor did any equivalent concept. The Christian concept of the will seems to be associated with the concept of responsibility. That's because the notion of will, a relatively new concept in human history, makes it easier to charge someone with responsibility.

The treatment of actions as private property came to dominate the art world as well. In reality, no work of art is created entirely by a single individual. Works of architecture and film are obvious examples. No one can say who built Takamiyama House, which has been subjected to repeated expansion and renovation. There is, I think, something uniquely endearing about the house's perpetual state of incompletion. To understand the appeal of a building like this one, we must distance ourselves from the ide-

4: REASSEMBLAGE OF ELEMENTS

ology of private ownership and instead consider the notion of "communism" in the dimension of action.

Objects as responsible actors and as knowledge itself

Kozo Kadowaki: The concept of a "work" of architecture has, to date, been closely linked to such notions as will and responsibility. However, architecture packaged by a particular architect as their own work is an extremely static, closed entity that does not admit of modification or participation. Your mention of the Daiju Weir got me thinking that whereas responsibility, will, and knowledge tend to be thought of as formal systems detached from physical objects, the Daiju Weir is the very embodiment of knowledge accumulated by local people, and its maintenance and preservation is a manifestation of responsibility. In that sense, we cannot really distinguish between human beings and objects as responsible actors.

Kokubun: "Objects" always require action in the form of maintenance of some sort, although lately the traditional Japanese word for "caring for" objects [*te-ire*, literally "taking a hand to"] isn't heard much. In a book I wrote earlier, *Ethics of Leisure and Boredom* [Asahi Press, 2011], I made a distinction between "dissipation" and "consumption." By "dissipation" I mean getting and using up things, whereas "consumption" connotes absorption of the concepts and meanings assigned to things. So unlike dissipation, which is limited by how many things we can get, consumption is limitless because it consists of information.

Kadowaki: Takamiyama House, too, seems

to have been amenable to any kind of input up to a certain point, but after around 1980 it stopped changing. That was because building construction became more systematically regulated, and renovations required a permit. Prewar houses were customarily built under a day-labor system where clients paid workers by the day and made revisions as they went along. After the war, though, the contract system became the norm, with plans and estimates prepared in advance. As a result, ours is a society in which it is difficult to carry out the maintenance of buildings.

Kokubun: This is a story I heard from a butcher I know who is still trying to keep his butcher shop going—but the makers of hooks for hanging meat or special refrigerators for small shops have nearly all gone out of business. Butcher shop equipment is only made for the large stores now. With the excessive standardization of the entire economy, many necessities are simply no longer made.

In the economist David Glaber's book *Bullshit Jobs: A Theory* [Simon & Schuster, 2018], he writes that only "bullshit jobs"—those that are meaningless—are on the increase, while our society seems to be eliminating jobs that are low-profile but important. There used to be professions with their own store of knowhow that served an intermediary function between different types of work, but the global economy has progressively done away with them. The consulting industry has burgeoned because that lost knowhow has to be supplied from somewhere.

Can human beings "start" something?

Kadowaki: How should we go about resisting the destruction of these intermediaries?

Kokubun: In his book *The Conquest of Happiness* [1930; Japanese translation by Sadao Ando, Iwanami Bunko, 1991], Bertrand Russell wrote, "Education used to be conceived very largely as a training in the capacity for enjoyment." In other words, humans do not know how to experience true enjoyment without training. The mass-production/mass-consumption/mass-disposal cycle is perpetuated because people cannot properly enjoy things. That is because people today are deprived of any opportunity for such training, and are therefore incapable of engaging in any enjoyment other than the kind ordained by a mass-disposal society.

Kadowaki: In times like these, perhaps what we need is design that enables objects themselves to teach us how to live with them. With this exhibition one of our aims is to encourage a familiarity with objects. We will be making things at the venue ourselves, but we want this to be an exhibition where objects arouse the creative urge in visitors so that they will want to participate too.

Kokubun: From a slightly different perspective, we might say that there is a need to question not only the notion of "completing" the making of something, but also the notion of "starting" it. Willpower is perceived as the impetus for starting something—but can human beings really *start* something? Our exhibition is meant to function perpetually in an intermediate phase, neither starting nor finishing. I believe that "not starting" will prove to be an important ethical concept for creative undertakings in times to come.

Intimacy with the uncanny

Kokubun: When you dismantle a building, then reassemble it, the parts become visible, don't they. Hannah Arendt found a special quality of 20th-century art in the experience it afforded of seeing objects as "uncanny" [*unheimlich*] when separated from their functional relationships [*Essays in Understanding 1930–1954*, Japanese translation by Jun'ichi Saito et al., published by Misuzu Shobo, 2002]. Perhaps she was thinking of Van Gogh's *Pair of Old Shoes* [1886]—a common pair of farmer's boots which, when isolated, exude a peculiar power. Though we believe ourselves to be intimate with the world, there is in fact a chasm between the world and us. The art of the 20th century thoroughly demonstrated this truth. That was a significant achievement, to be sure, but today, I think, the question confronting us is how to regain our intimacy with the world.

Kadowaki: I agree with you on that point. On the other hand, objects that resemble a house reconfigured in a different context are unquestionably "uncanny," and one of our aims is to trigger that sensation. It is certainly important to encourage a sensation of endearment in the everyday sense—but how should we maintain a critical perspective, then? It's hard not to be influenced by the 20th-century concept of the "uncanny" in art.

Kokubun: I think either perspective is valid. However, the appearance at a venue in Venice of something like an old Japanese house should strike one as uncanny (unheimlich) from the outset; it then becomes familiar (heimlich) through our exposure to its elements, the production process, and so on. Over the course of the history of thought and art to date, the process of the familiar (heimlich) becoming unfamiliar (unheimlich) has come to be viewed as significant. This exhibition, on the other hand, appears to be pushing along a vector in the opposite direction.

Kadowaki: I see what you mean. That vector should be evident in Takamizawa House itself. For example, the aluminum sashes used for the window frames were "uncanny" elements adapted from the aircraft industry to imitate the traditional wooden fixtures in Japanese houses, but everyday use made them familiar. Perhaps we are trying to repeat that process in Venice. In contemporary society, dramatic advancements in distribution have surrounded us with unfamiliar objects, in that we don't know the origins of things we use on a daily basis. You might say we are addressing the question of how to create a vector toward the familiar in everyday life based on an awareness of that reality.

Not even a single house is knowable

Kadowaki: Another central theme of this exhibition is "loss"—of parts, information, function, and so on. For example, when we try to convert Takamizawa House in its entirety to 3D data, the quantity of information is too great for us to deal with. In short, we cannot completely know a house—even a single house. A dismantled house could be seen as a metaphor for the inadequacy of our perceptions of the world—but simply reconnecting elements

that have lost their functional relationship will not produce a finished structure. If we wish to restore a structure full of such losses to everyday use, we must compensate for those losses with new creations. Losses are gaps through which a variety of actors may enter, and for that very reason I anticipate that the production of these creations will be a collaborative effort among diverse actors.

Kokubun: That's very intriguing. Every since Kant's time, Western philosophers have asserted that human beings can only know objects through the filter of our perceptions, and are unable to access the thing-in-itself. However, Quentin Meillassoux, a leading proponent of speculative realism, criticized this post-Kantian theory of knowledge as a kind of "correlationism" and caused a sensation by arguing that the intellect can access reality itself, via mathematics. Meillassoux's critique of correlationism is interesting as a philosophical challenge, but the notion that "we cannot know" is, I think, a legacy we cannot discard as long as we find ourselves living within the bounds of our intellect.

Kadowaki: Conversion of a house to 3D data is nothing more than a mathematical process. The quantity of data obtained by scanning the surface of objects is prodigious, yet the composition of the interior remains a black box. Even supposing we were able to obtain data for the interior as well, black boxes would surely remain here and there due to the limitations of the cognitive capacity of humans and computers. In that light, the effort of Google to digitize the entire world begins to sound extremely optimistic. Perhaps we have to return to a more humble stance in recognition of the fact that our communication will always be based on perceptions that are incomplete.

Kokubun: We can think of "knowing everything" as "making everything heimlich," but the unheimlich will never entirely vanish from the human experience. However, the unheimlich may become heimlich over time, and that, it seems to me, is precisely what we are addressing now.

4: REASSEMBLAGE OF ELEMENTS

行為のコミュニズム
國分功一郎

聞き手：門脇耕三（建築家・構法研究）＋岩瀬諒子（建築・ランドスケープ）＋元木大輔（建築家）

テクネーとともに続く手直し

國分功一郎：　まずは「竣工」概念と技術をめぐる展示コンセプトが面白いですね。思い出したのは、徳島の吉野川第十堰という堰のことです。国が吉野川に可動堰を建設しようとした際、2000年の住民投票でノーを突きつけた経緯があるんですね。2013年に僕が地元の東京都小平市で都道328号線建設反対の住民投票を呼びかけたときに参考にしたのが第十堰の事例でした。1994年に長良川で可動堰が建設されるときにも大きな反対運動が起きましたが、全国各地から集まった自然保護団体の行動に地元の人々がしらけてしまったそうです。吉野川ではこの例を反面教師にして、あくまでも地元の人たちで反対運動を展開したといいます。

もともと吉野川は渇水時に海水が流入して塩害が起きやすく、川の流れを変えるためにつくられた第十堰は世代を超えて手直しをしながら受け継がれてきました。ところが当時の建設省は、透過構造の第十堰は大雨になれば洪水を招くと主張して可動堰を建設しようとしました。大水になっても洪水は起きないと地元の人がいっても聞かない。だったら実験してみようと同じ構造の堰をつくって調べたら何の問題も生じなかったそうです。どうやら、川が増水すればフィルターのなかを通る水の量も増える仕組みになっているらしい。しかも堰はフィルター状になっているので、水がきれいになって出てくる。それに対し可動堰では水の流れが止まり、ヘドロ化してしまうわけです。吉野川は飲料用の原水ともなっており、地元の人々は可動堰建設に強い関心をもっていました。

この第十堰は技術について考えるうえでも興味深い事例で、『原子力時代における哲学』（晶文社、2019）という本でも取り上げました。マルティン・ハイデッガーは古代ギリシャの「フュシス（自然）」と「テクネー（技術）」という概念を使いながら、もともとフュシスがもっている力を人間の側に引き寄せて利用することをテクネーと定義します。水や土地が本来もっている力を利用する第十堰は、テクネーの素晴らしい事例です。それに比べて可動堰は水を止めるだけですから、はるかにローテクですよね。また、世代を超えて手直しされ続けているものには「完成」の概念がありません。まさしく「竣工」概念を問い直す事例でしょう。

何世代にもわたって手直しを続けていくと、地域に川と堰に関するテクネーの知識も蓄積されていく。じつは都道328号線をめぐっても、地域の人々はかつてはたしかに渋滞がひどく、バスが50分ぐらい遅れることもざらだったけれども、いまではそれもほとんど解消されていることを知っていました。

行為のコミュニズム

國分：　それからもうひとつ、僕は『中動態の世界――意志と責任の考古学』（医学書院、2017）を書いて以来、ずっと「行為のコミュニズム」ということを考えていました。近代は、ある行為を誰かに帰属させるという意味において、行為を私有財産化する時代だったといえます。それを支えていたのが「意志」という概念です。ジョルジョ・アガンベンは『身体の使用――脱構成的可能態の理論のために』（上村忠男訳、みすず書房、2016／原著＝2014）のなかで「意志は、西洋文化においては、もろもろの行動や所有している技術をある主体に所属させるのを可能にしている装置である」(113頁)と書いています。僕が『中動態の世界』で強く批判したのがこの「意志」なる虚構的概念です。驚くべきことに古代ギリシャには意志という言葉もなければ、それに相当する概念もありませんでした。プラトンの本にもアリストテレスの本にも、意志という概念は出てきません。われわれはある行為を自分の意志に従って行ったと思っていますが、他者や過去からなんの作用も受けずに、ゼロの状態から何かを行為することなど不可能です。ちょっと考えれば誰もがおかしいとわかる概念を日常的に使わなければ生きていけない文明を僕らはつくりあげてしまった。このことはおそらく責任の概念と関係している。人類史にお

いて比較的新しくできたこの概念を使えば、簡単に誰かに責任を負わせることができるわけです。なお、ハンナ・アーレントは、意志はキリスト教的な概念で、おそらくパウロやアウグスティヌスによってつくられたものだろうといっています。すると僕らは、クリスチャンではなくても、どこかキリスト教的なもののなかで生きているといえるかもしれません。

僕が意志という概念を批判しているというと、「無責任の哲学をやろうとしているのですか」と聞かれることがあるのですが、それは誤解です。責任（responsibility）とは応答（response）することです。ある問題に応答するときにその人は責任を果たしていることになる。けれども、本来応答すべき人が応答しないことがある。その時に、意志の概念を使ってその人に責任を強制するというのが、意志とペアになった責任の考え方です。こう考えると、責任がもともとの意味からずいぶんとかけ離れてしまっていることがわかる。意志によって強制する責任というのは、もはや堕落した責任というべきかもしれません。僕らはそのような堕落した責任概念が当たり前のものだと思っている。

話を戻すと、意志の概念が妥当性をもたないとすると、行為を個人に帰属させること自体が不可能になるわけですね。例えば、僕はいまこうやって話をしていますが、この話は誰かが考えたことを引用しながらしているわけだし、この話をしているのも対話の提案を受けたからです。話をするというこの行為は僕だけに帰属するとはとてもいい切れない。ひとつの行為はコミュニズム的に共有されていると捉えたほうがいいのではないか。モノの私有財産制やコミュニズムについてはこれまでさんざん考えられてきましたが、行為の次元でもそれを考えていく必要があるのではないか。そのためのひとつのヒントになったのが、中動態というインド＝ヨーロッパ語の態の存在でした。この失われた態がもつ概念を考えると、能動態（する）／受動態（される）という行為の分類の疑わしさが見えてきて、意志や自発性といった既成の概念が自明なものではなくなってきます。

近代における行為を私有財産とみなす考え方は、芸術をも支配してきました。しかし、これについてもあらためて疑ってみる必要があります。作品というのは誰かひとりによってゼロから創造されるものではない。建築や映画などはわかりやすい例でしょう。今回のプロジェクトに選定された《高見澤邸》は増改築が繰り返されてきて、誰がつくったものなのかわからない。そしてけっして竣工されないつくりかけの状態のなかに、独特の可愛らしさを秘めている。このような建築の魅力を理解するためには、私有財産制的思考を離れ、行為の次元におけるコミュニズムを考えていく必要があるのではないでしょうか。

責任主体としてのモノ、知識自体としてのモノ

門脇耕三： これまで建築の「作品」という概念は、お話しいただいたように意志や責任と近いところで組み立てられてきました。しかし、ある建築家が自分の作品としてパッケージした建築はきわめて静的かつクローズドで、変化や参加を許さない。われわれはそうした「作品」概念に居心地の悪さを感じていて、それがコンセプトの出発点になっています。

國分： 『中動態の世界』を読んだ建築家の方々からもコメントをいただくことがあって、あるときは建築家とクライアントの関係が能動／受動になっているとうまくいかず、2つのエージェントのあいだに中動態的な関係がなければいけないといわれ、なるほど、そういう受け取り方もあるのかと考えさせられました。さらにいえば、第十堰もそうですが、僕はひとりの作家による閉じた作品という切り口では捉えられないものとして、土木にすごく興味があるんですね。土木は作家という個人と結びつけられることはほとんどありません。けれども、水道や道路などのインフラがなければ、建築は建築として成り立たない。そうしたインフラが匿名の技術者たちによってつくられていることにも関心をもっています。

岩瀬諒子： 日本の公共工事や土木工事では、サービスを

提供する側と受け手側の隔たりが大きく、住民一人ひとりが主体的な関わりを築きづらい状況にあります。

自己責任の文化のあるヨーロッパ諸国に比べて、日本では何か問題が起こった時に、当事者の問題が行政へのクレームというかたちで責任転嫁されやすく、あらかじめできないことばかりが増えていく悪循環があります。このぎこちない能動／受動の関係を変えていきたいと考えていたため、お話を伺って我が意を得たりと感じました。現在、道路の設計にも取り組んでいますが、つくり手と使い手とをつなぐ媒体のようなデザインを目指しています。道路の下には電気・水道・ガスなどのインフラが通っていますが、多くの人はその存在を意識していません。当たり前に存在しているインフラも誰かの手によってメンテナンスされていることを意識化、可視化できないかと考え、沿道建物の建て替えやインフラ修繕のたびに張り替えられるアスファルト舗装の改修履歴をパッチワーク状にデザインしたり、マンホールの存在も再考したりと、人々の意識が道路とその下に向くように設計しています。

國分： 考えてみると、メンテナンスの可視化とは歴史の可視化ですよね。堰にしても道路にしても、いままではこうやってきたという地域の歴史を知るだけで、住民は関わり方も見えてくるし、関わりたいという気持ちも出てくる。僕の自宅近くの玉川上水でも、護岸調査をしたら川岸が崩れそうだという結論がでて、あるとき突然行政がコンクリートで固めてしまったんです。たしかに危険はあったのかもしれない。でも、景観は台無しでした。玉川上水の横の散歩道は大切な観光資源なのに。玉川上水がこれまでどのように使われて、どういうふうに維持されてきたか、どういうふうに享受されているのか、それについての地域の知識や意見をもっと聞くべきだったのではないかと考えさせられました。

門脇： 責任や意志や知識は、モノと切り離された形式的な体系だと思われているふしがありますが、お話を聞いていると、第十堰は地域の人が積み重ねてきた知識そのものに思えてきます。だとするならば、それが壊れないで維持さ

れていること自体が責任の現れではないか。そのように考えると、責任主体としての人間とモノは簡単に切り分けられなさそうです。

岩瀬： 石を積む技術も好例になりそうです。コンクリートやモルタルを使わない「空石積み」の風景は中山間地域の農業技術として継承されてきたものですが、実際には崩れないように何度も人の手で積み替えられており、長い時間スケールにおける動的平衡状態に本質を感じます。ところが現代の土木の現場では、担い手不足や「景観への配慮」などから、石積みのような化粧を施したコンクリート擁壁も多く普及しています。

ささやかな仕事とどうでもいい仕事

國分： モノにはメンテナンスという行為が不可避的に伴いますが、最近は「手入れ」という言葉もあまり使われなくなりましたね。以前書いた『暇と退屈の倫理学』（朝日出版社、2011）という本のなかで、僕は「浪費」と「消費」を区別しました。モノを受け取って享受する浪費と違って、消費は情報だけを受け取るので際限がない。大量生産－大量消費－大量投棄というサイクルを回し続けることで20世紀の経済は成長したわけですが、その限界は誰の目にも明らかです。そのときにあらためてモノを享受することの大切さが問われてくる。そのひとつの手段は手入れをすることだと思うんですね。そうすれば、修理やメンテナンスの仕事がいくらでも創出されるはずです。

門脇： 今回扱っている《高見澤邸》にしても、1980年くらいまでは融通無碍に手を入れられているのですが、ある時から変化しなくなる。それは建築工事が制度化され、許可がないと手を入れられなくなったからです。戦前の住宅は直営工事といって、クライアントが職人に日当を払い手を加え続けることが一般的な慣習でしたが、戦後になって工事前に図面と見積もりを出す契約請負型が普及しました。結果として、建築のメンテナンスがやりづらい社会になってしまったんですね。

國分： ある肉屋さんから聞いた話ですが、いまは肉屋の店舗を維持しようとしても、肉を吊るすためのフックをつくる業者や個人商店用の冷蔵庫をつくる業者がほとんどなくなっているという事情があるそうです。肉屋の設備をつくる業者はもう大型店舗向けのものしかつくっていないというのです。社会的に経済の規格化が猛烈に進んでいて、必要なものがつくられなくなっている。

経済学者のデヴィッド・グレーバーが『Bullshit Jobs: A Theory』（Simon & Schuster、2018）という本で書いていますが、いまは、どうでもいい仕事（Bullshit Jobs）ばかりが増えていって、どう考えても必要だろうというささやかな仕事が社会から放逐されつつあるのではないか。いまコンサルティング業界が大きなマーケットをもっていますが、なぜこういう仕事のニーズが増えたかを考えると、本来は仕事と仕事のあいだに中間領域があってそこに知識が蓄えられていたはずなのに、そういう領域をグローバル経済が破壊し続けた結果、失われたノウハウをどこかからもってこなくてはならなくなったからではないでしょうか。中沢新一さんは、東京都による築地市場の解体と豊洲新市場＝物流センターへの移転は、仲卸の仕事現場をはじめとする超合理的な「中間機構」的なものを放逐する無配慮な行為で、「そのとき東京という都市は、自分の保有してきた重大な『富』を、決定的に失うことになる」と訴えました（『現代思想 総特集＝築地市場』2017年7月臨時増刊号、青土社、61頁）。

中沢さんによれば、知識や知恵は中間的なもののなかにこそ蓄積される。けれどもグローバリゼーションが一番の標的としてきたのが中間的なものです。グローバリゼーションの特徴は、中間領域を破壊して、個人を直接的に世界経済市場に対峙させる点にこそある。このとき、たしかに中間領域からの解放を謳歌する人々もいるかもしれない。でも、そこでの行為の責任はすべて個人に背負わされる。そんなことに誰しもが耐えられるだろうか。そして中間的なもののなかにあった知識と知恵もまた破壊されてしまいます。

少し話が逸れますが、2011年のオキュパイ・ムーブメントの参加者たちは図書館をつくっていました。そこで大学の教員がレクチャーを行ったりしていたらしいのですが、介入した警察が最初に壊したのが図書館だったそうです。それは知識が人を結びつけることを直感的に警察が理解していたからかもしれません。

人間は何かを「始める」ことができるか？

門脇： 中間領域の破壊にはどのように抵抗すればいいとお考えですか。

國分： 繰り返しになりますが、いまはあらためてモノを享受することの大切さが問われていると思います。バートランド・ラッセルは『ラッセル 幸福論』（安藤貞雄訳、岩波文庫、1991／原著＝1930）のなかで、「教育は以前、多分に楽しむ能力を訓練すること（training in the capacity for enjoyment）だと考えられていた」と述べています（56頁）。つまり、トレーニングしなければ人は楽しむことができない。モノを楽しむことができないから、浪費ではなくて消費が続くことになり、大量投棄がなくならない。いまはトレーニングをする機会がことごとく奪われていて、誰もが大量投棄社会に都合のいい楽しみ方しかできなくなっているわけでしょう。

門脇： そのような時代にあっては、モノ自体がモノとの付き合い方を教えてくれるようなデザインが求められているのかもしれませんね。今回の展示はモノと親しむことを促すことも企図していて、われわれは会場でモノをつくっているのだけれど、訪れた人もそこに参加したくなるような、モノが制作を誘っているような展示にしたいと考えています。手入れもそうですが、いまは手仕事がどんどんなくなりつつある。建築の分野でも、図面を手で描くことはほとんどありませんし、模型製作も3Dプリンタなどに代替され始めていて、身体的な領域が消えつつある。ただ、そのことは年配の人や障がいのある人など、多様な身体の参加を可能にするとは思うんですね。つまり、制作への参加可能性を開くことと、手仕事の領域を増やすことはかならずしも

イコールではない。また、環境問題などを考えると、制作そのものが過剰に目的化するのもよくないのでしょうね。

國分： 別の観点からいえば、制作を終わらせる「竣工」だけではなくて、「始める」ということも僕たちは疑ってみる必要がある。意志は何かを始める契機とみなされています。意志の概念を批判的に検討していくと、はたして人間は何かを始めることができるのかという問題に行き着く。いま人間は「始める」という行為に囚われているのではないか。今回の展示はつねに中間にあるような、始まりも竣工もないものとしてある。「始めないこと」はこれからの創作における大事な倫理観になってくる気がしています。

門脇： このプロジェクトはもちろんわれわれがやろうと決めたことではあるのですが、みずからの強い意志の力で自発的に進めている感じはあまりないですね。多くの人やモノを巻き込んでいるので、途中からその渦と一緒に進んでいる感覚が強くなってきているというか。正直、最初はこんなに大変な思いをするとは想像していませんでした（笑）。

國分： ハイデッガーは「意志することとは忘却することだ」といっています。未来を志向して意志によって何かを始めるというのは、過去を切断してリセットすることであるわけです。意志とはつまり切断です。それに対して覚悟というのはこれまでの歴史といまある物事を引き受けることを意味する。意志と覚悟はしばしば混同されますが、大きく異なります。今回のプロジェクトにあるのは、覚悟のほうでしょう。

不気味なものに慣れ親しむ

國分： 建物を解体してつくり直すとなると、メンテナンスや歴史の可視化と同じように、パーツの可視化が起こりますよね。ハンナ・アーレントは──おそらくはハイデッガーの哲学を意識しながら──20世紀の美術の特徴を、モノを機能連関から取り外したときにそのモノが「不気味なもの」に見えてくるという経験に見出しています（『アーレン

ト政治思想集成 I』、齋藤純一ほか訳、みすず書房、2002、223頁）。おそらく、ゴッホの《古靴》（1886）などを想定してのことなのでしょうが、ありふれた農夫の靴でも、それだけを取り出すと異様な迫力をもって現前してくる。われわれは世界に慣れ親しんでいるつもりだが、じつは世界とわれわれのあいだには溝がある。20世紀の美術はそのことを徹底的に知らしめたわけです。それはそれで大事なことですが、いまは世界との慣れ親しみをどう回復するかということのほうが問われている気がします。自分と目の前にあるものとの連関を理解して可視化していくことの大事さ。ハイデッガーは「存在することは住むことだ」といって、切り離されてしまった世界のなかに人間がどうやって慣れ親しんで住むかを問うたわけですが、かつては保守的に見えた彼の問題意識をいまあらためて見直す必要があるのではないでしょうか。

門脇： その点には共感するところもあるのですが、異なる文脈の上で再構築された家の似姿をした「何か」がまさに「不気味なもの」であって、その感覚を呼び起こそうとする狙いもあるのです。日常的な感覚である愛着を増大させることは大切ですが、そこで批評的な視座をどうやって確保すればいいか、疑問が残ります。批評的な視座というのはモノと意志を切り離すことによって発見された20世紀的な産物なのでしょうが、それはいまだに魅力的で、後ろ髪を引かれる思いもあるんですね。

國分： おそらくどちらの側面もあると思うのです。ただヴェネチアの会場に日本の古い民家のような何かが現れれば最初から不気味なもの（unheimlich）に見えるはずで、それがエレメントや制作プロセスを通して慣れ親しんだもの（heimlich）になっていく。

これまでの思想史や芸術史の流れでは、見知ったもの（heimlich）が不気味になる（unheimlich）という回路が大事だと思われてきたけれど、展示は逆向きのベクトルに挑戦しているように見えるのです。

門脇： なるほど。いまのご指摘はたいへん腑に落ちました。そもそも《高見澤邸》にもそういう回路が見出せるは

ずで、例えば窓枠に使われているアルミサッシは、日本の伝統的な木製の建具を模して航空機産業から転用された不気味なものでしたが、日常に取り込まれることで慣れ親しんだものになっています。そのことをもう一度ヴェネチアでやろうとしているのかもしれません。物流が高度に発達した現代社会では、普段使っているものもどこから来たのかわからない。ですから、われわれは不気味なものに包囲されているともいえる。そのことを自覚したうえで、日常の回路をどうつくっていくかを問題化しているのがこのプロジェクトであるといえるかもしれません。

國分： おっしゃるように、手中の iPhone がどこからどうやって来たのか、その軌跡がわからないということはとても不気味なことですよね。僕たちはどんどん出所や由来がわからない不気味なものに取り囲まれていくし、制度もいろいろなものを隠して社会のなかに不気味なものをつくり出している。その結果、ある時突然玉川上水にコンクリートの護岸ができるという事態が起こるわけですが、事前に話し合いへの参加機会があって、経緯なり必然性なりがわかれば、もっと親しみのもてる選択肢を考えるはずです。

元木大輔： その視点でいうと、例えば生物界には車輪がありません。なぜなら道路がないからです。われわれには日常的でも、完全な平地がない自然界ではきわめて特殊な存在だということです。凹凸のない道路を整備して車輪をつくり、車幅が決まり、トラックの荷台のサイズが決まり、荷台に積む資材のサイズが決まり、それで組み立てた家のサイズが決まり、都市や郊外の風景が決まっていく。そうやってすでにあるもののプロセスを逆照射することで、周囲にある不気味なものたちを、もう一度日常的な回路に取り込むことができるかもしれません。

住宅一軒すら知ることができない

門脇： 今回は「欠損」も重要なテーマですが、プロジェクトを進めるうちに、ここにはさまざまな暗喩が潜んでいそうだという気持ちが強くなっています。例えば、住宅をす

べて 3D で情報化しようとしても、情報量が多すぎて制御できない。つまり、われわれは住宅一軒すら完全に知ることができない。こうした経験は、世界に対するわれわれの認識が不完全であることを教えてくれるわけですが、バラバラになった住宅は、そうした認識の不完全さを暗喩しているともいえる。でも、機能連関を失ったモノ同士を接合しても完全な構築物にはならず、欠損を内包した構築物を日常に引き戻すためには、その欠損を新たな創造によって埋め合わせなければいけない。この新たな創造は、おそらく解体前の住宅がそのままの形で日本にあっても起こらない種類のもので、欠損によって文脈が過剰に切断されたことではじめて見えてくるようなものになるでしょう。また、欠損はさまざまな主体が忍び込むことのできる隙間でもある。だからそこでの創造は、多様な主体による共同編集的な作業になるのではないかと期待しています。

國分： 面白いですね。いまの「住宅一軒すら知ることができない」という話を聞いて、少し前に哲学の領域で話題になった思弁的実在論のことを思い出しました。西洋の哲学ではカント以来、人間は対象を認識のフィルターを通してしか把握できず、モノ自体にはアクセスできないという考え方が強固にあります。しかし、カンタン・メイヤスーという思弁的実在論を代表する哲学者はカント以来の認識論を「相関主義」と呼んで批判し、知性は実在そのものにアクセスできるとしてセンセーションを巻き起こしました。メイヤスーは数理的な方法を採れば可能だというわけです。ただ、メイヤスーの相関主義批判は哲学的なチャレンジとしては面白いけれど、「知ることができない」は哲学にとっての捨てられない遺産で、知性の限界をふまえて生きていくうえでの嗜みとして大事だと思うんですね。

門脇： 住宅を 3D で情報化することも、数学的な処理にすぎません。モノの表面をスキャンして採れる情報量は膨大ですが、それでも内部の組成はブラックボックスとして残されてしまう。仮に内部の組成まで情報化できたとしても、人間やコンピュータの認知能力の限界によって、ブラックボックスはどこかに生じてしまうことでしょう。そう考え

ると、世界をすべて情報化しようとするGoogleの取り組みなどはきわめて楽観主義的に思えてくる。もう一度、われわれのコミュニケーションはつねに不完全な認識の上に成り立っているのだという素朴な場所に戻って来ざるをえないのかもしれませんね。

國分： 思弁的実在論を日本に紹介し、メイヤスーの本の翻訳も手掛けている千葉雅也君がいうには、メイヤスーは数理科学という「非人間的な」方法を使えば実在にアクセスできるといっているにすぎない。人間的なもの、つまり自然言語を使っているかぎりおそらくはアクセスできないわけです。メイヤスーのいっていることは同意できる部分も多いのですが、僕たちは自然言語を使って生きていて、その前提は乗り越えられない。むしろ彼の議論は、人間が使っている自然言語とは何かということをもう一度考え直すきっかけになっていると僕は考えます。「すべてを知る」ことは「すべてをheimlichにする」ことともいえますが、人間からunheimlichなものは消えてなくならない。ただ、unheimlichなものが時間をかけてheimlichなものになることもあるわけで、いまはそれこそが問われているように思われるのです。

Contributor Profiles

Norimasa Aoyagi
Born in 1975. Associate Professor, Department of Architecture and Urban Design, Ritsumeikan University. Architectural historian and cultural property preservation specialist. Author of *Architectural Design of Japan* (co-author, Gakugei Shuppansha, 2016); *Building Preservation Methodologies in Modern Japan: The Grand Horyuji Restoration and Preservation Principles of the Showa Era* (Chuo Koron Bijutsu Shuppan, 2019).

Aya Hiwatashi
Born in 1982. Lecturer, Department of Architecture, Kindai University. Urban historian. Author of *The Territorio of Venice* (co-author, Kajima Institute Publishing, 2016); *Venice and the Laguna* (Kajima Institute Publishing, 2017).

Naoyuki Matsumoto
Born in 1986. Research Associate, Institute of Industrial Science, University of Tokyo. Specialist in wooden structures and construction methods. Author of "Research on Wall Construction and Structural Performance in Modern Wooden Buildings" (doctoral dissertation, University of Tokyo, 2016).

Tetsu Makino
Born in 1981. Works for Kenbun Co., Ltd. Architectural historian. Major preservation and repair projects include seismic improvements for the Gotoh Museum Kokyoro and preservation plans for the Tekigaiso.

Jan Vranovský
Born in 1986 in Prague. Architect and graphic designer. He received a master's degree in architecture and urban design at The University of Tokyo, Japan (2016) and undergraduate degree in Architecture at Technical University of Liberec, Czech Republic (2013). Jan co-founded FRVR, a graphic design studio in Prague, and worked with Jun Aoki & Associates before starting his own studio in Tokyo, VVAA.

Hirofumi Nakamoto
Born in 1986. Videographer. President of Zushi Art Films. Teaches at university while making films and contemporary art. Works include *Silent Passengers* (2012), *IR PLANET* (2014), *Coves of Bodies* (2016), *The Spacecraft Diaries* (2016), *Visitors from the Riverside* (2017).

Yoshitake Doi
Born in 1956. Professor Emeritus, Kyushu University. Architectural historian, doctor of engineering, French government-certified architect. Author of *Language and Architecture: History and Concepts of Architectural Criticism* (Kenchiku Gijutsu, 1997); *Dialogue: Architecture and Time* (co-author with Arata Isozaki, Iwanami Shoten, 2001); *Perception and Architecture: Claude Perrault's "Five Kinds of Column" and a History of Its Interpretation* (Chuo Koron Bijutsu Shuppan, 2017); *The Sacred in Architecture: Religion and Modern Architecture as a History of Ideas* (University of Tokyo Press, 2020).

Masaya Chiba
Born in 1978. Associate Professor, Graduate School of Core Ethics and Frontier Sciences, Ritsumeikan University. Philosopher and writer. Author of *Don't Move Too Much: Gilles Deleuze and the Philosophy of Becoming* (Kawade Bunko, 2017); *Philosophy of Learning: For the Stupid to Come* (Bungei Shunju, 2017); *Meaningless Meaninglessness* (Kawade Shobo Shinsha, 2018); *Deadline* (Shinchosha, 2019). Co-translator of Quentin Meillassoux, *After Finitude: An Essay on the Necessity of Contingency* (Jinbun Shoin, 2016).

Takehiko Daikoku
Born in 1961. Professor, School of Information and Communication, Meiji University. Philosopher. Author of *Philosophy of "Media": Range and Limits of Luhmann's Social Systems Theory* (NTT Publishing, 2006); *What Is an Information Society? Prelude to Media Theory* (NTT Publishing, 2010); *Reconstructing Communication Theory: Body, Media, Information Space* (co-author, Keiso Shobo, 2012); *A Philosophy of Virtual Society: Bitcoins, VT, Post-Truth* (Seidosha, 2018).

Koichiro Kokubun
Born in 1974. Associate Professor, Graduate School of Arts and Sciences, University of Tokyo. Philosopher. Author of *The Principles of Deleuzian Philosophy* (Edinburgh University Press, 2020); *Spinoza's Method* (Misuzu Shobo, 2011); *The World of Chu-Dou-Tai: An Archaeology of Will and Responsibility* (Igaku-Shoin, 2017); *Philosophy in the Nuclear Age* (Shobunsha, 2019). Co-translator of Gilles Deleuze, *Qu'est-ce que fonder?* (Chikuma Gakugei Bunko, 2018).

執筆者・話者略歴

青柳憲昌
1975 年生まれ。立命館大学理工学部建築都市デザイン学科准教授。建築史・文化財保存。主な著書=『日本の建築意匠』(共著、学芸出版社、2016)、『日本近代の建築保存方法論──法隆寺昭和大修理と同時代の保存理念』(中央公論美術出版、2019) など。

樋渡彩
1982 年生まれ。近畿大学工学部建築学科講師。都市史。主な著書=『ヴェネツィアのテリトーリオ』(共著、鹿島出版会、2016)、『ヴェネツィアとラグーナ』(鹿島出版会、2017) など。

松本直之
1986 年生まれ。東京大学生産技術研究所助教。木質構造、建築構法。主な論文=「近代木造建築の壁構法と構造性能に関する研究──木摺漆喰壁の構成要素と水平力抵抗機構」(東京大学博士論文、2016) など。

牧野徹
1981 年生まれ。建文・建築文化研究所所属。建築史。主な保存改修=《五島美術館古経楼》耐震改修工事、《荻外荘》保存活用計画策定など。

ヤン・ブラノブセキ
1986 年、プラハ生まれ。建築家、グラフィックデザイナー。リベレツ工科大学卒業、東京大学国際都市建築デザインコース修士課程修了。青木淳建築計画事務所を経てグラフィックデザイン・スタジオFRVR共同設立。VVAA 主宰。

仲本拡史
1986 年生まれ。映像作家。逗子アートフィルム代表。大学で教員を務めながら、主に映画と現代美術の領域で作家活動を行う。主な作品=『無言の乗客』(2012)、『IR PLANET』(2014)、『肉体の入江』(2016)、『宇宙の舟』(2016)、『水際の来客』(2017) など。

土居義岳
1956 年生まれ。九州大学名誉教授。建築史。工学博士。フランス政府公認建築家。主な著書=『言葉と建築──建築批評の史的地平と諸概念』(建築技術、1997)、『対論 建築と時間』(磯崎新と共著、岩波書店、2001)、『知覚と建築──クロード・ペロー「五種類の円柱」とその読解史』(中央公論美術出版社、2017)、『建築の聖なるもの──宗教と近代建築の精神史』(東京大学出版会、2020) など。

千葉雅也
1978 年生まれ。立命館大学大学院先端総合学術研究科准教授。哲学者、作家。主な著書=『動きすぎてはいけない──ジル・ドゥルーズと生成変化の哲学』(河出文庫、2017)、『勉強の哲学──来たるべきバカのために』(文藝春秋、2017)、『意味がない無意味』(河出書房新社、2018)、『デッドライン』(新潮社、2019)ほか。主な訳書=カンタン・メイヤスー『有限性の後で──偶然性の必然性についての試論』(共訳、人文書院、2016) など。

大黒岳彦
1961 年生まれ。明治大学情報コミュニケーション学部教授。哲学者。主な著書＝『〈メディア〉の哲学──ルーマン社会システム論の射程と限界』(NTT出版、2006)、『「情報社会」とは何か?──〈メディア〉論への前哨』(NTT出版、2010)、『コミュニケーション理論の再構築──身体・メディア・情報空間』(共著、勁草書房、2012)、『ヴァーチャル社会の〈哲学〉──ビットコイン・VR・ポストトゥルース』『(青土社、2018) など。

國分功一郎
1974 年生まれ。東京大学総合文化研究科准教授。哲学者。主な著書=『スピノザの方法』(みすず書房、2011)、『ドゥルーズの哲学原理』(岩波書店、2013)、『中動態の世界──意志と責任の考古学』(医学書院、2017)、『原子力時代における哲学』(晶文社、2019) ほか。主な訳書=ジル・ドゥルーズ『基礎づけるとは何か』(共訳、ちくま学芸文庫、2018) など。

CO-OWNERSHIP OF ACTION:
TRAJECTORIES OF ELEMENTS

Supervisor:
Kozo Kadowaki

Contributors:
Kozo Kadowaki
Jo Nagasaka
Ryoko Iwase
Toshikatsu Kiuchi
Taichi Sunayama
Daisuke Motogi
Rikako Nagashima
Naritake Fukumoto
Kayoko Ota
Norimasa Aoyagi
Aya Hiwatashi
Naoyuki Matsumoto
Tetsu Makino
Jan Vranovský
Hirofumi Nakamoto
Yoshitake Doi
Masaya Chiba
Takehiko Daikoku
Koichiro Kokubun

Translator:
Alan Gleason

Jacket Photos:
Jan Vranovský

ふるまいの連鎖：
エレメントの軌跡

監修：
門脇耕三

執筆者・話者：
門脇耕三
長坂常
岩瀬諒子
木内俊克
砂山太一
元木大輔
長嶋りかこ
福元成武
太田佳代子
青柳憲昌
樋渡彩
松本直之
牧野徹
ヤン・ブラノブセキ
仲本拡史
土居義岳
千葉雅也
大黒岳彦
國分功一郎

翻訳：
アラン・グリースン

カバー写真：
ヤン・ブラノブセキ

The Japan Pavilion at the 17th International
Architecture Exhibition of La Biennale di Venezia 2020
"Co-ownership of Action: Trajectories of Elements"
Exhibition period: 29 August - 29 November 2020
Venue: The Japan Pavilion at the Giardini

Commissioner: The Japan Foundation

Curator: Kozo Kadowaki
Architects: Jo Nagasaka, Ryoko Iwase,
Toshikatsu Kiuchi, Taichi Sunayama, Daisuke Motogi
Designer: Rikako Nagashima
Researchers: Norimasa Aoyagi, Aya Hiwatashi,
Naoyuki Matsumoto, Tetsu Makino
Building System Design Laboratory at Meiji University
(Kozo Kadowaki, Makoto Isono, Kimihito Ito)
Editor: Jiro Iio
Advisor: Kayoko Ota
Photos: Jan Vranovský
Video: Hirofumi Nakamoto

Exhibition Design:
Schemata Architects (Jo Nagasaka, Yuhei Yagi)
Studio IWASE | Architecture+Landscape
(Ryoko Iwase, Kaoru Endo)
sunayama studio+Toshikatsu Kiuchi Architect
(Taichi Sunayama, Toshikatsu Kiuchi, Risako Okuizumi,
Kei Machida/Zu Architects)
DDAA (Daisuke Motogi, Riku Murai)
Graphic Design:
village®
(Rikako Nagashima, Kohei Kawaminami, Hiroyuki Inada)
Structural Engineering:
TECTONICA (Yoshinori Suzuki, Kakeru Tsuruta)
Mitsuhiro Kanada Studio at Tokyo University of the Arts
(Mitsuhiro Kanada)

Exhibition Construction:
TANK (Naritake Fukumoto, Ai Noguchi, Takashi Arai)
Takahiro Kai
Tsuguhiro Komazaki
Takashi Takamoto
Masayasu Fujiwara
Exhibition Design Management:
associates (Kozo Kadowaki, Akiko Kadowaki)
Local Coordinator:
Harumi Muto

With special support by
Ishibashi Foundation

Sponsored by
Stroog Inc.
JINS Holdings Inc.
Suikoukai Medical Corporation, Japan
KAMAWANU CO., LTD.
Window Research Institute

In cooperation with
under design Co., Ltd.
IWASAKI ELECTRIC CO., LTD.
NBC Meshtec Inc.
KUMONOS Corporation
DAIKO ELECTRIC CO., LTD.
Japan 3D Printer Co., Ltd.
Rotho Blaas

第 17 回ヴェネチア・ビエンナーレ国際建築展 日本館展示
「ふるまいの連鎖：エレメントの軌跡」
会期：2020 年 8 月 29 日 -11 月 29 日
会場：ヴェネチア・ビエンナーレ日本館（ジャルディーニ地区）

コミッショナー：独立行政法人 国際交流基金

JAPANFOUNDATION

キュレーター：門脇耕三
参加建築家：長坂常、岩瀬諒子、木内俊克、砂山太一、元木大輔
参加デザイナー：長嶋りかこ
リサーチャー：青柳憲昌、樋渡彩、松本直之、牧野徹
明治大学構法計画研究室（門脇耕三、磯野信、伊藤公人）
エディター：飯尾次郎
アドバイザー：太田佳代子
写真：ヤン・ブラノブセキ
映像：仲本拡史

展示設計：
スキーマ建築計画（長坂常、八木佑平）
岩瀬諒子設計事務所（岩瀬諒子、遠藤郁）
sunayama studio ＋木内建築計画事務所
（砂山太一、木内俊克、奥泉理佐子、町田恵／ズーアーキテクツ）
DDAA（元木大輔、村井陸）
グラフィックデザイン：
village®（長嶋りかこ、河南浩平、稲田浩之）
構造設計：
テクトニカ（鈴木芳典、鶴田翔）
東京藝術大学金田充弘研究室（金田充弘）
施工：
TANK（福元成武、野口藍、荒井隆志）
甲斐貴大
駒崎継広
高本貴志
藤原賢康
展示設計マネジメント：
アソシエイツ（門脇耕三、門脇章子）
現地コーディネーター：
武藤春美

特別助成：公益財団法人 石橋財団

協賛：
株式会社ストローグ、株式会社ジンズホールディングス、
医療法人翠光会（まつもと皮膚科クリニック、松本歯科クリニック）、
株式会社かまわぬ、一般財団法人 窓研究所

協力：
アンダーデザイン株式会社、岩崎電気株式会社、
株式会社 NBC メッシュテック、
クモノスコーポレーション株式会社、大光電機株式会社、
日本 3D プリンター株式会社、ロトブラース

ふるまいの連鎖：エレメントの軌跡

2020 年 8 月 10 日　初版第 1 刷発行

監修：
門脇耕三

発行者：伊藤剛士
発行所：TOTO 出版（TOTO 株式会社）
〒 107-0062 東京都港区南青山 1-24-3
TOTO 乃木坂ビル 2F
［営業］
TEL: 03-3402-7138
FAX: 03-3402-7187
［編集］
TEL: 03-3497-1010
URL: https://jp.toto.com/publishing

デザイン：長嶋りかこ + 稲田浩之／village®
編集：飯尾次郎／speelplaats co., ltd.
印刷・製本：株式会社サンニチ印刷